INTERAMERICAN INSTITUTE OF
INTERNATIONAL LEGAL STUDIES

THE
ANDEAN
LEGAL ORDER
A New Community Law

by

F.V. García-Amador

1978
OCEANA PUBLICATIONS, INC.
Dobbs Ferry, New York

Library of Congress Cataloging in Publication Data

García Amador y Rodríguez, F.V.
    The Andean legal order.

    At head of title: InterAmerican Institute of
International Legal Affairs.
    Translated from the Spanish.
    1. Law—Acuerdo de Cartagena countries. 2. Acuerdo
de Cartagena. I. Title.
Law   341.24'2   78-11916
ISBN 0-379-20285-9

Manufactured in the United States of America

PREFACE

The process of economic integration of the Andean subregion arises not only within the Latin American Free Trade Association (LAFTA), but furthermore continues to develop within its legal and institutional framework. However, despite the close linkage and relationship, the new Latin American integration process, given its objectives and mechanisms, relies on its own institutions and law.

The present study of the Andean law or legal order is based on both of these premises, as well as a third: that we are dealing not merely with the law of an economic integration process, but with a new and genuine "community law". This last premise seemed to us rather bold when we began our research, but today, after completing the study, we see it as a simple objective fact.

This conception of Andean law explains to a large extent the content of this study. After the first chapter, which offers a brief history of the Cartagena Agreement and an explanation of its objectives and mechanisms, including the acts of the subregional organs under which they are being implemented, the second chapter examines its linkage and relationship to the legal order of LAFTA. The third chapter is devoted to the Andean institutional framework, and points out the "community" oriented operations of the two principal organs of the Agreement—the Commission and the Board—and their relationship. The fourth chapter analyzes the system that the Agreement adopts for attributing competences, in such a way that one can fully appreciate the considerable extent to which competences *ratione materiae* are reserved to the subregional organs. The fifth and last chapter studies at length the nature and validity of subregional acts, a topic tied, more than any other, to the essential notion of community law. Here the ample practice of the organs of the Agreement joins with the equally abundant domestic practice of the member states, and both considerably enrich the material available for a study of the Andean legal order in its present stage of development.

The author wishes to take this opportunity to reiterate his sincere thanks for the invaluable cooperation he has received during these past two years from members of the Legal Unit of the Permanent Secretariat of the Cartagena Agreement, especially the personal assistance offered to him during the two visits he made to headquarters of the Board.

I take the pleasure of acknowledging the contribution to the translation into English of the original Spanish version of this book. First, to Mr. Frank Monisera, who worked on the first draft, and to the Misses Judy N. Readon and Julia C. Allen, then students from Mount Holyoke and Hampshire Colleges, respectively, who also worked on the draft. Mr. Roberto Alvarez was responsible for the final version of the text. The English version was completed during the author's tenure as Visiting Professor at the University of Miami School of Law.

The author also wishes to thank again the Inter-American Institute of International Legal Studies for having sponsored the publication of the original Spanish version, as well as the Instituto para la *Integración de América Latina* (INTAL) for its cooperation with that publication.

F.V. García-Amador

Coral Cables, Florida
June, 1978

TABLE OF CONTENTS

Chapter III

THE ANDEAN INSTITUTIONAL FRAMEWORK ....

Chapter IV

COMPETENCES OF THE SUBREGIONAL ORGANS ....

Chapter V

NATURE AND VALIDITY OF THE SUBREGIONAL ACTS 147

APPENDICES

Chapter I

A BRIEF HISTORY OF THE
SUBREGIONAL INTEGRATION AGREEMENT;
ITS OBJECTIVES AND MECHANISMS

This first chapter serves two purposes: first, to review the most recent and direct historical antecedents of
the Subregional Andean Agreement, including those related
to its signature and other acts and procedures leading to
its entry into force, and second, to explain in general
terms the objectives and mechanisms of the Agreement, as
well as the results obtained as of the present. Complementing this second purpose is an explanation at the end of the
chapter of other aspects of the process of subregional integration.

1. Brief History of the Subregional Agreement

Although the intention that eventually led to the formalizing, in 1969, of the Subregional Integration Agreement,
has antecedents in the origins of Latin American economic
integration, no concrete or effective initiative appeared
until the Bogota Declaration, which was signed in the
Colombian Capital on August 16, 1966 by the presidents of
Colombia, Chile, and Venezuela and the personal representatives of the presidents of Ecuador and Peru. [1]

---

1. The antecedents referred to are those related to
the need of suitability for special measures for countries
of "medium development" (or "insufficient market") as well
as those granting special treatment for countries of "relatively less economic development" in the Montevideo Treaty
which created the Latin American Free Trade Association
(LAFTA). See, among other sources, Colombia, Departa-
mento Nacional de Planeación, Antecedentes y Principales
Características y Mecanismos del Acuerdo Subregional Andino, doc. ONP-285-UIE-Junio 1969. The document is
reproduced in the publication of the Institute for Latin
American Integration (INTAL), Derecho de la Integración,
No. 5, octubre 1969, p. 117.

a) The Declaration of Bogotá and the Declaration of the Presidents of America (1967)

The initiative referred to, as was described in the above-mentioned Bogotá Declaration, consisted in the following decision:

> ... to promote joint action to obtain with LAFTA the approval of specific measures which will fulfill the goals contained in this declaration, and especially to promote joint action for the adoption of practical formulas that will provide an adequate treatment in accordance with the conditions of our countries, which are characteristic of those with relatively less developed economies, or of insufficient market. These are the indispensable means to attain a harmonious and balanced development of the region within the spirit of the Montevideo Treaty. 2/

Consistent with the concern shown in the above passage of the Declaration, its authors formulated various recommendations among which the outstanding ones are that complementation agreements and temporary concessions should be made, in which exclusively less developed countries and countries with insufficient markets would participate; that agreements should be signed between the countries in these two categories and more developed countries, whose advantages would not be extended to the other more developed countries of the latter category; and that a system of programmed tariff reductions be established, based on the different degrees of development between countries and sectors. The Declaration also contains recommendations for border integration, physical integration, multinational projects and monetary policy.

---

2. The complete text of the Bogotá Declaration may be found in the publication of the Cartagena Agreement and INTAL, Historia Documental del Acuerdo de Cartagena, 1974, p. 245. It is also included in INTAL's publication, Boletín de la Integración, Agosto de 1966, p. 22.

Further, in the Bogotá meeting a program of action was agreed upon, which included the creation of a mixed commission of government officials whose duty, among other things, would be to submit proposals to fulfill the provisions of the Declaration, and a development corporation in charge of direct promotions as well as technical assistance to the private sector for projects of common interest. 3/

Another new and very important step toward Andean Subregional integration was taken by the presidents of American states, in the summit meeting held at Punta del Este, Uruguay from April 12-14, 1967. In the Declaration of Presidents of the Americas, with regard to the Latin American Free Trade Association (LAFTA) the following was recommended, among other things:

> To promote the conclusion of temporary subregional agreements, with provision for reducing tariffs within the subregions and harmonizing treatments toward third nations more rapidly than in the general agreements, in keeping with the objectives of regional integration. Subregional tariff reductions will not be extended to countries that are not parties to the subregional agreement, nor will they create special obligations for them.

This first definition of "subregional agreements" is completed by this other passage from the Declaration:

> The countries of relatively less economic development will have the right to participate and to obtain preferential conditions in the subregional agreements in which they have an interest. 4/

---

3. The first of the institutions alluded to was the Mixed Commission which negotiated the subregional agreement, and the second is the present Andean Development Corporation, created by another instrument, as will be seen in section 4 of Chapter III.

4. The complete text of the Declaration of Presidents is reproduced in Inter-American Institute of International Legal Studies, Instruments Relating to the Economic Integration of Latin America (2d. ed., 1968), p. 395.

It was thus, at the highest political level, that a decision to further the subregional agreements conceived in the Bogotá Declaration was agreed upon and with them to promote, within the framework of LAFTA, 5/ the processes of economic integration capable of ensuring a more harmonious and balanced development within the region through the more accelerated and dynamic integration of a group of countries with insufficient markets and of countries relatively less developed.

b) Complementary resolutions of LAFTA organs

By decision of the presidents, in August and September of the same year the Council of Ministers of LAFTA met in Asunción, Paraguay, and approved two resolutions intended to make the fulfillment of the Punta del Este pledges feasible. One of these was Resolution 202, of September 2, 1967, which placed the Conference of Contracting Parties of the Montevideo Treaty in charge of establishing the standards to which subregional agreements whould be subject, and indicated to them the principles to which the standards should conform. 6/

The second was Resolution 203, of the same date, which approved the bases for a subregional agreement that had been presented by Chile, Colombia, Ecuador, Peru and Venezuela, delegated to the Standing Executive Committee of LAFTA the authority to verify that the subregional agreement to be signed was compatible with the bases approved in the same resolution and with the principles 1 to 10 in Article 2 of Resolution 202, and placed the Conference of Contracting Parties in charge of analyzing in its regular

---

5. In this connection, the Declaration explicitly states that "all of the provisions set forth in this section fall within or are based on the Treaty of Montevideo".
6. The complete text of Resolution 202, (Standards for Subregional Agreements) appears in Inter-American Institute of International Legal Studies, Instruments of Economic Integration in Latin America and the Caribbean (Oceana Publications, Inc., 1975), vol. I, p. 166.

meetings the progress of the subregional agreement and its adequacy in achieving the main objectives of the Montevideo Treaty. 7/ The bases presented by the six countries had been approved by the above-mentioned Mixed Committee at its meeting in Caracas on August 13-16, 1967, in which Bolivia was beginning to participate in the process of Andean integration. 8/

The next step was taken when the Conference of Contracting Parties of LAFTA, in its Resolution 222 (VII) of December 17, 1967, approved the "Regulations to be Applicable to the Subregional Agreements". As will be seen in Chapter II, this resolution contains the fundamental regulations or principles governing relations between the present Subregional Andean Agreement and the legal and institutional structure of LAFTA. Thus, for example, this resolution considers the question of "compatibility" of subregional agreements and that structure, the hierarchical relations between the provisions contained in the former and the rights and obligations arising from the latter, the transitory nature of said agreements, and the required approval of these agreements by the Standing Executive Committee. Along another train of thought, Resolution 222 (VII) determines the questions and aspects regarding which subregional agreements should contain provisions, the scope or effect of tariff exemptions provided for under them, and preferential treatment for relatively less developed countries. From the institutional point of view, it provides for the establishment of an executive organ to administer each agreement. Finally, it should be noted that this resolution formulates a definition of subregional agreements which, up to a certain point, complements the one formulated in the Declaration of Presidents transcribed

---

7. For complete text of Resolution 203 (Bases for a Subregional Agreement between Chile, Colombia, Ecuador, Peru and Venezuela), including the text of said bases, see ibid, p. 162.

8. In the course of this and other meetings, the Mixed Commission also worked out the Agreement Establishing the Andean Development Corporation, signed in Bogotá on February 7, 1968. For complete text of the Agreement see ibid., p. 270.

The subregional agreements are those by means of
which the countries of LAFTA subscribing thereto
shall be able to promote the process of economic integration in a balanced and more accelerated form than
that derived from the commitments undertaken within
the framework of the Montevideo Treaty.

Various other norms of Resolution 222 (VII), some of which
were just referred to, complement this definition. 9/

    c) <u>Signature, declaration of compatibility, approval</u>
        <u>and entry in force of the Agreement</u>

Once the preceding steps had been taken by LAFTA
organs, the Mixed Commission resumed its activities, one
of which consisted of convening a committee of experts,
pursuant to the instructions approved for this purpose, to
draft the final text of the proposed subregional agreement.
The Committee met in Bogotá from January 8 to March 29,
1968, and prepared a first draft. Because of the difficulties
that arose within the Commission, the draft was transmitted
to the governments to be studied, which brought out the existing discrepancies regarding the degree of acceleration
that should be applied to the regional integration process.
The negotiations were also prolonged by the participation
of the industrial sector whose proposals definitively exercised considerable influence in the second draft agreement.
This draft was worked out by the Committee of Experts
between June 3 and July 4, so that it would be considered by
the Mixed Commission at its sixth meeting, which took place
in Cartagena, Colombia, in the same month of July.

At this meeting the discrepancies and difficulties arose
again, perhaps even to a greater degree. Nevertheless the
draft was approved, although with reservations to some articles on the parts of Peru and Venezuela and with the request
from Ecuador that the meeting be declared in recess for
sixty days to permit its new government to issue a definitive
statement. Finally, the Mixed Commission resumed its

---

    9. For the complete text of Resolution 222 (VII), see
<u>ibid.</u>, p. 169.

sixth session on May 5, 1969, again in Cartagena, where the Subregional Integration Agreement was approved on the 25th of that month. The Agreement was formally signed on the following day--May 26, 1969--in the city of Bogotá. 10/

As a result of the provision on this particular matter in the above-mentioned Resolution 203 of the Council of Ministers of LAFTA, Article 110 of the Agreement stipulated that it would be submitted to the consideration of the Standing Executive Committee of the Association so that a declaration of compatibility with the principles and objectives of the Montevideo Treaty and with Resolution 203 itself could be made. The Agreement was submitted to that Committee on June 10, 1969, which examined it in three special sessions (Nos. 513, 514 and 515) held in the course of the following month. At the conclusion of the third session, on July 9, the Committee passed its Resolution 179, which resolved:

> To declare that the Agreement on Subregional Integration signed in Bogotá on May 26, 1969, by the

---

10. Venezuela abstained from signing the Agreement and so was given the opportunity to sign before December 31, 1970, without being affected by the adherence procedure provided in Article 109. However, its representative could be sent as an observer of the intervening sessions of the Commission created by the Agreement. On February 13, 1973, Venezuela signed the Agreement, and the "Additional Instrument for the adherence of Venezuela to the Cartagena Agreement" was deposited in the LAFTA Executive Secretariat on November 29 of the same year. For a detailed exposition of the different levels of the negotiations leading to the Agreement, see Inter-American Institute of International Legal Studies, Derecho de la Integración Latinoamericana, Ensayo de Sistematización (Depalma, Buenos Aires, 1969), pp. 361-398. For the negotiations between the Commission of the Agreement and the Government of Venezuela, which culminated in the former's approval of the conditions of adherence for Venezuela, see infra, subsection 1, d) of Chapter II.

plenipotentiaries of Bolivia, Colombia, Chile, Ecuador and Peru, of which the text is included in this resolution, is compatible with the Montevideo Treaty and conforms to the general principles stated in Resolution 202 (CM-II/VI-E), to the bases approved by Resolution 203 (CM-II/VII-E), and to the norms established in Resolution 222 (VII) of the Conference. Consequently, it gives its approval to the Agreement. 11/

The Agreement took force when the third "act of approval" of the member states was notified to the Executive Secretary of LAFTA, which is the other condition established in Article 110. 12/

d) Decision 102: withdrawal of Chile from the Agreement

At present there are two additional instruments to the Subregional Integration Agreement. One is the Additional Instrument for the Adherence of Venezuela, signed on February 13, 1973; the other is the Additional Protocol of Lima to the Agreement, signed on October 30, 1976 by the governments of five of the six Member States: Bolivia, Colombia, Ecuador, Peru and Venezuela. Both instruments introduced amendments to the original Agreement,

---

11. For the complete text of Resolution 179, see Inter-American Institute, op. cit., in note 6, p. 173.

12. Peru was the third country to notify its approval of the Agreement to the Executive Secretariat of LAFTA, on October 16, 1969. The remaining approvals of the Agreement are arranged in chronological order below: Decree 1245, August 30, 1969, Colombia (as will be seen in subsection 4, b) of Chapter V, a Colombian approbatory instrument of a legislative nature also exists in Law 8 of March 21, 1973); Decree 428, July 30, 1969, Chile; Decree-law 17851, October 14, 1969, Peru; Executive Decree 1932, October 24, 1969, Ecuador; Decree-law 08,985, November 6, 1969; and Law 3, September 3, 1973, Venezuela. The text of the original five approbatory instruments appear in the Historia Documental del Acuerdo de Cartagena, p. 184 et seq.

as will be seen in due course. 12-a/ The Protocol of Lima
was not signed by the six Member States due to the "cessation by Chile of the rights and obligations derived from the
Cartagena Agreement", which was agreed upon through
Decision 102 of the Commission of the Agreement. The
events which preceded this Decision will be described
briefly below, without prejudice to the observations regarding some interesting juridical and institutional aspects
posed, in light of the pertinent provisions of the Cartagena
Agreement, by the way in which Chile ceased to be a
Member State. 12-b/

In this connection, perhaps it would be fitting to begin
by making reference to the refusal by Chile to sign the Additional Protocol, whose signature was recommended by
the Commission to the Governments of the Member States
through the Decision 100 referred to. This Protocol was
signed by the other five countries on August 4, 1976, and a
clause was included therein by which Chile was granted a
period of sixty days in which to sign it.

Notwithstanding the concessions made by the five
countries (Declaration of Sochagota, Colombia, on August
14), 12-c/ both with respect to the Common Regime of
Treatment of Foreign Capital... (Decision 24) and to the
tariff levels, after the expiration of the period referred to
(October 3) for the signature of the Additional Protocol,
Chile reiterated its position, and for this reason a situation

---

12-a.   The Lima Protocol is the instrument whose
signature was recommended to the Member States by the
Commission of the Agreement thorugh its Decision 100,
adopted at its Sixteenth Special Session (February-March-
April 1976). The only difference between the two lies in
the fact that the Protocol extends to three years--in place
of the two provided in Decision 100--the time periods
contemplated in the Agreement with respect to Industrial
Programming and the Common External Tariff.
    12-b. See some of these observations in section 4
of Chapter II.
    12-c. See complete text of the Declaration in La
Crónica, Lima, Peru, August 16, 1976.

similar to the one that had been foreseen in a second Declaration, issued by the same five countries in Cali on September 27, had arisen. The pertinent parts of this second Declaration are cited below: 12-d/

    1. To present a new appeal to the Government of Chile to contribute to the full reestablishment of normalcy of the Andean integration process through the firm ratification of the Additional Protocol within the period contemplated for its signature.

    2. To reiterate their willingness to arrange with Chile, as a result of the reestablishment of that normalcy, a special procedure of a temporary nature for the fulfillment of the obligations and the exercise of the rights emanating from the Cartagena Agreement, its Protocols and Additional Instruments, the decisions of the Commission, the resolutions of the Board and other norms issued by the principal organs of the Agreement.

    The countries are also willing to establish the conditions and the time periods which would make it possible for Chile to again become part of the Agreement.

    3. To affirm their complete willingness to adopt the machinery which will enable the declarant countries to continue their progress toward attaining the objectives contemplated in the Cartagena Agreement, even in the eventuality that Chile should not accept the proposed terms of the first two parts of the Declaration.

Thus, instead of the signature by Chile of the Additional Protocol modifying the Cartagena Agreement, what was signed this time by the six countries on October 5 was

---

12-d. See the complete text of the Declaration in La Crónica, Lima, Peru, September 28, 1976.

a new Additional Protocol to the Agreement, also modifying it, whose substantive provisions are as follows:

Article 1. A Special Commission is created between Bolivia, Colombia, Ecuador, Peru and Venezuela, on the one hand, and Chile on the other, for the purpose of agreeing, within the period of twenty-four days from the date of the present Protocol, on a special regime, for a definite period, which shall subject them to the rights and obligations derived from their status as Member States of the Cartagena Agreement.

Article 2. If by the completion of the period indicated in the preceding article an agreement between the Parties should not be reached, they then agree, by virtue of this Instrument, to Chile's withdrawal from the Cartagena Agreement, renouncing all its rights and ending its obligations derived from that Agreement, its Protocols, Decisions and Resolutions, from the thirtieth of October, nineteen hundred seventy six, except the rights and obligations emanating from Decisions 40, 46, 56 and 94, which shall remain fully in force.

As can be seen, unlike the alternatives which were contemplated in the Declaration of Cali, the new Protocol does not contemplate the acceptance by Chile of the Protocol modifying the Cartagena Agreement which the other five countries had signed on August 4.

Furthermore, what the new Additional Protocol provided for was, on the one hand, the establishment of a "special regime" which would define the juridical and institutional situation in which Chile would continue in the Andean Group for a period to be determined and, on the other hand, the "withdrawal" of Chile from the Cartagena Agreement (with the consequences stipulated in the Protocol as to its rights and obligations) if it would not be possible to agree on the "special regime".

Considering that it was not possible to agree on the "special regime", on October 30, 1976, "The

11

Representatives of the Member States in the Commission
of the Cartagena Agreement, on the one hand, and the
Plenipotentiary Representative of the Government of Chile,
on the other" signed a Joint Declaration. By this instrument (in one of whose preambles Article 2 of the mentioned
Additional Protocol of October 5 is transcribed) it was
agreed to create a Joint Andean-Chilean Commission, composed of the Commission of the Agreement of Cartagena,
on the one hand, and a Plenipotentiary Representative of
the Government of Chile, on the other, in order to (a) see
to the application of Decisions 40, 46, 56 and 94 in relations
between the Parties; (b) promote agreements on cooperative
programs in productive, commercial, financial and technological matters, as well as in other areas where this is
possible, preserving for the Member States the principles,
juridical structure and objectives of the Cartagena Agreement; and (c) establish the procedure for its functioning.

On the same date that the Joint Declaration was issued
the Commission of the Cartagena Agreement met, for the
first time without the presence of the representative of the
Government of Chile. In this second part of its Twentieth
Regular Session, the Commission approved several decisions, the first of which--Decision 102 ("Cessation by Chile
of the rights and obligations derived from the Cartagena
Agreement")--incorporates the stipulation in Article 2 of the
Additional Protocol of October 5 in the following manner: 12-e

Article 1. Beginning October 30, 1976, all the
rights and obligations derived from the Cartagena
Agreement, its Protocols, Decisions and Resolutions,
except for the rights and obligations emanating from
Decisions 40, 46, 56 and 94, which remain fully in
force, are without effect for Chile.

The cessation of rights and obligations referred
to in the preceding paragraph include the advantages

12-e.   Cf.   Acta Final, Vigésimo Período de Sesiones Ordinarias, 4 de Agosto y 30 de Octubre, 1976, Lima,
Perú.

received and granted by Chile in accordance with the liberalization program and the rights and obligations emanating from Decisions 57 and 91 of the Commission.

Article 2. The Commission shall agree with the Government of Chile on the form in which the application of Decisions 40, 46, 56 and 94 of the Commission shall be administered in relations with that country.

Article 3. This Decision shall enter into force on October 30, 1976.

In the course of this meeting the Chairman of the Commission reported on the Additional Protocol of Lima to the Cartagena Agreement, which was also signed on October 30 by the Plenipotentiary Representatives of the Governments of Bolivia, Colombia, Ecuador, Peru and Venezuela, and to which reference has already been made at the beginning of this subsection.

2. Objectives and Mechanisms of the Agreement

Both the Bogotá Declaration and the Declaration of the Presidents of America as well as the resolutions of the LAFTA organs point out the primary goals and purposes which subregional agreements seek. Obviously, these goals and purposes are much more fully developed and precise when examined through the objectives and mechanisms of the Cartagena Agreement. 13/ The Agreement refers specifically to both of these in its Chapter I, which follows:

Chapter I: Objectives and Mechanisms

Article 1. The present Agreement has as its goals: to promote a balanced and harmonious

---

13. Decision 1 of the Commission created by the Subregional Integration Agreement designates the latter as the "Cartagena Agreement". Although it has not been officially sanctioned, the term "Andean Pact" is often used.

development of the member states, to accelerate this development through economic integration, to expedite their participation in the integration processes as stipulated in the Montevideo Treaty, and to create a climate favorable to the conversion of LAFTA into a common market, all of these designed to secure the progressive improvement of the living standards of the peoples of the subregion.

Article 2. A balanced and harmonious development must be conducive to an equitable distribution of the benefits resulting from integration of the member states by effecting a reduction of the existing discriminations that aggravate them. The achievements of the process should be periodically assessed, taking into account, among other factors, its effect on the expansion of global exports of each state, the conduct of its trade balance with respect to the subregion, the development of its gross territorial product, the generation of new employment, and its capital formation.

Article 3. To achieve the goals set by the present Agreement, the enumerated operations and measures shall be employed, inter alia:

a) Coordination of economic and social policies, and unification of domestic law in pertinent fields;

b) Joint programming, intensified subregional industrialization processes, and execution of Sectoral Programs of Industrial Development;

c) Greater acceleration in the trade liberalization program than that adopted generally within the LAFTA framework;

d) A common external tariff, attained by progressive stages through a minimum common external tariff;

e) Programs directed toward stimulation of development in the agricultural and livestock sector;

14

f) Channelling of resources from inside and outside the subregion to provide investment financing necessary to the integration process;

g) Physical integration; and

h) Preferential treatment to be accorded to Bolivia and Ecuador.

Article 4. For the better achievement of the present Agreement, the member states shall undertake the necessary efforts to seek adequate solutions for the problems arising from the land encirclement of Bolivia.

Articles 1 and 2 are excessively explicit. They essentially deal with the promotion of balanced and harmonious development of member states which will lead to an equalized distribution of the benefits of integration so as to attenuate the existing differences between them, to accelerate the development or growth of all countries by means of economic integration, and to contribute to the effort to convert LAFTA into a common market. These major objectives, through which a higher standard of living for the inhabitants of the Subregion is sought will be attained through the methods and mechanisms enumerated in the other two articles transcribed above and explained below.

3. Coordination of Economic Policy and Development Planning (Ch. III); Industrial Programming (Ch. IV)

As for the methods and mechanisms referred to in Article 3 a) above, Chapter III of the Cartagena Agreement contains the stipulations corresponding to the "coordination of economic policy and development planning". In this respect the strategy for development of the Subregion begins to crystallize with the following fundamental goals:

a) Acceleration of the economic development of the Member States on an equitable basis;

b) Increased generation of employment opportunities;

c)   Improvement in the position of Member States
     and of the Subregion as a unit in matters of for-
     eign trade and balance of payments;

d)   Overcoming of infrastructure problems which
     are presently hindering economic development;

e)   Reduction in the existing discrimination of
     development levels among the Member States;
     and

f)   Achieving a maximum utilization of scientific
     and technological progress, and activation of re-
     search in these fields.

The above commitment is strengthened and supplemented by another one to undertake at once a coordinated
procedure in national development planning in specific
sectors as well as by harmonizing their economic and social policies, with the objective of achieving a concerted
planning system for integrated development of the area.
These processes will be employed simultaneously and in
coordination with the formation of the subregional market,
through the following machinery, inter alia:

a)   A system of industrial programming;

b)   A special system for the agricultural-livestock
     sector;

c)   Plans for physical and social infrastructure;

d)   Coordination of exchange, monetary, financial
     and fiscal policies, whether use of subregional
     capital is to be made within or outside of the
     area;

e)   A common trade policy with respect to third
     countries; and

f)   Harmonization of planning methods and tech-
     niques.

In order to bring about the coordination and harmonization described in Article 26, the Commission, at the proposal of the Board, and at the latest by December 31, 1970, should establish the necessary permanent procedures and machinery (Article 29). 14/

The next provision of the Agreement, in Chapter III, deals with the "common system for treatment of foreign capital and, among others, on trademarks, patents, licenses and royalties", which the Commission, at the proposal of the Board, was to approve and submit to the consideration of the member states   before December 31, 1970. These countries committed themselves to adopting the necessary provisions to implement this system within six months after its approval by the Commission (Art. 27). The latter complied with its mandate through the well-known Decision 24, adopted in December 1970. 15/ The member

---

14. The Commission established these mechanisms and procedures in December 1970, by means of Decision 22, whose Article 5 was amended by Decision 53, adopted in August 1972, and other decisions which are examined in section 3 of Chapter III.

15. The Commission made certain adjustments to Decision 24 in its Decisions 37 and 37-A, adopted in June and July 1971, respectively; and later   additions   were made in Decision 70, adopted because of Venezuela's adherence to the Agreement. As indicated below, more recently new and important changes have been introduced to Decision 24. Moreover, the Commission has adopted various decisions complementing Decision 24. Decision 40, adopted in November 1971 which approved the agreement to avoid double taxation between Member States and States outside the subregion, both provided in Art. 47 of Decision 24. Decision 47, adopted in December 1971 on the minimum percentage of state or mixed enterprise participation referred to in Article 36 of Decision 24. Decision 48, adopted in December 1971, established norms applicable to investments made by the Andean Development Corporation in any Member State, in conformity with Art. 1 of the Transitory Provisions of Decision 24. Decision 84, adopted in June 1974, established the bases for a subregional technological policy. Decision 85, adopted in the same month and year, approved the Regulation for application of norms governing industrial property.

countries in turn successively adopted the provisions of
Article 27. 16/

One of the members of the Board of the Cartagena
Agreement has summarized the central elements of Andean
policy in the matter of private foreign investments and,
therefore, of the common system in the following terms:
(a) creation of a reporting system on capital flows and technology transfers; (b) use of selective criteria in evaluating
investment decisions; (c) establishment of a reasonable
system for promoting and protecting national enterprises;
(d) nonacceptance of legal clauses or provisions limiting
national sovereignty in the resolution of conflicts with investors and opposition to the establishment of international
obligations in connection therewith; (e) gradual transformation of the foreign enterprise into one with national participation and, finally national control; (f) adaptation of legislation on industrial property to the needs of developing
countries and elimination of restrictive practices of a mo-
nopolistic or oligopolistic nature which are often tied to a
foreign investment or to the marketing of patented technology; and (g) creation of economic conditions and institutions
propitious to the organization of regional enterprises and
to the realization of a joint effort in the technological field.
It is essentially a matter of favoring community business
undertakings according to the statute of the Andean multinational enterprises (Decision 46) whose purpose is to encourage the organization of vigorous regional enterprises,
as well as to structure a joint effort in the program of
technological development. 17/

---

16. For the national instruments complementing these
provisions of Art. 27 of the Agreement, see infra, subsection 3, a) of Chapter V.
    17. Cf. Germánico Salgado: "El Grupo Andino y la In-
versión Extranjera" in Comercio Exterior, México, February 1973, p. 157. A great deal has been written on the
Common Regime. Among others, see Furnish, D.B., "The
Andean Common Market's Common Regime for Foreign Investments", in Vanderbilt Journal of Transnational Law
(1972), vol. 2, p. 313; Oliver C., "The Andean Foreign Investment Code" in American Journal of International Law,
1972, vol. 66, p. 763; Mauricio Guerrero, "El Régimen

In the course of the Sixteenth Special Session of the Commission, the Representative of Chile reiterated his opinion that Decision 24 should be revised for the purpose of eliminating certain rigidities which it noted, especially in three points, to wit: (a) the limit in the transfer of profits set forth in Article 37; (b) the period of time and conditions for transformation of the foreign enterprise into a mixed enterprise; and (c) the prohibition from admiting foreign capital for acquiring shares owned by national investors. With respect to the first of these matters, the observation was made that Article 37 admits exceptions to the general rule, and it was added that this problem could be considered in the Regulations that were being prepared. 17-a/

During the Twentieth Regular Session the Commission adopted Decision 103, which contains important changes in

---

17 (cont.). Común de la Inversión Extranjera en el Grupo Andino", in INTAL, La Dimensión Jurídica de la Integración (América Latina), 1973, p. 222.

17-a. Cf. Acta Final del Decimosexto Período de Sesiones Extraordinarias, Feb. 28-March 3, March 30 and April 6-9, 1976, p. 7. See also the position of Chile in Appendix IV. Venezuela expressed its willingness to analyze constructively the request of Chile that it be authorized, within the rights and obligations contracted in the juridical framework of the Cartagena Agreement, to establish a regime whereby it would be excepted from applying Decision 24 to direct foreign investments. In this connection, Venezuela considered that the Working Group of the Commission should examine, in addition to the questions posed in that request, the specific conditions under which Chile would obtain such authorization, the treatment given to subregional capital, the treatment given to Latin American capital and the capitalization of resources of international financial institutions that lend their assistance to the integration efforts of the developing countries. Bolivia, Chile and Ecuador adhered to this statement and expressed their feeling that the authority that could be granted should not be restricted to Chile but extended to the Member States. Ibid., pp. 10-11.

the Common Regime of Treatment of Foreign Capital. 17-b/
The Commission of the Agreement met again at the end of
November and held its Twenty-first Regular Session, among
whose agreements and decisions arose Decision 109, by
which the Commission introduced new changes in the Common Regime. This same meeting also adopted Decision 110,
relating to the investments of the mixed enterprise (Art. 52
of Decision 24). In this connection, the Commission agreed
to examine the treatment which would be granted to such
investments.

In Article 28 the Agreement contemplates the uniform
regime to which multinational enterprises shall be subject,
which the Commission, at the proposal of the Board, had to
approve and propose to the member countries before December 31, 1971. During the same month and year, the
Commission approved the "Uniform regime on multinational
enterprises and regulations of the treatment applicable to
subregional capital" (Decision 46). Regarding this decision,
it has also been observed that it establishes a special legal
and economic regime, reserved for multinational enterprises under subregional control which differs in essence
from the one established by Decision 24 for enterprises
under the control of foreign investors. This distinction is
important because current economic and political literature
refers to foreign enterprises as multinational. 18/

Within the same period ending December 31, 1971,
and also at the proposal of the Board, the Commission was
to approve directives which would serve as a basis for the

17-b. The changes introduced by Decision 103 and
109 are incorporated in the "codified text" of Decision 24
reproduced in the Appendices.

18., Cf. Gustavo Fernández Saavedra, "El Régimen
Uniforme de la Empresa Multinacional en el Grupo Andino",
INTAL, Derecho de la Integración, October 1972, No. 11,
p. 23. See also Manuel J. Cárdenas Z. "La Empresa Mul-
tinacional dentro del Acuerdo de Cartagena", Revista de la
Cámara de Comercio de Bogotá (1973), No. 77, p. 133.

coordination of laws governing industrial development in these countries. Within the said period the Commission approved the "Directives for the harmonization of legislation on industrial development" (Decision 49). In a third paragraph, the same article deals with these countries' commitment to adopt measures to implement the uniform system and the directives with six months of their approval by the Commission. 19/

In Chapter III of the Agreement a further task is assigned to the Commission and the Board: at the latter's proposal, the Commission was to agree on a program of coordination of instruments and machinery regulating the foreign commerce of member states which they would implement before December 31, 1972. Matters relating to the common external tariff are exempt from this program, which is governed by the provisions of Chapter IV (Art. 30). In the fulfillment of this mandate the Commission first adopted Decision 31 in March 1971, entrusting the Board with developing a proposal for adopting the common tariff nomenclature of the member states (NABANDINA), which should be based on the Brussels Tariff Nomenclature. Second, the Commission adopted Decision 51, approving NABANDINA, which is contained in the Annex of that Decision. 20/ Chapter III of the Agreement concludes with a stipulation that reiterates the member states commitment relating to the measures necessary to ensure the fulfillment of the above articles of that chapter, except that the commitment now consists specifically of taking such measures in connection with national development planning and the formulation of economic policy (Art. 31).

The methods and mechanics provided in Article 3 b) transcribed above are provided for in Chapter IV (Industrial

---

19. With respect to Decision 46, six of the member states have taken the steps cited here, as indicated in subsection 3, a) of Chapter V. However, none has taken the same steps with respect to Decision 49.

20. Starting in September of the same year the Commission introduced amendments and clarifications to this Annex (Decision 58 and 75).

Programming) of the Cartagena Agreement. In the first article the Member States pledge themselves to undertake a process of industrial development of the subregion through joint programming to achieve the following goals, among others: (a) greater expansion, specialization and diversification of industrial production; (b) maximum utilization of available resources of the area; (c) stimulation of greater productivity and more efficient utilization of production factors; (d) utilization of large industry; and (e) equitable distribution of benefits (Art. 32). For the above enumerated goals, the Commission, at the proposal of the Board, must approve Sectoral Programs of Industrial Development, to be jointly implemented by the Member States (Art. 33).

The following article indicates the aspects and matters in which these sectoral programs must contain clauses. To this date, the Commission has approved only the Sectoral Program of Industrial Development of the Metalworking Sector which is treated in the Annex of Decision 57, with the amendments introduced by Decision 57 a, adopted in July and September 1972 respectively, and the Sectoral Development Program of the Petrochemical Industry, which is treated in Decision 91 and its Annexes. The remaining articles of Chapter IV confer upon the Commission and the Board certain functions and powers to ensure the implementation of industrial programming, including those recommending the establishment of multinational enterprises for the installation, expansion or complementarity of specific industries (Art. 38) and also give the Commission powers to maintain adequate coordination with the Andean Development Corporation and to negotiate the collaboration of any other national and international institutions whose financial and technical contributions may be deemed desirable for the goals of planning and industrial development of the subregion (Art. 40). 20-a/

With respect to the industrial programming considered in the Cartagena Agreement, a member of the Board

_____

20-a. See in the Appendices the changes introduced to the mechanism of industrial programming by the Lima Protocol, to which reference is made in note 12-a.

has pointed out that the difference in the level of development of the participating countries are well known, principally in the industrial sector, that the size of national markets limits the possibilities of advancing in the process of substituting imports and taking advantage of technological progress, and that, above all, experience shows that eliminating trade barriers as the only instrument of integration can lead to the placement of investments in a position adverse to balanced development among participating countries. For these reasons, a series of mechanisms have been designed to direct the industrialization process through joint investment programming, specialization and location of plant so as to best serve the interests of the countries and the Subregion as a whole. The Sectoral Programs of Industrial Development occupy a predominant place within those mechanisms. They attempt to rationalize production in the most dynamic industrial sectors through collective agreements governing the products included in each program, through existing specialization practices, through coordination of investments and the methods needed to ensure their financing. Such programs will be implemented jointly by all member states in such way that the entire subregional market will be available for production as scheduled and a fair distribution of the net benefits of the system will be obtained. Each program will include regulations for the elimination of taxes and for the application of the Common External Tariff to the products covered. 21/

The role played by industrial programming in the process of Andean economic integration can be illustrated by the ideas expressed by another member of the Board of

———————

21. Cf. F. Salazar Santos, "Una Visión General del Grupo Andino", presented to the Jornadas Hispano-Andinas, Madrid, June 1973, published in doc. J/VE/6, May 23, 1973, pp. 14-15. For information of the contents and operation of this mechanism of the Cartagena Agreement, see also Mauricio Guerrero, "La programación conjunta del desarrollo industrial subregional y el primer programa sectorial de la industria metal mecánica", en INTAL, Derecho de la Integración, March 1973, No. 12, p. 33.

the Cartagena Agreement, who asserts that the existence of integrated industrial planning, based on community goals, with the ability to direct the exploitation of new production scales and counteract trends toward concentration resulting from market forces is a decisive element in the operation of formulas for the integration of developing countries. In his opinion, the first of three conditions that must be met by integrated industrial planning is that such planning "must be in keeping with community goals and must be a community initiative. A simple transaction based on general or sectoral development plans does not satisfy that requirement due to the lack of the proper framework of community interests, which are, in short, the rapid and coordinated development of each and every one of the countries within the community. Community initiative does not constitute supranationality, since it cannot impose on national governments; it represents only the consideration in the negotiations of an overall view, which must always be borne in mind in any integration under-taken. The fulfillment of this condition demands the presence of community entities with defined powers of initiative and proposal, even in the field of planning". 22/ Thus, he em-phasizes not only that the industrial programing stipulated in the Cartagena Agreement is a decisive element in the process of subregional integration as it concerns developing countries, but also the necessity that there be--as in the Andean scheme--community goals, initiative and organs.

4. Liberalization Program (Ch. V) and Common
   External Tariff (Ch. VI)

The program of trade liberalization provided in Arti-cle 3 c) of the Cartagena Agreement is regulated in detail in Chapter V ("Liberalization Program"). It deals in fact with the matter most thoroughly regulated in the Andean Pact, regarding which the mandates to the two subregional organs are numerous and important. First of all, the

---

22. Cf. Germánico Salgado, "The Economic Integra-tion of the Developing Countries and the Role of a Joint In-dustrial Programing" in Journal of Development Planning (United Nations), 1975, No. 8.

Liberalization Program has as its goals the elimination of charges and restraints of all kinds encumbering the importation of goods originating in the territory of the member states (Art. 41). The following article defines "charges" as custom duties and any other charges of equivalent effect, whether fiscal, monetary or exchange, that are imposed on imports, and "restraints of all kinds" as any measure of administrative, fiscal or exchange character, imposed by unilateral decision of a member state, which impedes or hinders importation, and exempts from this concept those situations covered in Article 53 of the Montevideo Treaty. (Art. 42). 23/

The Board is authorized to determine at its own initiative or upon request of a party, when necessary, whether a measure constitutes a "charge" or a "restraint" (Art. 43). As of the present time no occasion has arisen for the Board

---

23. In order to understand fully the scope of Article 42 of the Cartagena Agreement, Article 53 of the Montevideo Treaty is transcribed below:

No provision of the present Treaty shall be so construed as to constitute an impediment to the adoption and execution of measures relating to: (a) the protection of public morality; (b) the application of security laws and regulations; (c) the control of imports or exports of arms, ammunition, and other war equipment and, in exceptional circumstances, of all other military items, in so far as this is compatible with the terms of Article 51 and of the treaties on the unrestricted freedom of transit in force among the contracting parties; (d) the protection of human, animal and plant life and health; (e) imports and exports of gold and silver bullion; (f) the protection of the nation's heritage of artistic, historical, and archaeological value; and (g) the export, use, and consumption of nuclear materials, radioactive products or any other material that may be used in the development of exploitation of nuclear energy.

to decide on this matter. 24/ Surely the crucial aspect of
the Andean Liberalization Program is rooted in its "automatic and irrevocable" character and in that it "governs
the entire realm of products to achieve its complete liberalization by no later than December 31, 1980;"the Program
will be applied, by use of its different methods, to different
categories or types of products specifically mentioned (Art.
45). Moreover, restraint of all kinds must be eliminated
by December 31, 1970, except those applying to goods reserved to the Sectoral Programs of Industrial Development,
which restraints will be eliminated whenever liberalization
is effected pursuant to the respective program, or to the
provisions of Article 53. Bolivia and Ecuador are not required to eliminate restraints of all kinds until they initiate
compliance with the Liberalization Program for each
product (Art. 46).

No later than December 31, 1970, the Commission,
at the proposal of the Board, was to prescribe what products
were to be reserved for the Sectoral Programs of Industrial
Development provided for in above-mentioned Article 45,
and prior to December 31, 1973, it was to approve the
Sectoral Programs related to the reserved products (Art.
47). As indicated above, up to the present time the Commission has only approved programs involving the metalworking sector (Decisions 57 and 57-a) and the petrochemical
sector (Decision 91). 24-a/ Previously, in December of

---

24. In conformity with Article 44 of the Agreement,
on the matter of taxes, rates and other internal duties and
charges this provision from Article 21 of the Montevideo
Treaty applies: "With respect to taxes, rates and other
internal duties and charges, products originating in the
territory of a contracting party shall enjoy in the territory
of another contracting party, treatment no less favorable
than that accorded to similar national products".
24-a. The period contemplated in Article 47 of the
Agreement, as well as in other provisions relative to industrial programming, has been extended to three years by the
Lima Protocol. On this and other amendments to the original
Agreement see the pertinent provisions of the Protocol, the
text of which is reproduced in the Appendices. In this connect

1970, the Commission had approved the list of products reserved for Sectoral Programs of Industrial Development (Decision 25, Annex). By means of Decision 59, adopted in September 1972, the Commission substituted the Annex of Decision 25 with another in which the list of these products was expressed in terms of NABANDINA.

The LAFTA program provides that goods included in the first stage of the Common Schedule described in Article 4 of the Montevideo Treaty will be liberated from all charges and restraints within 180 days following the date that the Cartagena Agreement becomes effective, and prior to December 31, 1971 the Commission, at the proposal of the Board, will establish the Liberalization Program to be applicable to goods included in the remaining stages of the Common Schedule. (Art. 49). 25/ The lack of action on the part of the Commission with respect to this mandate is due to the fact that the LAFTA Common Schedule did not include additional stages to the first one.

As for goods not produced in any country of the Subregion, nor reserved for Sectoral Programs of Industrial Development, prior to December 31, 1970, the Commission, at the proposal of the Board, was to prepare a schedule and select those which would be reserved to be produced in Bolivia and Ecuador, establishing, with respect to these latter two, the conditions and duration of the reservation (Art. 50). In fulfillment of this mandate, in December 1970 the Commission approved, first, the schedule which

---

24-a. (Cont.) reference should also be made to Decision 105, by which the Commission established a procedure for consideration of the proposals of industrial development (of the Board), consistent with the new periods fixed by the Lima Protocol.

25. The Common Schedule prescribed in Article 4 of the Montevideo Treaty is that which contains products whose duties, charges and other restrictions have been agreed upon collectively by contracting parties to be eliminated completely within the period mentioned in Article 2 (12 years), fulfilling the minimum percentages and the process of gradual reduction established in the provisions of the Treaty (Arts. 7 and 5, respectively).

appears in the Annex of its Decision 26, 26/ and later the one in Annexes I and II of its Decision 28, which is a schedule of products reserved for production in Bolivia and Ecuador; this schedule is expressed in terms of NABANDINA in Decision 62.

Article 52 of the Agreement establishes the means by which goods not included in Articles 47, 49 and 50 will be liberated from charges, and Article 53 establishes the means to carry out the Liberalization Program of those goods which had been selected for Sectoral Programs of Industrial Development but were not included in them within the time period of Article 47. Acting in conformity with the last paragraph of Article 53, the Board adopted Resolutions 5, 7, 11, 11-a and 17 which refer to the case of goods, which had been reserved for Sectoral Programs but were not included in them, applying the corresponding liberalization procedures. In relation to Article 52 the Commission, this time acting with a mandate implicit in this article, approved the initial points of liberalization in October 1970 (Decision 15, Annex) 27/ and also approved in December of the same year the schedule of goods not included in Articles 47, 49 and 50 of the Agreement for the treatment provided by for them in Article 52 referred to above (Decision 27, Annex). 28/

26. The Annex of Decision 26 was replaced by the one in Decision 60, adopted in September 1972, in which the list of these products is expressed in terms of NABANDINA.

27. By means of Decision 23, adopted in December of the same year, the Commission approved the document of the Board which contained the points of departure for the tariff elimination regime expressed in terms of NABALAC, in accordance with the charges approved in the Annex to Decision 15.

28. The Commission adjusted Decision 27 in July 1971 by means of Decision 38, and again in November of the same year by means of Decision 41. Later, the Commission replaced the Annex to Decision 27, with the one in Decision 61, adopted in September 1972, in which the list of these products is expressed in terms of NABANDINA.

The following three articles contain other substantive stipulations. Through them member states will abstain from altering the level of charges and from introducing new restraints of any kind on imported goods originating in the Subregion, which result in a less advantageous situation that the one in existence at the time of the acceptance date of the Agreement, save for the exceptions specifically indicated. (Art. 54).

Up to December 31, 1970, each member states could present to the Board a schedule of goods currently being produced in the Subregion as exceptions to the Liberalization Program and the procedures for establishing an external tariff. The exception schedules may not include products listed in the Common Schedule (Art. 55). The incorporation of a product on the schedule of exceptions of a member state prevents it from enjoying the advantages granted to the product by the Agreement. However, a member state may withdraw products from its schedule of exceptions at any time, in which case it must immediately adjust them to the Liberalization Program and the External Tariff in force for such products. In duly qualified cases, the Board may authorize a member states to incorporate on its schedule of exceptions products which, although having been reserved for Sectoral Programs, had not been so programmed (Art. 56).

The inclusion of products on exception schedules does not affect exported products originating in Bolivia or Ecuador which have been the object of substantial trade between the respective country and Bolivia or Ecuador during the preceding three years, or which appear to be of imminent commercial importance. The same applies in the future to those products originating in Bolivia or Ecuador which were included on any member states schedule of exceptions and with respect to which arise certain or immediate prospects for exportation from Bolivia or Ecuador to the country which had made them an exception from the reciprocal liberalization program. The Board is responsible for determining when significant trade has existed or whether there is a definite prospect for it (Art. 58). The Board exercised this power when requested to do so by the Government of Ecuador (Resolution 44, May 6, 1975).

The Andean Pact governs complementary agreements by stipulating that member states shall endeavor to conclude them with other contracting parties of LAFTA in those sectors of production susceptible to complementation, in conformity with the Montevideo Treaty and the respective Resolutions (Art. 59). 29/ Chapter V concludes with the following general provision, perfectly explainable as shall be seen shortly: 30/ "The commitments adopted under the Montevideo Treaty in compliance with the LAFTA Liberalization Program shall prevail over the provisions of the present chapter to the extent that the former may be more advanced than the latter." (Art. 60).

As a recapitulation, the various features of the Andean Liberalization Program are the following: (a) the regulations established in the Sectoral Programs for Industrial Development will apply to the products included in the same program; (b) those products already included in the LAFTA common schedule were totally liberated by April 1970, 180 days after the entry in force of the Agreement; (c) those goods not produced in any of the subregional countries will be freely traded starting February 28, 1971, after a reservation has been made for Bolivia and Ecuador and with those methods provided in Articles 50 and 51, and (d) all other products are subject to annual successive reduction of 10%, the first of which occurred in December 31, 1971, starting at the lowest extent level for each product in the external tariff of Colombia, Chile, and Peru or on their national schedules on May 26, 1969,

_____

29. The Montevideo Treaty regulates the complementary agreements in its Article 17. The Conference of Contracting Parties regulates this Article by its Resolution 99 (IV). The Commission of the Cartagena Agreement adopted Decision 8 for the "Coordination of the Member States in view of the Complementary Agreements of LAFTA".

30. See infra, Section 3 of Chapter II.

the date of the signing of the Agreement. Restraints of all kinds other than charges were eliminated in December 31, 1970, with the exceptions provided by Article 46. A certain number of products are temporarily excepted from liberalization according to the rules established in Articles 55, 56, 57, 102 and 103, but all products without exception must be totally liberated from charges and other restraints within a pre-established period of time. 31/

The second mechanism covered under this section, "whose first step will be the adoption of a minimum common external tariff", as provided in Article 3 d) of the Andean Pact, is an essential medium for the adequate protection of subregional production and, along with the total liberalization of trade, an indispensable step towards creating a customs union in the Subregion. In the first provision of Chapter VI (Common External Tariff), member states pledge themselves to make the tariff fully operative by no later than December 31, 1980 (Art. 61). Prior to December 31, 1973 the Board was to have drafted a common external tariff schedule for consideration of the Commission for approval within two years. The same provision established December 31, 1976, as the date when member states were to begin a process toward adoption of the common tariff by reconciling the charges levied by their domestic tariffs on imports from outside the Subregion; on an annual automatic and parallel basis, and in such a manner as to make it fully operative by December 31, 1980 (Art. 62). 31-a/

---

31. Cf. op. cit., Note 21, p. 11. The different provisions of Decision 70 of the Commission, which contain the conditions for Venezuela's adherence to the Cartagena Agreement and the provisions of the additional instrument subscribed to in connection therewith, must be borne in mind when considering these characteristics of the Liberalization Program.

31-a. The already mentioned Lima Protocol also extends to three years the period contemplated in the Cartagena Agreement for approval of the Common External Tariff by the Commission. See Article 2 of the Protocol, the text of which is reproduced in the Appendices.

As for the Minimum Common External Tariff, the Cartagena Agreement also establishes procedures and time periods for its preparation, approval and application. Thus, prior to December 31, 1970, the Commission, at the proposal of the Board, was to approve the common tariff, and beginning December 31 of the following year the member states were to begin reconciling the charges levied on imports from outside the Subregion with those established in the Minimum Common External Tariff in those cases where the former are lower than the latter, and this procedure was to be effected on an annual, horizontal and automatic basis, enabling it to become fully operative by December 31, 1975 (Arts. 63 and 64). The Commission approved the tariff in December 1970 by Decision 30. 32/

The Agreement contains, moreover, some special rules, one of which applies to products subjected to the Sectoral Programs of Industrial Development, regulated by the provisions that these Programs establish concerning the common external tariff. Furthermore, when in compliance with the Liberalization Program a product becomes liberated from charges and other restraints, it is immediately and fully subject to the charges established in the Minimum Common External Tariff or the Common External Tariff, as the case may be. 33/ In the case of products not produced in the Subregion, each country may defer the application of common charges until the Board verifies that production has begun in the Subregion. However, if in the judgment of the Board the new production is

---

32. The Commission amended Article 2 of Decision 30 by Decision 33, adopted in March 1971. By means of its Decision 104, the Commission replaced the charges of the Common Minimum External Tariff indicated in Decisions 30, 64, 79 and 81 by those indicated in the Appendix of that Decision 104.

33. To achieve the ends of the last provision, prior to the above-mentioned Decision 30 the Commission adopted the Minimum Common External Tariff for products in the first section of the Common Schedule, by means of Decision 12, adopted in June 1970.

not sufficient to satisfy normal demand in the Subregion,
it will propose to the Commission the methods necessary
to balance the need for protection of the subregional product with the need to insure a normal supply (Art. 65).   In
applying this article of the Agreement, as well as Article
12 of Decision 70 by means of Resolution 42 of April 1975,
the Commission included new commodities on the schedule
of products not produced in the Subregion.

The remaining articles of this chapter of the Agreement confer new and important powers and functions on the
two subregional organs. Thus, the Commission, at the
proposal of the Board, may modify common tariff levels
when it deems such action suitable, in order to satisfy the
needs of the Subregion as well as to consider the special
status of Bolivia and Ecuador, or even to adjust these levels to those fixed in LAFTA's Common External Tariff
(Art. 66). The Board may also propose to the Commission
any measures it considers necessary to achieve normal
conditions and take other action by itself or by soliciting
the help of the Commission. To cover temporary short-
ages affecting it, any member state   may raise this question with the Board, which will verify the situation within
a reasonable period of time depending on the urgency of
the case. Once the Board acknowledges the existence of
the problem and so informs the affected country, the latter
may take such steps as a provisional reduction or suspension of the charges of the External Tariff, within the limits
necessary to correct the problem (Art. 67). 34/ In the

---

34.   The Board has taken the opportunity to adopt
various resolutions for the application of the second part
of Article 67, enumerated below: Resolution 3 (April 1972);
Resolution 4 (June 1972); Resolution 6 (September 1972);
Resolution 8 (March 1973); Resolution 12 (July 1973); Resolution 13 (August 1973); Resolution 14 (October 1973);
Resolution 15 (December 1973); Resolution 19 (February
1974), extending the provisions of Resolution 15; Resolution
21 (February 1974); Resolution 22 (February 1974); etc.
Up to the present, the latest applications of Article 67 of
the Cartagena Agreement are Resolution 47 (June 1975),
Resolution 53 (September 1975) and Resolution 54 (October
1975).

following and final article the member states pledge themselves to refrain from unilaterally altering any charges established during the various stages of the External Tariff, and they promise to enter into necessary consultations with the Commission before concluding tariff agreements with countries outside the subregion. Furthermore, they agree to coordinate the agreements under this chapter with their commitments under the Montevideo Treaty.

Accordingly, the Common External Tariff will also cover all products and will be adopted gradually and automatically, so as to be in full force within the same time period provided for the fulfillment of the Liberalization Program. The Cartagena Agreement establishes a methodology for the adoption of said tariff and for its administration with the flexibility necessary to adjust the common charges to changes in production conditions to the special conditions of Bolivia and Ecuador, and to emergency situations that may arise due to deficiencies in subregional supplies. The Common External Tariff will be the instrument par excellence of subregional trade policy and therefore, no member state may unilaterally alter the charges established in its varous stages. As an intermediate mechanism for facilitating the adoption of the tariff and progressively creating a subregional margin of preference and for establishing adequate protection of subregional production, the so-called Minimum Common External Tariff affords uniform minimum protection over such production. 35/

5. Other Objectives and Mechanisms of the Agreement

Once those objectives and mechanisms that, up to a certain point, are considered to be the outstanding ones of

35. Cf. op. cit. in note 21. The above cited Decision 70 also contains provisions related to Venezuela's compliance with the Minimum Common External Tariff; the Additional Instrument subscribed to explicitly for in connection with Venezuela's adherence to the Cartagena Agreement also contains provisions related to this mechanism.

the Cartagena Agreement have been explained, it is perhaps sufficient to describe the rest of them only generally.
Moreover, in examining the competencies and powers of
the subregional institutions and the nature and validity of
their acts there will surely be an opportunity to become
acquainted with other provisions or aspects of the Agreement related to these other objectives and mechanisms.

a) Measures on agriculture and livestock (Ch. VII)

This system is based on the pledge of member states
to harmonize their national policies and to coordinate
their plans for agro-livestock development with the objective of adopting a common policy for this sector. This
pledge proposes, among other things, to raise the standard
of living of the rural population, increase production and
productivity, substitute subregional imports, and diversify
and increase exports (Art. 69). To achieve these goals or
objectives subregional organs must take certain measures
(Art. 70) 36/ and, in particular, both the Commission and
the Board are entrusted to negotiate the measures necessary to accelerate the agro-livestock development of Bolivia and Ecuador and increase their participation in the expanded market (Art. 71). Along another line of thinking,
the Agreement provides for saving clauses to protect the
agro-livestock sector subject to Article 28 of the Montevideo Treaty, 37/ the resolutions complementing it, and the

---

36. Through Decision 43, adopted in December 1971,
the Commission approved the first measures for increasing
trade in agro-livestock products. Further, in Decision 66,
adopted in December 1972, it substituted the Annex of Decision 16 in order to express it in terms of NABANDINA.
At more recent date, in applying the same Article 70, the
Andean System of Agro-Livestock Health was created by
Decision 92. By its Decision 106, the Commission extended to February 25, 1977, the periods referred to in
Articles 21 and 25 of Decision 92.

37. This article of the Treaty reads as follows:
"Providing that no lowering of its customary consumption
or increase in antieconomic products is involved, a contracting party may apply, within the period mentioned in

future provisions amending or replacing them (Art. 72). The following articles, the last two of the chapter, establish the procedure to be followed before the subregional organs, as well as their powers with respect to the saving clauses (Art. 73), and provide that the Commission, at the proposal of the Board, shall, prior to December 31, 1970, prepare the list of agro-livestock products for purpose of the application of Articles 72 and 73 (Art. 73). 38/

b) Competitive commercial practices (Ch. VIII)

The Cartagena Agreement governs this matter by first providing that the Commission, at the proposal of the Board, shall, prior to December 31, 1971, adopt the rules essential to forestall or to remedy any unfair business practices within the Subregion such as dumping, undue price manipulation, maneuvers intended to impede normal supply of raw materials, and others of similar effect. The Board is entrusted with surveillance over the application of these rules in any particular cases of complaint for purpose it must bear in mind the need to coordinate these measures with the provisions of Resolution 65 (II) of the Conference of Contracting Parties of LAFTA and those which complement or amend them (Art. 75). Until the Commission adopts the above-mentioned regulations, the

---

37 Cont. ...Article 2, and in respect of trade in agricultural commodities of substantial importance of its economy that are included in the liberalization program, appropriate nondiscriminatory measures designed to: (a) limit imports to the amount required to meet the deficit in internal production; and (b) equalize the prices of the imported and domestic product. The contracting party which decides to apply these measures shall inform the other contracting parties before it puts them into effect".

38. By Decision 16, adopted in October 1970, the Commission approved the list of agro-livestock products. Finally, Decision 93 was approved, in application of the entire Chapter VII; it created a Central Office of Commercial Information on Agro-Livestock Products.

Board will apply Resolution 65 of LAFTA at the request of
the affected country (Art. 76). 39/ Finally, member
states may not adopt corrective measures without prior
authorization from the Board. The same article charges
the Commission with the issuance of procedural rules for
the application of the rules of this chapter of the Agreement
(Art. 77).

    c)   <u>Saving Clauses (Ch. IX)</u>

    The Cartagena Agreement authorizes each member
state that should find itself in the circumstances described in Chapter VI (Saving Clauses) of the Montevideo
Treaty, caused by factors external to the Liberalization
Program of the Agreement, to invoke safeguards consonant
with that chapter and the pertinent resolutions (Art. 78).
However, when the imposition of this subregional Liberalization Program causes or threatens to cause grave dam-
ages to the economy of a member state or a significant
sector of its economic activity, said country may, with
prior authorization of the Board, apply corrective measures in a nondiscriminatory manner. 40/ When necessary,
the Board may propose measures of collective coordination
to overcome prejudice that may have been caused (Art. 79).
In another provision the Agreement describes the action to
be taken when a monetary devaluation in one member states
alters normal competitive conditions (Art. 80). Other
articles prohibit the application of saving clauses of any

---

39. Decision 45, adopted in December 1971, approved
the "Regulations for preventing and correcting practices
that might interfere with competition within the Subregion".
In exercising the power provided in Article 75 of the Agreement and in accordance with the provisions of Decision 45,
the Board dismissed the application of the corrective measures referred to in Article 5 of that Decision which were requested by the Government of Peru (Resolution 59).

40. In Resolution 20, adopted in February 1974, the
Board declared that it could not accelerate Peru's request
for the application of saving clauses.

kind to the importation of products originating within the subregion included in Sectoral Programs for Industrial Development, as well as the application of Articles 79 and 80 of the Agreement to the importation of products originating in other LAFTA countries, when incorporated in the Liberalization Program of the Montevideo Treaty (Art. 81).

d) Origin (Ch. X)

This chapter of the Cartagena Agreement has not substantive provisions on the matter considered. It charges the Commission with the adoption, at the proposal of the Board, of any special measures necessary to classify the origin of merchandise (Art. 82). The Commission has not as yet adopted any such measures. The remaining provisions of the chapter define the roles of the two subregional organs in this matter. Thus, the Board is responsible for establishing specific requirements of origin for the products that will require it and also for determining when these requirements will be necessary on a Sectoral Program of Industrial Development. [41] Within the year following the fixing of specific requirements, member states may request a review by the Board, which must give its summary opinion. In this respect, the Board is also authorized to amend at any time these requirements on its own initiative or at the request of a party so as to adapt them to the technological and economic progress of the subregion. (Art. 83).

In adopting and establishing special norms or specific requirements, as the case may be, the Commission and the Board will make sure that these do not create obstacles to enjoyment by Bolivia and Ecuador of the advantages deriving from application of the Agreement (Art. 84). Finally,

---

41. In fulfillment of this mandate the Board, in April 1973, adopted Resolution 1, establishing specific requisites for origin of the products contained in the Annex of the same. In January 1974, in Resolution 18, and in October 1975, through Resolution 56, the Board established requirements of origin for other products included in the respective annexes of these other two resolutions.

the Board will supervise the compliance with these norms and requirements within subregional trade and must propose any measures necessary to solve problems of origin that hinder the achievement of the goals of the subregional agreement (Art. 85). 42/

e) Physical Integration (Ch. XI)

The first article in this chapter of the Andean Pact has no provisions as precise as those which member states have contracted in other matters. In this regard, said article limits itself to saying that they will undertake concerted action to solve infrastructural problems that unfavorably affect the process of economic integration of the subregion, and that this action will take place principally in the fields of energy, transportation and communications and will contain, in particular, the measures necessary to expedite border trade among the member states. Toward this end, these countries propose to establish multinational entities or enterprises, where feasible and desirable, to expedite the execution and administration of said projects (Art. 86). Nevertheless, prior to December 31, 1972, the Board was to draft initial programs in the fields mentioned, and present these for the consideration of the Commission, including the items indicated in the Pact (Art. 87). In particular, such programs and those for sectoral industrial development must contain measures for collective cooperation to satisfy the infrastructural requirements essential for their execution and give special consideration to the situation of Ecuador and the landlocked condition of Bolivia (Art. 88). 43/

---

42. In application of Articles 83, 84 and 85 the Board adopted, in March 1973, Resolution 9, acceding to a request of Ecuador, and later, in June and December 1973, respectively, Resolutions 10 and 16, both delaying the effects of the former. Later resolutions, Nos. 23 and 33 of June 1974 and January 1975 respectively, cover the same matter.

43. In compliance with this mandate, the Commission adopted, in August 1972, its Decision 56 which regulates in detail international highway transportation. Through its Decision 56-a, adopted in July 1973, it approved the forms prescribed in Article 46 of the previous resolution. In June

Obviously, the latter is closely related to the pledge contracted in Article 4 of the Agreement, transcribed at the
beginning of this section.

f) Financial matters (Ch. XII)

The Cartagena Agreement contains imprecise provisions in this area also. After indicating that member
states should coordinate their national policies in financial
and payment matters to the extent necessary to expedite
achievement of the goals of the Agreement, this chapter
provides that, to this end, the Board should present proposals to the Commission on certain matters, among them
the problems of double taxation, 44/ and, from the institutional point of view, the strengthening of the multilateral
clearing system of reciprocal balances in effect among the
Central Banks of LAFTA, to fulfill subregional commerce,
and the eventual creation of a Subregional Compensation
Payments Fund, and a system of reciprocal credits (Art.
89). The second and final article establishes that when a
member state encounters difficulties with its fiscal income
as a consequence of compliance with the Liberalization
Program of the Agreement, the Board may propose measures to remedy such problems to the Commission when requested by the affected state. In its proposals, the Board
will keep in mind the degree of economic development of
the member state (Art. 90).

6. Special Regime for Bolivia and Ecuador (Ch. XIII)

This special regime reflects the "preferential" treatment of Bolivia and Ecuador provided in Article 3 (h) of the
Cartagena Agreement transcribed at the beginning of this
section. The purpose of the regime is explained clearly
in the first article of this chapter: "In the progressive
elimination of the differences presently existing in the development of the Subregion, Bolivia and Ecuador shall

---

43 Cont. ... of the same year it created the Council
on Physical Integration (Decision 71).
44. In relation to this matter the Commission adopted
its Resolution 40, mentioned in note 15.

enjoy special treatment to permit them to achieve a more accelerated rate of economic development, through effective and immediate participation in the advantages of area industrialization and liberalization of trade. To achieve this aim, the organs of the Agreement shall propose and adopt the necessary measures, in conformity with its rules" (Art. 91). 45/

The Agreement continues in numerous and thorough provisions to define what comprises the preferential treatment that the two countries will receive according to the relevant mechanism or activity. Thus, the chapter is divided into the following sections: Section A - Harmonization of Economic Policies and Coordination of Development Planning; Section B - Industrial Policy; Section C - Commercial Policy, which is obviously the most detailed of them all; Section D - Common External Tariff; Section E - Financial Cooperation and Technical Assistance, and Section F - General Provisions. These last two must be quoted even though this was not done in the case of the corresponding ones of previous sections of the chapter. One of them states that in its periodic evaluations and annual reports the Board must give special and individual consideration to the status of Bolivia and Ecuador within the subregional integration processes, and propose to the Commission any

---

45. In subsequent articles of the chapter various functions and powers, as well as specific mandates, are conferred on subregional organs. In accord with the pertinent provisions, the Commission and the Board have adopted decisions and resolutions, according to the case, several of which have been cited above, relating to other mechanisms of the Agreement. It will suffice to mention these others: Decision 34, adopted in March 1971, which approved the margins of preference for products of special interest to Bolivia and Ecuador; Decision 65, adopted in September 1972, expressing those margins of preference in terms of the NABANDINA; Resolution 17, adopted in June 1974, excepting Bolivia and Ecuador from all restrictions relating to the importation of the products indicated in Annex I of the resolution.

measures deemed adequate to improve their development potentials substantially and to activate their participation progressively within the industrialization of the area (Art. 107). The second article states that wherever no provision is made in the Agreement as to special treatment for Bolivia and Ecuador, the principles and provisions of the Montevideo Treaty and the LAFTA Resolutions favoring the relatively less economically developed countries are to be considered as incorporated therein (Art. 108). It is needless to emphasize the importance of the supplementary role which these two provisions play with respect to those of the preceding section of Chapter XIII of the Agreement.

7. Other Aspects of the Subregional Integration Process

The process of Andean subregional integration is not limited to the objectives and mechanisms provided in the Cartagena Agreement. Far from it, this process has been extending itself to other areas, such as educational, scientific and cultural integration, cooperation in health, and socio-labor integration. Below is a summary description of the means by which such integration processes are being brought about.

As far as the first area referred to is concerned, the ministers of education of the Subregion signed the "Andrés Bello" Agreement on Education, Scientific and Cultural Integration of the Countries of the Andean Region on January 31, 1970. The Agreement proposes to accelerate the overall development of the countries by joining forces in education, science and culture with the intent that the benefits derived from this cultural integration will ensure the harmonious development of the region and the conscious participation of the people as activator and beneficiary of the process (Second Article). With this purpose and the other specific objectives combined in the third article in mind, the successive chapters of the Agreement consider concerted or unilateral actions to be taken to promote the knowledge and circulation of persons and cultural assets (Chapter II), to interchange experience and regional technical cooperation (Chapter III), to coordinate educational systems (Chapter IV) and concerted actions in other matters or subjects (Chapter

V). The Agreement establishes its own institutional structure whose main organ is the Meeting of Ministers of Education. Other organs or agencies charged with over-seeing the application and fulfillment of the Agreement are: Chiefs of Planning Board; the Coordination Office established by the Ministry of Education of the host country of the next Meeting of Ministers; the Mixed Commissions and the Ministries of Education. Chapter VI defines the respective integration, functions and powers. 46/

In the area of health, the Ministers of Health signed the "Hipólito Unanue" Agreement on Health Cooperation of the Andean Area. The purpose of this Agreement is to improve human health in these countries, for which coordinated action will be initiated to make the aims of the Agreement a reality (Art. 1). Signatory governments will give priority to the solution of the problems that affect area countries similarly; Article 2 enumerates many of these problems. Article 3 does the same with respect to the measures which the governments propose to take in order to achieve their ends; some of these measures are the individual responsibility of each government while others must be developed collectively; some involve research study and technical assistance while others require action directed toward the solution of specific problems such as the illicit use and traffic of addictive drugs. From the institutional point of view the Agreement contains one Meeting of Ministers of Health each year to study the problems mentioned and formulate programs, and a Coordinating Committee of the Agreement from the I Meeting of Ministers of Health of the Andean Area to act until definitive agencies are set up; the Committee will rely on a full-time secretariat until that time. 47/

---

46. The complete text of the Agreement appears in Historia Documental del Acuerdo de Cartagena, p. 537.

47. For the complete text of the Agreement, see ibid. p. 547. In the field of health cooperation there is a Health Council, created by the Commission of the Cartagena Agreement. See, in this connection, infra, section 3 of Chapter III.

With respect to the third area referred to above, the Ministers of Labor (and the Bolivian Ambassador to Venezuela as representative of Bolivia), signed the "Simón Rodríguez" Agreement on Socio-Labor Integration on October 26, 1973. The Agreement aims to adopt strategy and programs directing the activity of the subregional and national agencies so as to attain the objectives of the Cartagena Agreement leading to overall improvement in the standard of living and work conditions of the countries of the Andean Group (Art. 2). The only chapter on substantive matters considers "priority matters and immediate measures". The former includes harmonization of labor and social security legal rules and the establishment of a regime to facilitate the mobility of the labor force; the measure includes the adoption of basic regulations governing social security and protection of migrant workers (Chapter II). The organs charged with overseeing the implementation of the Agreement are: the Conference of Ministers of Labor; the Commission of Delegates; the Coordinating Secretariat, and other agencies with the Conference of Ministers--the supreme organ--may decide to create (Art. 5). The remaining provisions of Chapter III of the Agreement define the functions which each of these agencies will perform. 48/

---

48. For the complete text of the Agreement, see _ibid._, p. 552.

Chapter II

LINKAGE AND RELATIONSHIP WITH THE
LEGAL ORDER OF LAFTA

In the historical sketch of the Cartagena Agreement and the explanation of its objectives and mechanisms presented in the preceding chapter, the close linkage and relationship between the process of subregional integration and that of the Latin American Free Trade Association (LAFTA) became evident. This linkage and relationship clearly presents juridical and institutional aspects of fundamental interest to the present study.

1. The Question of "Compatibility"

Before continuing with the examination of the above-mentioned aspects in the following section, it would be well to begin this one by analyzing an aspect that relates more to a previous question of the "compatibility" of the Cartagena Agreement with LAFTA's basic agreement--the Montevideo Treaty--as well as "its protocols and other instruments which constitute the legal structure of the Association", in the words of the repeatedly mentioned Resolution 222 (VII). In spite of the formal acceptance, in principle, of the compatibility of subregional agreements, by virtue of the Declaration of Presidents and subsequent resolution of the competent organs of LAFTA, it is interesting to note the reasons why this question arose and the criteria or motives which contributed to its resolution.

Furthermore, with the declaration of the compatibility of the Cartagena Agreement (Resolution 179 of the Standing Executive Committee of the Association) the question has been resolved only with respect to the original organic instrument of the Andean integration. As will be seen, this is a question which can be raised in regard to any other future subregional agreements including certain aspects of the Andean Pact itself or the secondary legal order generated by it.

a) Statement of the problem; the most-favored-nation clause

As was indicated in a detailed study of the question, from a legal point of view the issue is "to know how to prevent the commitments assumed by a group of countries that sign an agreement for subregional integration from contravening the commitments assumed by those same countries in conjunction with countries that comprise the process of total integration." [1] Above all, it should also be noted that, in contrast to what occurs in regard to other agreements, the Montevideo Treaty does not provide for subregional agreements. The second group of commitments mentioned above alludes, in particular, to the most-favored-nation clause, stipulated in Article 18 of the Treaty in the following terms:

> Any advantage, benefit, franchise, immunity, or privilege applied by a contracting party in respect of a product originating in or intended for consignment to any other country shall be immediately and unconditionally extended to the similar product originating in or intended for consignment to the territory of the other contracting Parties.

How does one overcome, then, this evident (or in any case "apparent") "incompatibility" between the commitment contracted in the Montevideo Treaty by all the contracting parties and the one contracted by a group of them under the Cartagena Agreement, e.g., special tariff reductions which have not been extended to other members of LAFTA?

The study of Cárdenas and Peña quoted above discusses the various formulas that were tried, especially within LAFTA itself, with this purpose, such as the one calling for "unanimous renunciation" by the contracting parties of

---

1. Cf. Emilio Cárdenas and Félix Peña, "Los Acuerdos Subregionales y el Tratado de Montevideo", INTAL, Derecho de la Integración, No. 2, October 1968, p. 10.

46

the exercise of all rights deriving from the most-favored-nation clause, the one formalizing this renunciation through a protocol amending the Treaty, in accordance with Article 60 thereof, and the one concerning a "functional interpretation" of Article 18. 2/

The functional or teleological interpretation, which the above-mentioned authors favor, seems to have a solid basis in light of the Montevideo Treaty itself. For one thing, the clause referred to is not for absolute application in the context of the Treaty, since the Treaty authorizes exceptions in cases which expedite border trade (Art. 19) and in those involving concessions to countries with relatively less economic development (Art. 32, a). Moreover, an old Latin American doctrine is invoked which confirmed another exception, that is, the Bello Clause, in favor of adjoining nations, or, rather, nations within a region. 3/ From this order of ideas a "Latin American interpretation" of the clause is conceived, in contrast to the more rigid interpretations traditionally sustained by the United States and the European countries. It is maintained that such an interpretation is justified, furthermore, in view of the statements of objectives contained in the preamble of the Montevideo Treaty and in its Article 54. 4/

---

2. Ibid., pp. 15 - 16.

3. By virtue of the so-called Bello Clause the privileges granted by Latin American countries in their reciprocal trade would not be extended to third countries benefitting from the most-favored-nation clause. For an analysis of this clause, see F. Orrego Vicuña, "Estudio sobre la Cláusula Bello y la crisis de la solidaridad latinoamericana", América Latina y la Cláusula de la Nación más Favorecida, a book edited under the direction of the same author (Study Group of the Carnegie Endowment for International Peace), Santiago, Chile, 1972, pp. 33 et seq.

4. Article 54, more explicit in this regard than the preamble of the Treaty, states that "the contracting Parties shall make every effort to direct their policies with a view to creating conditions favorable to the establishment of a Latin American common market. To that end, the /Standing Executive/ Committee shall undertake studies and

Looking at the question from other perspectives, the thesis in favor of compatibility appears equally well-founded. For example, given the purpose of the clause (which is to "establish and maintain at all times among the interested nations a fundamental equality without discrimination"), one can maintain that the scope of its application in the Montevideo Treaty should relate to the various aspects of the Treaty's program for trade liberalization. And in fact, it is in connection with this program, contained in Chapter II of the Treaty, that consideration is given to the gradual elimination (Art. 2) of duties, charges and restrictions applied to imports of goods originating in the territory of any contracting party (Art. 3) which are brought about through legal negotiations (Art. 4), from which result National Schedules and a Common Schedule. This program is built on the cornerstone of the principle of reciprocity (Arts. 10 and 13) and in this regard, true reciprocity in actions is assured through the procedures provided to correct any disadvantages that might arise (Arts. 11 and 12). Therefore, because they are closely linked to the liberalization program of LAFTA, which they propose to further accelerate, the subregional integration agreements are bound to the principle of reciprocity. 5/

b) Analogy to the complementary economy
agreements

Another argument, from an even more convincing point of view than the preceeding one, lies in the analogy between the question of the compatibility of the subregional

---

4 (cont.) consider projects and plans designed to achieve this purpose, and shall endeavor to coordinate its work with that of other international organizations. "

5. Cf. loc. cit. in note 1, pp. 17-18. For a more detailed examination of this aspect of the question, see F. Peña, "La Claúsula de la Nación más Favorecida en el Sistema Jurídico de la Asociación Latinoamericana de Comercio", in ibid., No. 9, October 1971, pp. 17-18, and also in the work cited in note 3, pp. 191-193.

agreements and the question that has already been raised, also in regard to Article 18 of the Montevideo Treaty, about the complementary economies agreements referred to in paragraph b) of Article 16 of that instrument. 6/ Despite this provision of the Treaty, in Resolution 99 (IV) of the Conference of Contracting Parties the latter expressly agreed that those who did not participate in a complementary economies agreement should benefit only from the resulting liberalization by granting adequate compensation, that is, through duly insuring the principle of reciprocity, from which only the group of relatively less developed countries would be excluded. Certainly, if the automatic and rigorous application of the most-favored-nation clause were upheld, as had occurred in two earlier resolutions, all the member countries of LAFTA could enjoy the benefits derived from a complementary economies agreement. Therefore, one may conclude with complete logic that identical reasoning is possible regarding the applicability of the clause to the subregional agreements, since these are related to the program of trade liberalization thus complementing the minimum program provided for in the Montevideo Treaty. 7/

Elaborating on this last point, one should bear in mind the more general observation that has been made, to emphasize "the minimum character of all its commitments" (those of the Montevideo Treaty), which can be broadened to achieve the final objectives of a customs union and common market, according to the provisions of the Treaty itself... From the foregoing it may be concluded that subregional agreements constitute, with respect to the member states, a broadening of the commitments established

---

6. Article 16, paragraph b), reads as follows: "/The contracting Parties/ may negotiate mutual agreements on complementary economies by industrial sectors".

7. Loc. cit. in note 1, p. 18. For a more thorough consideration of the question of the compatibility of complementary economic agreements, including Resolutions 15 (i) and 16 (II) referred to above, see F. Peña, loc. cit. in note 5, pp. 12-14, and also in the book cited in note 3, pp. 180-183.

by LAFTA, bringing them closer to the indicated final objectives, always within the basic framework of the Montevideo Treaty, which in this case is further developed in a way applicable to that subregion. Since they constitute a special improvement of the structure of the Treaty, the compatibility of subregional agreements with that basic instrument has been recognized without reservation by the Council of Ministers of LAFTA. It is obvious that this situation was only made possible thanks to the 'treaty-framework' characteristics of the Montevideo Treaty. 8/ Concerning the "minimum character" attributed to the commitments established in the Treaty, it should be remembered that the first of the norms in Resolution 222 (VII), cited again below, which states, in defining the subregional agreements, that through them "LAFTA countries which suscribe to them will be able to promote the process of economic integration in a more balanced and accelerated form than that stemming from the commitments assumed within the framework of the Montevideo Treaty".

From another point of view, it has been said, also with complete justification, that, as occurred with the complementary economic agreements, "it would be unjust to have the benefits derived from the subregional agreement extended, by virtue of the unrestricted play of the most-favored-nation clause, to other members of LAFTA not participating in the subregional agreement and consequently not making any sacrifice as is required of the members of that agreement." 9/ This consideration explains the following norm of Resolution 222 (VII): "The stipulated (tariff) exemptions in a subregional agreement shall not be made extensive to the contracting parties who are nonparticipants in these subregional agreements, neither will they create for them any special liabilities." This, together with the previous considerations, has made it possible, having surmounted the difficulties and doubts

---

8. Inter-American Institute of International Legal Studies, Derecho de la Integración Latinoamericana, Ensayo de Sistematización (1969), p. 1045.
   9. Ibid., p. 1046.

that at first arose, for the thesis favoring compatibility to be accepted.

c) Conditions to which compatibility is subject to and those relative to amending the Agreement

The observation just made is confined, on the one hand, to the repeated and well-deserved acceptance of sub-regional agreements by the organs of LAFTA since the Declaration of Presidents on April 14, 1967, in the sense that these agreements are compatible in principle with the Montevideo Treaty and, on the other hand, to the declaration of compatibility issued by the Standing Executive Committee regarding the Cartagena Agreement itself. In other words, not all subregional agreements, by the mere fact of their identity as such, nor the legal order generated by the process of Andean integration will necessarily be compatible with the Treaty and the other instruments of the legal structure of LAFTA. 10/

Now, it is precisely because the case is not one of automatic and unconditional compatibility that the presence of both substantive requirements and procedural norms is noted in the regulations which the organs of LAFTA have placed on subregional agreements, and in the Cartagena Agreement itself. As will be remembered, these regulations are contained, specifically, in Resolution 222 (VII)--"Norms of Subregional Accords"--one of which reiterates in the following terms the requirement of approval by one of the designated organs:

Each subregional agreement, in order to become enforceable, shall require the approval of the Standing Executive Committee, which shall decide by an

_____

10. See, for example, Celso Lafer, "Un análisis de la compatibilidad de los Artículos 27 y 28 del Pacto Andino con el ordenamiento jurídico de la ALALC", en INTAL, Derecho de la Integración, No. 6, April 1970, especially pp. 104 et seq.

affirmative vote of at least two thirds (2/3) of the contracting parties and always provided that no negative vote is cast. The Committee shall decide within a period of no more than thirty days from the presentation of the subregional agreement.

This norm formalizes the delegation by the Council of Ministers to the Committee of the "authority to verify the compatibility of the subregional agreement suscribed to..." (Res. 202 and 203). This procedural requirement is also present in the Cartagena Agreement in the sense that, when referring to its validity or entry into force, it begins by stating that: "The present Agreement shall be submitted for consideration by the Standing Executive Committee of LAFTA, and once the Committee has declared it compatible with the principles and objectives of the Montevideo Treaty and Resolution 203 (CM-II/VI-E)..."

It would seem to be a logical corollary to the norm and rule just referred to, both those contained in the resolution of the LAFTA organs and in the corresponding provision of the Cartagena Agreement, that proposed amendments of the latter are subject to the same requirement of a declaration of compatibility by the Standing Executive Committee of the Association. The resolutions are silent on the subject, and the Agreement is limited to granting its Commission the authority "to propose to the member states any reform of the present Agreement" (Art. 7, j) 11/. Therefore, with no stipulation of a special procedure, a requirement for action on the part of the competent organ can and should be presumed for the purpose of determining if the amendment or amendments in question are "compatible with the Montevideo Treaty, its protocols, and other instruments which constitute the legal structure of the Association", as stated by Resolution 222 (VII). It would also seem presumable that the requirement

---

11. In Annex I, paragraph 2, of the Agreement this matter is included among those which the Commission must decide "by a two-thirds affirmative vote and without a negative vote. "

in question does not apply to each and every amendment
made to the Agreement but rather to those which, by their
nature and scope, seem to justify a declaration of compatibility with the legal structure of LAFTA. 12/

The determination of whether a particular amendment falls into one or the other of the two categories just
indicated would not necessarily have to depend on the sole
judgment of the member states of the Agreement or of
the subregional organ which proposes it to them. First,
Resolution 203 and later 222 established a procedure by
virtue of which the Conference of the Contracting Parties
of LAFTA "shall examine in its regular sessions the progress of the subregional agreement and its adequacy to the
principal objectives of the Treaty of Montevideo", for the
purpose of which the parties to subregional agreements
shall present for the consideration of the Conference,
through the executive organ of the agreement (in the present
case the Board) "the most complete information possible
concerning the functioning of the agreement". 13/

---

12. As will be seen in the next subsection, in the
instrument itself which amended the Agreement due to the
accession of Venezuela, the requirement of the declaration
of compatibility was stipulated.

13. Subsequently, Resolution 179 of the Standing Executive Committee stated that, for the purposes set forth
in Resolutions 203 and 222, the Commission established by
the Cartagena Agreement would inform the Conference annually of the functioning of the Agreement. In compliance
with this statement, said Commission has proceeded to
present a report covering each annual period, which relates
the decisions adopted and the other activities accomplished
under the Agreement during the period in question. See,
as an illustration, the Report Submitted to the XIV Regular
Session of the Conference of High Contracting Parties to
the Montevideo Treaty on the Functioning of the Cartagena
Agreement, which covers the period October 31, 1973 to
November 1, 1974, docs. COM/XVI/dt 5/Rev. 1 (November 5, 1974) or ALALC/C/XIV/doc. 16 (November 19,
1974).

Therefore, through this close and permanent communication between the two institutional structures, the solution to the problem of the application of the requirement in question is considerably facilitated.

d) Conditions relative to accession; the case of Venezuela

Another situation should be mentioned which also demands the requirements of compatibility and of consequent action on the part of the Standing Executive Committee of LAFTA. This is the situation created by "accession" to the subregional Agreement. According to its Article 109, it "shall remain open to accession by the other contracting parties of the Montevideo Treaty..." and in another paragraph the following is added: "The conditions for accession shall be defined by the Commission, bearing in mind that the acceptance of new members must be adjusted to the goals of the Agreement". 14/ Apart from the fact that in this last sentence the question of compatibility is implied, Resolution 202 already explicitly provided that "Subregional agreements shall contain norms of accession compatible with the objectives of the Montevideo Treaty". Resolution 222 (VII) complemented this stipulation to the effect that "The rules for accession to subregional agreements, which must be compatible with the Montevideo Treaty, shall be established by the Standing Executive Committee". The above-mentioned Article 109 of the Agreement contains a specific provision on the relatively less economically developed countries, according to which those that fall in that category "which adhere hereto shall have the right to treatment similar to that accorded in Chapter XIII to Bolivia and Ecuador". It is strange to note that in neither of the two mentioned resolutions was the case of this category of countries considered for the purposes discussed here. However, it was considered in Resolution 179 of the Executive Committee, which contains the declaration of compatibility of the Cartagena Agreement by stating specifically that in such a case the countries adhering to the Agreement "shall have full right to

---

14. This material is also included in Annex I, paragraph 13, of the Agreement.

treatment similar to that which is established therein /in the Agreement/ for the benefit of Bolivia and Ecuador". 15/

The Committee again considers this category of countries in its Resolution 165, by which it complied with the mandate to establish norms on accession, which was given to it in Resolution 222 (VII). Resolution 165 begins by reiterating that subregional agreements will be open to adherence by the other contracting parties of the Montevideo Treaty (First). A nation that wishes to adhere to one of these agreements must notify the Committee, which shall refer it to the competent authority of the subregional agreement, so that the authority and the party wishing to adhere may take the steps necessary to begin negotiations (Second). When these negotiations are completed, the competent authority shall forward the results to the Committee, which by a 2/3 vote must rule, within a period of 30 days, on the compatibility of the terms of accession with the objectives of the particular subregional agreement (Fourth). 16/ Once this declaration of compatibility is made, the accession shall be formalized, within a period of 30 days, by the adherent depositing the instrument of accession with the secretary of the competent organ of the subregional Agreement, the pertinent communications being made to LAFTA's Executive Committee (Fifth).

Concerning the relatively less economically developed countries, Resolution 165 states that their "admission" shall not be subject to the procedure described in the Fourth and Fifth articles. In these cases, "accession" shall be

---

15. In regard to Resolution 179, see *supra*, note 11 of Chapter I.
16. Note that reference is not made to compatibility with the Montevideo Treaty and other instruments of the juridical structure of LAFTA because the object of Resolution 165 is not that but the compatibility of the "terms of accession" vis-à-vis a given subregional agreement which the Committee has already declared compatible according to what the resolutions of the Association's organs and the Cartagena Agreement itself in its Article 110 provide on the subject.

formalized by depositing the instrument of the adhering party with the secretary of the competer organ of the subregional agreement, following notifications of the Executive Committee by the above-mentioned party and organ, at least 15 days prior to the date of deposit, in which they state that the negotiations conducted to such end and in accordance with article eight of Resolution 222 (VII) have been satisfactorily concluded (Sixth). In these cases Resolution 165 adds yet another provision: that if the negotiations cannot be concluded satisfactorily, the party wishing to adhere and the competent organ of the agreement may, unilaterally or jointly, present their difficulties to the Committee so that it can investigate whether this and other applicable resolutions have been complied with and, if it deems it advisable, formulate recommendations aimed at the completion of the negotiations. 17/

Negotiations between Venezuela and the Commission of the Cartagena Agreement with a view to that country's accession to the subregional instrument were carried out in accordance with the pertinent provisions of Resolution 165. They began on March 17, 1972 and ended February 13, 1973, the date on which the Government of Venezuela signed the Agreement. On the same date, on the one hand, the representatives of the governments of Bolivia, Colombia, Chile, Ecuador, Peru and Venezuela signed an "Additional Instrument to the Cartagena Agreement for the Accession of Venezuela", and on the other hand, the Commission adopted Resolution 70, in which the conditions for the accession are defined. Both the "Additional Instrument" and Decision 70 were forwarded at the proper time to the Executive Committee of LAFTA, together with the Final Act of the Eleventh Special Session of the Commission, which contains a record of the result of the negotiations. According to this Act,

---

17. See other accessory provisions of Resolution 165 in the complete text of the resolution, contained in doc. ALALC, CEP/Resolution 165, December 19, 1968. The same text, almost complete, is also found in INTAL, Boletín de la Integración, Año IV, January 1969, No. 38, p. 23.

Venezuela's accession would be completed for all effects
and purposes, when that country deposited its instrument
of accession with LAFTA's Executive Secretary and when
the Additional Instrument signed by the six countries entered into force. 18/

It may have been noted that the mandates given, respectively, to the Executive Committee of LAFTA to establish norms for accession to subregional agreements and to
the Commission of the Cartagena Agreement to define the
specific conditions for accession to that Agreement, are
concurrent stages in the accession process. Both pursue
the common purpose of seeing to the compatibility of the
accession process, but while Resolution 165 confines itself
strictly to the procedural norms to be followed when a contracting party of the Montevideo Treaty wishes to adhere
to a subregional agreement, Decision 70, on the other hand,
delineates in detail the substantive or fundamental conditions for accession, in this case specifically for Venezuela,
such as conditions for participation in the Liberalization
Program and for compliance with the Common Minimum
External Tariff. This explains why, despite the intervention of both the Executive Committee and the Commission

---

18. This "Additional Instrument", because it was an
instrument intended to modify the Cartagena Agreement,
contained a clause (Art. 12) conceived in the same terms
as those used in Article 110 of the Agreement, and therefore
its entry into force was made subject to a declaration of
compatibility by the competent organ of LAFTA, as well as
the approval of each member state. But in contrast to the
pertinent provisions of the Agreement, according to the
Instrument, it "shall enter into force when all of the member states and Venezuela have communicated their approval
to the Executive Secretariat of LAFTA". In contrast to the
Agreement, which is silent on the matter, the Instrument
provides that it shall be deposited in the Executive Secretariat itself. The Final Act of the negotiations for the accession of Venezuela ("Consensus of Lima") and its Annexes
A (the Additional Instrument) and B (Decision 70) are reproduced in full in the Appendices.

in an act of accession, there is in practice no duplication
of functions in the actions of these two organs.

2. Transitory Nature of the Agreement and Limits to the Capacity to Adhere to It

The question of "compatibility" is only the first of the
aspects that should be kept in mind in studying the close
linkage and relationship which exist between the legal order
of the subregional Agreement and that of LAFTA. Now, it
is precisely through this question that the most prominent
feature of this linkage and the relationship becomes evident:
i. e. , what has been described as the "derivative" character of the former of these agreements, in the sense that it
"derives from the general legal order of LAFTA, as a
particular application to the subregion". 19/ This conception has merited wide acceptance in both the academic
world and the official sector, 20/ since it faithfully reflects
the position of the subregional legal order in regard to the
Montevideo Treaty and the other instruments by which
LAFTA is governed, without implying, as will be seen
further on, a situation of absolute dependence or subordination.

This situation of dependence or subordination, whose
most ostensible expression stems from the need for a declaration of compatibility (which is equivalent to an act of

---

19. Inter-American Institute, op. cit. , p. 1047.
20. For example, the Round Table on the "Juridical
and Institutional Problem of the Andean Subregional Agreement" held at the Central University of Venezuela from
May 11 to 15, 1970, under the auspices of the above-
mentioned Inter-American Institute "agreed that the two
legal orders /the subregional and the LAFTA/ are closely
related and that they are in complete harmony and are fully
compatible. The Subregional Agreement forms a substantive part of the Montevideo Treaty framework and therefore
has a derivative character..." (Mimeo). See also the
position assumed by some countries in regard to approval
of the Cartagena Agreement in subsection 2 a) of Chapter
V.

"approbation" by the competent organ of LAFTA), 21/ is also evidenced by the "transitory" nature of the Cartagena Agreement. The "transience" of subregional agreements is stated in the Declaration of Presidents, in one of the passages transcribed in the appropriate context, 22/ and is reiterated, also specifically, in Resolution 202 and 222 (VII). The Agreement, for its part, likewise admits it in one of the clauses relating to its duration, in stating that it "shall remain effective as long as the goals achieved within the general framework of the Montevideo Treaty do not surpass those established herein". (Art. 110). This clause, in contrast to those which figure in the three previous sources, explains the purpose of this other characteristic of the Cartagena Agreement.

In effect, subregional agreements have a purpose and are justified only under the conditions described in the above-mentioned clause of Article 110. Even more explicitly, in the Bases for a Subregional Agreement presented by the interested countries to the Council of Ministers of LAFTA and approved by it through its Resolution 203, "the transitory nature of the regimes of exceptions to be provided by this agreement is strongly emphasized in them (the Bases), in the sense that these special regimes shall cease to be applied to the extent that they are identical to the more general commitments assumed within LAFTA to achieve a common market".23/ Now, it has been observed that the "transience" of the Cartagena Agreement should be interpreted within the scope of its conception. Thus, in the work of the Committee of Experts which prepared the draft of the Agreement, the conclusion was reached that what was referred to in the Bases of the Subregional Agreement was trade liberalization and the common external tariff, but not some permanent effects that

---

21.   Remember, in this connection, that in its Resolution 179 the Standing Executive Committee did not limit itself to a declaration of compatibility but added this other sentence: "Consequently, the Committee gives its approval". See the complete text of the first paragraph of the resolution in subsection 1 c) of Chapter I.

22.   See supra, subsection 1 a) of Chapter I.

23.   See supra, subsection 1 b) of Chapter I.

the Agreement would produce, such as joint planning, co-ordination of development plans, sectoral programs of industrial development, and others. 24/ However, it is evident that the term of validity or duration of the subregional Agreement itself has been made dependent on the future, though uncertain, event foreseen in the above-mentioned clause of its Article 110. 25/

Another manifestation of the dependent or subordinate relationship of the Cartagena Agreement to the Montevideo Treaty is based on the accession clause contained in Article 109 of the Agreement, according to which it will remain "open to accession by the other Contracting Parties of the Montevideo Treaty only". This is, like others examined earlier, a clause that was already contained in the norms developed by the organs of LAFTA and, especially, in Resolution 165 of the Standing Executive Committee, both cited herein. By virtue of this clause, which presents aspects different from those already examined, the capacity to adhere to the subregional Agreement is subject to the condition of being a Contracting Party of LAFTA, that is to say, in order for a state not fulfilling this condition to be able to adhere to the Agreement, it would first have to adhere to the Montevideo Treaty, in accordance with Article 58 of the latter. In contrast to other analogous or similar situations, in the case of the Agreement, given the procedure and conditions which must be observed for admitting new members into the "Adean Group", 26/ the relation of

---

24. See Informe del Comité de Expertos a la Sexta Reunión de la Comisión Mixta, July 1968, cited in Inter-American Institute, op. cit., pp. 1049 and 1077-78.

25. Obviously, the term or duration of the Cartagena Agreement is also affected by another factor, which is its denunciation, provided for in Article III, which is examined further on and in a different context.

26. As occurs with the expression "Andean Pact", although without official sanction, there is frequent use of the expression "Andean Group" in referring to the group of countries or subregional association governed by the Cartagena Agreement.

dependence or subordination under consideration is undeniable.

3. Normative Dependence and Hierarchical Relationships

A new manifestation of the linkage and relationship
under consideration is the normative dependence--since
perhaps it would not be in order to speak here also of
"subordination"--found in certain areas of the Cartagena
Agreement in respect to the legal structure of LAFTA, in
particular regarding the Montevideo Treaty, which permits
one to maintain that the subregional instrument, and in
general Andean law as a whole, are not a self-sufficient
legal order.   Thus, for example, according to Article 44
of the Agreement, "The provisions of Article 21 of the
Montevideo Treaty shall be applicable in cases involving
matters of tax, assessment and other internal liens".   Its
Article 108 differs in scope, since it only tries to remedy
omissions in the special regime provided in its Chapter
XIII (Special Regime for Bolivia and Ecuador) by stating
that, "Whenever no provision is made in this Agreement
as to special treatment for Bolivia and Ecuador, the principles and provisions of the Montevideo Treaty, as well
as the LAFTA Resolutions favoring the Relatively Less
Economically Developed Countries, shall be considered as
incorporated therein".

Finally, Article 114 of the Agreement should be
mentioned, specifically a provision of that article which
falls within the context of those being cited, without prejudice to other equally important provisions of that article
which will be pointed out later.   Under the article, the
Montevideo Treaty and the resolutions of LAFTA "shall
be applied in a supplementary manner".   As can be understood, by means of this provision the application of any
norms from LAFTA's juridical structure is authorized
when there are none applicable in the subregional

Agreement, and with this, the role of the former in complementing Andean law is legally valid. 27/

This relationship of normative dependence of the subregional legal order to the LAFTA order necessarily influ-
ences their hierarchical relationship. First of all, the
provision relative to the supplementary nature of LAFTA's
legal structure, cited in the previous paragraph, would
seem to indicate that, as a "special" order, the provisions
of the Andean legal order supersede, in regard to the subregion, those of LAFTA; 28/ i. e., the latter provisions
will only be applicable either when the subregional order is
silent on the matter, or when the concrete application of
some of them is stipulated. If this second exception were
not accepted, the thesis of the primacy of the subregional
order would not be consistent with the general basic norm
expressly established by the organs of LAFTA and contained
also in the Cartagena Agreement. In fact, Article 114 itself begins by stating that "The clauses of this Agreement
shall not affect the rights and obligations derived from the
Montevideo Treaty and the LAFTA resolutions... " 29/
Furthermore, this stipulation is perfectly explicable in
light of the fundamental requirement of compatibility: a
subregional accord can hardly be considered compatible
with the legal structure of the Association if it contains
provisions which affect the rights and obligations emanating
from the above-mentioned instruments of the Association.

Besides this general stipulation, the Agreement
contains others which have been mentioned and which are

---

27. This provision of Article 114 appears for the
first time in Resolution 202, and later in the Bases presented to the LAFTA Council of Ministers, which are mentioned above and which said Council approved in its Resolution 203, and lastly in one of the norms established by
Resolution 222 (VII).
28. Inter-American Institute, op. cit., p. 1048.
29. This other provision of Article 114 also appears
in almost the same terms, in the sources mentioned in
note 27.

applicable to specific matters or situations. Thus, according to its Article 60, "The commitments adopted under the Montevideo Treaty in compliance with the LAFTA Liberalization Program shall prevail over the provisions of the present chapter /Chapter V/ to the extent that the former may be more advanced than the latter". Here the exception is also perfectly explicable: How could the provisions of subregional liberalization programs continue to prevail over commitments adopted under the LAFTA program once the latter were more advanced than the subregional program, when one of the fundamental purposes of the subregional agreements, as declared by the Presidents, is precisely the establishment of a "provision for reducing tariffs within the subregions and harmonizing treatments toward third nations more rapidly than in the general agreements..."? 30/ A second concrete situation, equally as explicable as the other exception, is that provided for in Article 72 of the Agreement, which declares trade in agricultural and livestock products "fully subject" to Article 28 of the Montevideo Treaty and the pertinent resolutions of the LAFTA organs. 31/

In another train of thought, a hierarchical relationship, of extreme importance, does also exist in regard to the scope or effect of tariff reductions made at the subregional level. As will be remembered, in the preceding section the problem of tariff reductions was examined

---

30. See the complete text of this passage of the Declaration of the Presidents in subsection 1 a) of Chapter I. When defining subregional agreements Resolution 222 also conceives of them in terms of their ability to "promote the process of economic integration in a balanced and more accelerated form than that derived from the commitments undertaken within the framework of the Montevideo Treaty".

31. The complete text of Article 72 of the Cartagena Agreement states: "trade in agro-livestock products, based on the Liberalization Program of this Agreement, even after the expiration of the periods stipulated in Article 2 of the Montevideo Treaty, shall be fully subject to its Article 28, to the Resolutions which complement it, and to any future measures that may be adopted to amend or substitute these".

from another angle: that of exceptions of the most-favored-nation clause contained in Article 18 of the Montevideo Treaty. What is of interest now is the norm contained in Resolution 222 (VII), which was cited in the appropriate context and which has already been enunciated in analogous terms in the Declaration of the Presidents: "Subregional tariff reductions will not be extended to countries that are not parties to the subregional agreement, nor will they create special obligations for them". In short, given its "special" character, the Agreement is autonomous within the Subregion as regards tariff reductions and other bene-fits agreed upon. However, this autonomy does not author-ize the creation of special obligations for the other contract-ing parties of LAFTA. 32/

4. Entry into Force and Denunciation of the Andean Pact; Execution of New Agreements

The provisions contained in Article 110 of the Carta-gena Agreement were examined in due course in connection with the requirement of a declaration of compatibility by the Standing Executive Committee of LAFTA and with the transitory nature of the Agreement, i.e. , with the duration of its enforcement which can be affected by the scope of commitments acquired within the general framework of the Montevideo Treaty as compared to those established in the

---

32. These situations are not the only ones which create hierarchical relationships between the two legal orders. By way of illustration, this other norm of Reso-lution 222 (VII), which is self-explanatory, should be mentioned: "Insofar as possible the subregional agree-ments shall incorporate regulations for the identification of the source of the products included therein. The general rules and specific requirements established by the Associ-ation shall prevail with respect to products covered by a subregional agreement that are simultaneously incorporated into liberalization programs of the Montevideo Treaty".

Agreement. 33/ The same provisions present other aspects of equal interest from the dual point of view of the entry into force and the duration of the subregional instrument.

In regard to the former, Article 110 states that once a declaration of the compatibility of the Agreement has been made, "each member state shall approve it in conformity with its respective legislative procedures and forward the corresponding ratification instrument to the Executive Secretariat of LAFTA". Here arises the question of the true nature of the "act of approval" of said countries. Or to state it more explicitly, the question of whether or not said act implies the formal requirement of legislative intervention and sanction. Thus, for example, at the Round Table held at the Central University of Venezuela, already referred to, it was maintained that the Cartagena Agreement forms a substantive part of the framework of the Montevideo Treaty and has therefore a "derivative" nature, and that consequently "it had not been necessary to subject it to legislative approval in the various member states, the original ratification of the Montevideo Treaty sufficing for this purpose, in application and furtherance of which the Subregional Agreement was developed".

Strictly speaking, the "derivative" character of the Andean Pact and its very close linkage and relationship to the legal and institutional framework of LAFTA are not necessarily the only factors or circumstances which may be resorted to in order to avoid the legislative process. Note, in this respect, as occurred in innumerable international treaties and agreements of the post-war period, that instead of providing for "ratification" it provides for "approval" or "acceptance", which are terms that permit the government which is willing and able to avoid the formalities and delays involved in the ratification process to expedite the "act of approval" referred to in Article 110

---

33. Article 110 adds that the Agreement "shall become effective upon communication of approval of three States to the Executive Secretariat of LAFTA."

through simple executive action. 34/ In practice, difficulties with this method have arisen only in Colombia, when Decree 1245, the instrument through which that country originally approved the Cartagena Agreement, was challenged as unconstitutional. The Colombian Supreme Court declared that said decree, "due to a flaw in its drafting, conflicts with constitutional law" because it considered that "the government did not abide by the Constitution from the moment that it failed to submit the Andean Pact to congressional consideration". 35/

Provisions relative to the denunciation and its effects are included in Article 111 of the subregional Agreement. The complete text thereof follows:

---

34. The International Law Commission of the United Nations, in its reports to the General Assembly on treaty law, observed that the procedure of "acceptance" and the more recent one of "approval", "are used above all in the case of treaties which because of their form or their basis are not of the types which normally require parliamentary ratification under the constitutional provisions in force in many States. In some cases, to make it easier for States whose constitutional procedures are different to become parties to the treaty, the treaty provides for either ratification or acceptance. However, in general it may be said that 'acceptance' is used as a simplified process of 'ratification'... The observations made in the previous paragraph apply mutatis mutandi to 'approval', a term whose introduction into conventional procedure is much more recent than that of 'acceptance'". Cf. A. G. Docs. Off.: Twenty First Session, Suppl. 9, A/G 309, Rev. 1, p. 33.

35. For many other interesting aspects of the Colombian case, including the case of the Government before the Supereme Court, presented by the Attorney General (Procurador General), see infra, subsection 2 b) of Chapter V, regarding acceptance of the Cartagena Agreement in the national law of the various member states.

Any member state desiring to withdraw from this Agreement shall communicate with the Commission. As of that date, the rights and obligations deriving from its status as a member shall cease, with the exception of those benefits received and granted pursuant to the Subregional Liberalization Program, which shall remain in force for five years following the date of withdrawal.

The period of time indicated in the preceding paragraph may be reduced in duly justified cases, by decision of the Commission and at the request of the interested member state.

The provisions of Section g) of Article 34 shall be applicable with respect to the Sectorial Programs of Industrial Development.

The preceding provisions are very explicit and require only a few brief comments. For example, it has been observed that "denunciation of the Agreement does not imply, then, total release from the obligations acquired during the term of membership; besides the effects which continue during the stipulated period, membership in LAFTA by the member who denounces the Agreement implies the maintenance of commitments acquired within the framework of the Montevideo Treaty". [36]

On the other hand, under Article 34, Section g), referred to in Article 111, Sectoral Programs of Industrial Development must contain, among others, stipulations on "the periods of time during which the rights and duties related to the Program must be continued in case of denunciation of the Agreement". As may be observed, denunciation has different effects depending on whether one is dealing with benefits received and granted (which continue for a period that may even be reduced by decision of the Commission), or with the rights and obligations derived from

---

36. Cf. F. Villagrán Kramer, "Sistematización de la Estructura Jurídica del Acuerdo de Cartagena", INTAL, Derecho de la Integración, No. 12, March 1973, p. 13.

Sectoral Programs of Industrial Development, which must be maintained for the full length of the period stipulated in the Program in question.

Considering the provisions relating to the denunciation of the Cartagena Agreement and the effects arising therefrom, the way in which Chile ceased to be a member state of the Andean Group would justifiable cause surprise. As will be remembered, in virtue of Decision 102 of the Commission, 36-a/

> Article 1. Beginning October 30, 1976, all the rights and obligations derived from the Cartagena Agreement, its Protocols, Decisions and Resolutions, except for the rights and obligations emanating from Decisions 40, 46, 56 and 94, which remain fully in force, are without effect for Chile.
>
> The cessation of rights and obligations referred to in the preceding paragraph include the advantages received and granted by Chile in accordance with the liberalization program and the rights and obligations emanating from Decisions 57 and 91 of the Commission.
>
> Article 2. The Commission shall agree with the Government of Chile on the form in which the application of Decisions 40, 46, 56 and 94 of the Commission shall be administered in relations with that country.

It is evident that for the withdrawal of a country from the Andean Group the Cartagena Agreement only provides for its denouncement. In this connection, therefore, the adoption of Decision 102 departs considerably from the procedure established in Article 111 of the Agreement.

With respect to the third and last question to be considered under this section, the Andean Pact provides

---

36-a. See subsection 1 b), Chapter I.

for the conclusion of new agreements, always with a view toward, and in accordance with, its objectives and mechanisms as well as those of the Montevideo Treaty. In one case it considers agreements or commitments with third countries and limits the contractual capacity of the member states. This is the case dealt with in Article 68, according to which these countries commit themselves to holding the necessary consultations with the Commission before concluding agreements of a tariff nature with countries outside the Subregion. In two other cases the Pact provides for agreements or commitments between the member states themselves, as in Article 53, which stipulates that said countries "may agree on a selective elimination of products /those included in the regime of Article 52/, provided it is at a more accelerated rate", and in Article 57, which stipulates that, during the second half of 1974, member states will conduct negotiations for the purpose of finding formulas that will permit them to obtain a gradual withdrawal of products from their exception schedules within the period ending December 31, 1985. The third type of authorized agreement is that considered in Article 59, regarding the other contracting parties of LAFTA; that is, complementarity agreements which try to coordinate the parties in suitable production sectors, in conformity with the provisions of the Montevideo Treaty, and the respective resolutions.

5. "Sui Generis" Characteristics of the Cartagena Agreement

As one can understand, the "Agreement on Subregional Integration", as it is termed in its own preamble, is not a customary treaty, convention or agreement. Far from it, despite its essentially conventional or contractual nature, it presents singular elements and characteristics that justify considering it an instrument with sui generis characteristics. It is undeniable that this is due, for the most part, to the very close linkage and relationship that it had with the Montevideo Treaty and, in general, with the legal and institutional framework of LAFTA. This linkage and relationship is due, in turn, to one of the most outstanding features of the Montevideo Treaty: that of constituting a true traité-cadre.

a) "Traité-cadre" Character of the Agreement

The outstanding note or characteristics of the Montevideo Treaty, which begins to explain the sui generis
character of the Cartagena Agreement, was first mentioned
in the provisional edition of Derecho de la Integración Latinoamericana by the Inter-American Institute of International Legal Studies, which has been cited repeatedly.
Here is the essence of the thesis sustained in that publication of the Institute. 37/

... Since the Treaty is not the only legal instrument
regulating the functioning of the Association--from
a substantive and adjectival point of view--and there
are also various other instruments created by that
treaty, it may be maintained in general, that one is
dealing with an international treaty which has features classified by doctrine as pertaining to a traité-
cadre, a treaty-framework, which contains essential
and basic norms while at the same time permitting
progressive application, complementation, improvement and projection into new circumstances by
means of other instruments, usually elaborated by
the organs, which are, in LAFTA's case, the
Protocols, Acts and Resolutions.

Consistent with this conception of the Montevideo
Treaty, as soon as the Cartagena Agreement was concluded, it was considered in the above-mentioned publication
"an extension of the commitments established by LAFTA,
bringing them closer to the indicated objectives /the customs union and the common market foreseen in the Treaty/,
always within the basic framework of the Montevideo Treaty, which in this case receives an additional boost through
the development of that Subregion". 38/ These considerations flow from those made at the beginning of section 2,
in the sense that the Cartagena Agreement, as well as the

---

37. Problemática Jurídica e Institucional de la Integración de América Latina, Ensayo de Sistematización
(1967), p. 739.
    38. Cf. op. cit. in note 8, pp. 1041 and 1045.

Andean legal order as a whole, "derive from the general legal order of LAFTA, as a special application to the Subregion", and at the same time clarify observations made in the same and subsequent sections regarding the linkage and relationship existing between the two orders.

Now, the Cartagena Agreement itself may be characterized, within its subregional scope naturally, as a new traité cadre. It was recognized and defined as such by the authors of the draft agreement in their report, which was unequivocally approved by the Joint Commission of the Bogotá Declaration. 39/

> If one realizes that the life of the Subregion cannot proceed now and forever under the provisions of the Agreement, if one considers that this is only the framework or source of future rights and obligations, and if one keeps in mind the unsuccessful experiences of other bodies, this will explain why the Committee of Experts devoted its time to analyzing the subject until it obtained a clear understanding of what, organically and functionally, the Subregional Agreement should be.

This characterization also leaves no room for doubt. On the one hand, after examining in the preceding chapter the objectives and mechanisms of the Agreement, one could appreciate the various instruments whose adoption is considered in it, such as those relating to the Common Regime of Treatment of Foreign Capital (Art. 27). On the other hand, as will be appreciated again and at length in Chapters IV and V, the Andean Pact confers competence ratione materiae and grants authority or powers to the subregional organs capable of generating, like the various instruments already referred to, new rights and obligations for the member states as required to achieve the goals to which the Agreement is dedicated.

------

39. Informe del Comité de Expertos a la Quinta Reunión de la Comisión Mixta, Acta Final de la Reunión (February 5 to 10, 1968), Annex 5, doc. DE. Bo/Co. Mx/V/ dt. 1, p. 4.

b) Other characteristics

The Cartagena Agreement offers other characteristics, although not as significant as the one above, which also deserve attention. One of these is that it "may not be signed with reservations" (Art. 109). Here we are not dealing with a peculiarity of the subregional instrument, since the Montevideo Treaty as well as numerous other treaties and agreements contain the same clause. The reason for making reference to such a prohibition is that, despite its necessity for preserving the integrity of economic integration instruments, in some treaties it takes the form of a tacit clause, as in the case of the instruments governing Central American Economic Integration. 40/ As for the fact that Article 109 seems to refer only to the signatories, obviously the clause is also applicable in cases of accession by other contracting parties of the Montevideo Treaty that did not sign the Agreement.

Another characteristic of the subregional agreement, much more prominent than the preceding one, is based on provisions relative to accession (besides those which were just alluded to) which constitute, as has been indicated, a limitation of the capacity to adhere to it. The remaining provisions were closely examined in subsection 1, d), in relation to the question of compatibility, so the only observation called for in the present context is to note the peculiarity of the presence of provisions of such a similar nature and scope. Departing considerably from law and the usual common practice in this area, the Agreement not only provides for conditions on accession and entrusts a subregional organ (the Commission) with defining them but it also, in the same Article 109, establishes a program of treatment similar to the one stipulated in Chapter XIII (applicable to

---

40. In fact, because some of these instruments are the constitutive instruments of international bodies, and because all regulate matters in which the participating states cannot be permitted exemptions from the obligations they establish, the inadmissibility of reservations, though not expressly stipulated in any of them, has been considered understood in all negotiations and has always been respected. Cf. Inter-American Institute, Derecho Comunitario Centroamericano (San José, Costa Rica, 1968), p. 331.

Bolivia and Ecuador) for relatively less economically developed countries which adhere to it. This remark should
be accompanied by the observation that according to the
regime for subregional agreements created by the organs
of LAFTA, as was earlier mentioned, such agreements
"shall contain norms of accession compatible with the objectives of the Montevideo Treaty".

In this and in the previous chapter the two substantive
provisions concerning the entry into force of the Cartagena
Agreement, contained in Article 110, were examined. 41/
These provisions are the ones concerning the declaration of
compatibility which must be made by the competent LAFTA
organ (this competence is stipulated not only in the Agreement but also in Resolution 203 of the Association's Council
of Ministers), and the one concerning approval on the part
of the member states. What is of interest now is the system
for the entry into force created by the need for these requirements. Given the "derivative" character of the subregional instrument, at first one would think that it would
enter into force "on the day in which the competent LAFTA
authority declares it compatible with the instruments mentioned in Article 2 of Resolution 203". 42/ This, naturally,
would have fulfilled one of the two requirements: the compatibility of the subregional agreements with the Montevideo
Treaty and, in general, with the legal structure of LAFTA,
a concern which has been expressed ever since the Declaration of the Presidents and been reiterated time and again
by the organs of the Association.

---

41.   See supra, subsection 1 c) and section 4 of
Chapter I.
42.   Cf. Inter-American Institute, op. cit. in note 8,
p. 1048. The explanation is based on the fact that the text
of the draft subregional Agreement quoted, although it was
the final text, was amended at the last minute to add the
requirement of approval by the member states; this is the
text that was discussed in the first session of the Sixth
Meeting of the Joint Commission, in July-August 1968.
Cf. Acuerdo de Integración Subregional, Anexo al Acta
Final of said session, Article 101, p. 50.

Nevertheless, despite its "derivative" character, the proposed subregional agreement contained substantive commitments considerable in scope and, furthermore, submitted the countries of the subregion to a new institutional framework, appreciably more dynamic than that of LAFTA. This explains why, in fact, an "act of approval" is required from the member states, together with the declaration of compatibility. In any case, what we are interested in emphasizing now is the peculiarity of the system adopted for putting into effect the Cartagena Agreement: necessitating the concurrence of these two requirements or conditions, thus departing drastically from the system normally followed in international practice. 43/ But it has already been noted that there are ample reasons to justify the participation of the competent organ of the Association in the system adopting the Agreement.

Neither is the duration of the subregional Agreement, for its part, subject to the norms usually observed in international practice on this subject. As has been seen, this is an intrinsically "transitory" instrument, as are all subregional agreements, whose existence is justified so long as it is given the conditions established in the norms which the competent organs of LAFTA have prescribed and which the Agreement itself incorporates; that is, it shall remain in effect or last "as long as the goals achieved within the general framework of the Montevideo Treaty do not surpass those established herein" (Art. 110). Thus the observation

_____

43. Even though the Vienna Convention on the Law of Treaties states that "a treaty shall enter into force in the manner and on the date prescribed or agreed to by the negotiating States", the only thing provided for and regulated in this regard in the Convention itself is "the consent of the State to obligate itself" (Art. 24). As demonstrated by the International Law Commission's commentary on Article 21 of its project, the cited provision of the Convention refers more to aspects or steps of the entry into force of treaties which have nothing to do with intervention or participation by international organizations in the process. Cf. document cited in note 34, p. 43.

made above, in the sense that the extent of the effectiveness or duration of the Agreement depends on a future but uncertain event. This type of "transience" in subregional agreements, therefore, at least is not due to the motives or circumstances which usually limit the duration of international treaties or agreements. 44/

Because of its close relationship to the topic, it would be well to reiterate a few brief observations regarding the Agreement's provisions on its denunciation, with the purpose of pointing out the characteristics that it presents in that respect. In the first place, denunciation does not imply for the denouncing member state a total renunciation of all its rights nor a total release from all its obligations. Secondly, upon petition of the denouncing country a subregional organ (the Commission) is authorized to reduce the five-year term for which said rights and obligations remain in effect, and, thirdly, when dealing with Sectoral Programs of Industrial Development, the duration of the rights and obligations following from them shall be maintained for the periods established in those programs. As can be seen, this set of provisions concerning the denunciation of the subregional Agreement also creates a system which departs sufficiently from the one usually followed in this connection in international practice. 45/

---

44. It is true that, as the International Law Commission observes, "Many treaties provide that they shall be in effect for a stipulated period of time or until a given date, or even until a stipulated result is produced; according to other treaties, their termination depends on a resolutive condition". Cf. document cited in note 34, p. 82. Therefore, what may really be considered novel in the subregional Agreement is not exactly the fact that its termination is subject to the fulfillment of a condition, but rather the originality of the condition itself.

45. Neither the Vienna Convention nor the project of the International Law Commission provided for denunciation as one of the causes of termination of a treaty, nor does it refer to its effects, perhaps because normally these effects are to completely release the parties to the treaty, immediately or after a date stipulated therein.

Normative dependence and the hierarchical relations between the Cartagena Agreement and the Montevideo Treaty, and in general between the subregional and the LAFTA legal orders, present new characteristics, in a way more significant than those already mentioned. On the first topic --the normative dependence of the subregional Agreement-- F. Orrego Vicuña has observed that "both by virtue of its provisions and the intention of its parties, the Agreement does not have a legal life of its own, independent of that of its basic framework: the Montevideo Treaty; if the latter should expire, the Subregional Agreement would automatically expire". 46/ In the same train of thought it has been added that "the Montevideo Treaty has, then, two important functions to discharge in relation to the Cartagena Agreement. First to complement this special structure when the compatibility of ends and objectives requires it, and second: to serve as a normative frame to resolve cases in which the integration of law within the framework of the Agreement is necessary". 47/ This does not prejudice, naturally, affirming that "despite its derivative character the Agreement enjoys a necessary autonomy and has the legal personality indispensable for the achievement of its objectives. 48/

In regard to the second topic--hierarchical relations-- as might have already been appreciated, these relations are extremely complex. From a purely legal point of view, the question cannot be posed in the absolute terms that are normally used to describe relations of this type between two international treaties or agreements; that is, in terms of knowing, in case of conflict between their respective norms, which one will prevail. Far from it, it has already been seen that, according to the matter at hand,

---

46. "La incorporación del ordenamiento jurídico subregional al derecho interno, análisis de la práctica chilena", in INTAL, Derecho de la Integración, No. 7, October 1970, p. 52.

47. Cf. Villagrán Kramer, loc. cit. in note 36, p. 16.

48. Conclusions of the Round Table of Caracas, which have been referred to above. See note 20.

either the Treaty or the Agreement shall predominate. Thus, for example, when the matter involves the question of "compatibility", or any other matters over which the primacy of the legal order of LAFTA is expressly (or tacitly) established (as, for example, Art. 60 of the Agreement), its norms will prevail. In the same way, subregional norms which result in rights, obligations and commitments exclusively for the member states will prevail, as long as, naturally, they are not incompatible with LAFTA's legal order (Art. 114 of the Agreement), or as long as, when dealing with subregional tariff reductions or benefits, these are not extended to non-member countries or do not create any obligations for them (Art. 113). It would seem that this is the only way of focusing on and resolving the relationships and problems of hierarchy between the two legal orders.

Chapter III

THE ANDEAN INSTITUTIONAL FRAMEWORK

Despite the very important role played by the organs of LAFTA in the initial stages of subregional agreements, and even in the progress of such agreements through the annual analysis which has been entrusted to the Conference, it was always intended that the agreements would be endowed with their own autonomous organs. 1/ In the case of the Cartagena Agreement, given the character and scope of its objectives and mechanisms, it is logical furthermore, that the institutional framework established should differ considerably from that of LAFTA, both in regard to the structure and functioning of the organs created by the Agreement as well as to the competencies or powers with which those organs are invested. Both aspects may be understood in the course of this chapter and the next one, and more fully still in the chapter following that, where the nature and validity of the acts of the subregional organs will be examined.

1. Organs of the Agreement: The Principal
Organs

Chapter II of the Andean Pact deals with "Organs of the Agreement", and begins by declaring that "the principal organs of the Agreement are the Commission and the Board (Junta). The auxiliary organs shall be the Committees as defined under Section C of this Chapter" (Art. 5). To these organs should be added the Andean Development Corporation, the financial body of the Subregion, referred to in Section E. The Councils created by the Commission--that is, the procedures and mechanisms for reconciling policies and coordinating the development plans referred to in

---

1. Thus, one of the norms of cited Resolution 222 (VII) states that "The contracting parties in a subregional agreement shall establish the executive organ to take charge of administration of the agreement".

Article 29 of the Agreement--and the Meetings of Ministers, as well as other institutions, also form part of the Andean institutional framework. The projected tribunal or sub-regional jurisdictional organ should be mentioned, although it has not yet been created. This and the next section deal with the structure and functioning of the principal and auxiliary organs mentioned in Article 5.

a) Structure and functioning of the Commission

The Commission is the chief organ of the Agreement and is composed of a plenipotentiary representative from the government of each member state (Art. 6); it has a president who remains in office one year; the office is held by each representative in turn, in alphabetical order by country, with the first president being chosen by lot (Art. 9). The Commission meets in regular sessions three times a year, and in special sessions whenever convened by its president at the request of any member state or the Board. Its meetings are held at Board headquarters 2/ but may take place elsewhere; the sessions must have a quorum of at least two-thirds of the member states, attendance at meetings is compulsory and non-attendance is considered abstention (Art. 10).

In its Regulations (Decision 6) the Commission supplemented these provisions with others, among which should be mentioned the following: the Commission may invite international organizations and governments not members of the Agreement to appoint representatives as observers or advisers and to participate in the meetings when invited to do so (Art. 4). Without prejudice to mentioning further other provisions referring to relations between the Commission and the Board, it is interesting to emphasize at this point two which are certainly not usual but whose presence reveals a decided intention to assure the effectiveness

---

2.   In conformance with the procedure stated in Article 18 of the Agreement, following the signing of the Agreement, Lima, Peru, was designated as headquarters of the Board.

of the Andean legal order. These are provisions contained in Chapter VI of the Regulations of the Commission, entitled "Obligations of the Representatives". According to the first one, those in the Commission are expected to present in due course the instruments by which the various obligations arising from the Agreement are put into force in their respective countries, and, according to the second, it is their responsibility to see that the obligations imposed in their respective countries by the Agreement are complied with (Art. 26).

According to Article 6 of the Cartagena Agreement, cited above, "the Commission shall express its will in the form of 'Decisions'," and to this effect Article 11 establishes a complex system of voting, as may be seen in the text of said article reproduced below.

> Article 11. The Commission's Decisions must be adopted by affirmative vote cast by two-thirds of the member states. Exceptions to this general rule are as follows:
>
> a) Matters covered in Annex I of the present Agreement, in which Commission decisions must be adopted by a two-thirds affirmative vote with no negative vote. The Commission may incorporate new matters in said Annex by an affirmative vote of two-thirds of the member states; 3/

---

3. Annex I includes the following matters: "1. Delegate to the Board whatever duties are considered appropriate; 2. Approve the modifications to the present Agreement; 3. Amend the proposals of the Board; 4. Approve the norms necessary to make possible the coordination of development plans and the harmonization of economic policies of the member states; 5. Approve the harmonization program for instruments regulating the foreign trade of member states; 6. Approve the physical integration programs; 7. Accelerate the Liberalization Program, by products or product groupings; 8. Approve the joint agricultural development programs; 9. Approve and modify the list of agricultural products dealt with in Article 74; 10. Approve the measures

b)   Cases enumerated in Annex II, where the Board
proposals must be approved by an affirmative vote
cast by at least two-thirds of the member states,
with no negative vote. The proposals receiving an affirmative vote of two-thirds of the member states, but
which are subject of a negative vote, must be returned
to the Board for consideration of the reasons originating the said negative vote. Within a period of not less
than two nor more than six months, the Board may
renew its proposal for Commission consideration
with the amendments deemed desirable and, in such
event, the amended proposal shall be considered as
approved if it receives an affirmative vote of two-
thirds of the member states, and no negative vote; or
if a negative vote is cast by the same state voting previously against it, it shall not be counted; 4/

c)   Matters related to the special treatment to be accorded to Bolivia and Ecuador, listed in Annex III.
In these cases, the Commission Decisions shall be
adopted by an affirmative vote of two-thirds, provided

---

3.   (Cont). for joint cooperation established in Article 79; 11. Modify the number of items referred to in Articles 55 and 102; 12. Reduce the number of matters included in the present Appendix; 13. Establish the conditions
for adherence to the present Agreement".
4.   Annex II lists the following matters: "1. Approve
the list of products reserved for Industrial Development
Sectorial Programs; 2. Approve the Industrial Development
Sectorial Programs; 3. Approve the rationalization and
specialization programs referred to in Article 36; 4. Approve the Common Minimum External Tariff and the Common External Tariff in accordance with terms stated in
Chapter VI, establish the conditions for their application,
and modify the common tariff levels; 5. Approve the list of
products not produced in any country of the Subregion; 6.
Approve the special norms regarding source".

that one of these is cast either by Bolivia or Ecuador; and 5/

d) Appointment of Board members, to be approved by unanimous vote.

As may be noted, in contrast to the voting system of the Conference of Contracting Parties of LAFTA, in which the general rule is the veto, in the Subregional Agreement the general rule is a two-thirds majority of the member states and the veto is the exception. 6/ Nevertheless, it is undeniable that the subjects or matters excepted from the rule of the unqualified majority are so many and of such importance at times that, strictly speaking, it cannot be said that this system of voting excels to a considerable extent the LAFTA system. 7/

---

5. Annex III lists the following matters: "1. Approve the list of products for immediate liberalization according to Article 97(b); 2. Fix margins of preference and indicate terms of enforcement for the lists of products of special interest for Bolivia and Ecuador /Art. 79(d) and (e)/; 3. Determine the form and the terms in which Bolivia and Ecuador will liberalize products reserved for Industrial Development Sectoral Programs and which may not have been included in them /Art. 100(b)/; 4. Revise the liberalization terms for the products referred to in items (c) and (f) of Article 100; 5. Determine the minimum tariff levels that Bolivia and Ecuador may adopt for products of interest of the other member states /Art. 104/; 6. Approve the lists of products not produced, reserved for production in Bolivia and Ecuador, and fix the conditions and reservation terms /Art. 50/".
6. Cf. Instituto Interamericano de Estudios Jurídicos Internacionales, Derecho de la Integración Latinoamericana, Ensayo de Sistematización (Buenos Aires, 1969), p. 718 and 814.
7. Neither the Commission's Regulations nor its practice has introduced substantive changes in the voting system established by the Agreement. The Regulations merely add that each representative shall be entitled to one vote and that, in counting the two thirds, any fraction shall be converted to the nearest whole number. (Art. 22).

b) Structure and functioning of the Board

The Board, for its part, "is the technical organ of the Agreement, consisting of three members /whose appointment and removal is the responsibility of the Commission, according to Article 7 c)/, and it may act only in the concerted interest of the Subregion as a unit". The members are elected for three-year terms and may be reelected; in case of a vacancy, the Commission must immediately proceed to designate a replacement, who will also have a three-year term (Art. 13). The Board members may be nationals of any Latin American state; they are answerable to the Commission for their actions, must act in the common interest, must refrain from any action incompatible with the nature of their duties, may not exercise any other professional activity, whether remunerative or not, for the duration of their terms, and may not seek or receive instructions from any government or from any national or international entity (Art. 14).

Besides its character of "technical organ", the Board performs "the functions of Permanent Secretariat of the Agreement" and maintains direct contact with the governments of member states through the organs designated by each for this purpose (Art. 15, i). Along this line, the Board proposes to the Commission the organic structure for its technical divisions and any reorganizations it may deem desirable, hires and dismisses technical and administrative staff, and entrusts the performance of specific tasks to experts in certain fields (Art. 15 n), o), p). In the contracting of technical and administrative staff, who may be of any nationality, the Board must consider solely the qualification, competency, and reputation of the candidates, and shall, insofar as not incompatible with the above criteria, fill the positions so as to effect as broad a geographical subregional distribution as possible (Art. 16). In connection with the provisions mentioned in this and the previous paragraph, reference should be made to those concerning the Coordinator of the Board, which are contained in the Regulations which the Commission prescribed for the Board (Decision 9). This function, which the members exercise in turn for one year, constitutes the legal representation of the Junta and other internal functions conferred by the Board (Arts. 8 and 9).

In regard to the voting system, "The Board shall always act with the unanimous expression of all members, but it may present for consideration of the Commission any alternative proposals, also unanimously approved". (Art. 17). The Regulations add that, "in the same way, the Board may modify its proposals while they are being discussed by the Commission". (Art. 10). The Regulations again require the unanimity of members in adopting "Resolutions", which, as will be seen in Chapter V, are the instruments through which the Board expresses its will in matters in which it has decision-making powers, as stipulated in the text of the Agreement or delegated by the Commission (Arts. 11 and 12). Considering that the voting system is also of foremost importance when dealing with an organ which has been assigned such a prominent role in the Andean institutional framework, it is evident that the system adopted is too rigid; a rigidity which has been attenuated to a very modest degre, and only concerning the mechanisms of proposals, by permitting the Board to present for consideration alternative proposals.

c) Institutonal equilibrium between the two organs

Having described the main features of the structure and functioning of the two principal organs of the Cartagena Agreement, 8/ the question arises especially after pointing out the considerable differences between the Andean and the LAFTA institutional framework, as to which type of institutional system the former should be identified with or assimilated to the extent that this is feasible, as this stage of its exposition. In this respect the most exact characterization, as well as one of the most authoritative, obviously continues to be the one made by the Committee of Experts

---

8. For a brief but sufficiently complete legislative history of the provisions of the Agreement examined at this time, see Inter-American Institute, op. cit., p. 799 et seq.

that drafted the subregional agreement, in referring to the Commission and the Board. Here are the relevant passages. 9/

The former is similar to the traditional conferences or plenary sessions with governmental representation. The latter, on the other hand, departs from the single powerless executive and the inter-governmental secretariat. The draft agreement defines the Board as a technical community organ composed by three members designated by the Joint Commission. Five delegations gave their assent. Peru reserved its vote on the question of formation of the standing Executive Board.

Because of their differentiated structure and competence, these organs ensure a system of institutional equilibrium which responds satisfactorily to the objectives of the Agreement. The adoption of advanced goals for subregional planning and coordinated development would serve no purpose if a legislative authority and a technical community authority were not established to serve them, each with the hierarchy, strength and functionality necessary for the continual solution of the problems inherent in such a vast, complex and difficult operation.

Also, the security offered to the subregion and its countries by the equilibrium between the governmental force and the community force, between the political aspects of the former and the technical aspects of the latter, should be noted.

This characterization of the Andean institutional system found immediate support. Thus, in the publication of the Inter-American Institute of International Legal Studies

---

9. Informe del Comité de Expertos a la Quinta Reunión de la Comisión Mixta. Acta Final de la Reunión (5 al 10 de febrero de 1968), Anexo 5, doc. De. Bo/CO. Mix/V/ dt. 1.

which has been repeatedly referred to, it was noted that, in accordance with the principles stated in the Report of the Committee of Experts, "a genuine community institutional system would be established in the subregional sphere", in support of which were cited, furthermore, statements to the same or similar effect prepared by the Advisory Promotional Committee and by the President of Colombia in a letter addressed on April 4, 1968, to the presidents of the other Andean countries. 10/

It is evident that the instituional system of the Andean Pact departs considerably from that of the Montevideo Treaty. Whereas the latter is essentially "intergovernmental" because all its principal organs are of that character, the system instituted by the Pact is essentially a "community" system; that is to say, that while the LAFTA system, even in its present stage of development, lacks an organ which represents the common interests of the region, in the Andean Group this organ does exist, making it possible, with the existence of the intergovernmental organ, for subregional interests to be linked with the national interests of the respective member states. All this, of course, is subject to certain reservations which cannot be overlooked due to the not altogether "community" elements apparent in the Andean institutional framework as a whole, some of which have been already referred to.

---

10. Cf. op. cit., p. 803. See also F. Peña, "Proyecciones Institucionales del Grupo Andino", INTAL, Revista de la Integración, Mayo 1968, No. 2, p. 153. More recently one of the members of the Board reiterated some of the concepts originally expressed by the Committee of Experts, in the following terms: "The Commission and the Board should seek equilibrium, coordination and harmony in their work. In the Commission the national interests of each of the member states are represented. The Board is the spokesman for the general interests of the Subregion, that is, for the economic community that it is creating". Cf. F. Salazar Santos, "Aspectos Jurídicos de la Integración Andina", INTAL, Derecho de la Integración, No. 13, Julio 1973, p. 151.

d) Functional relations between them

In the Andean instituional system the close relations between the different subregional organs play a key role. These relations, are expressly provided for and regulated in the Cartagena Agreement and in the regulations of the organs. As will be observed, in the pertinent provisions of these instruments these relations often shape the exercise of competencies on powers assigned to the organs; this occurs most frequently between the Commission and the Board, which are based on the system of principle of "instituional equilibrium", referred to by the Committee of Experts mentioned in the previous subsection.

This "institutional equilibrium" is principally evident in the mechanism of proposals which the Board must make to the Commission. According to Article 15 c) of the Agreement, the Board must "prepare proposals for the Commission, conducive to expediting or accelerating compliance with the Agreement, in order to achieve its goals within the shortest possible time". Subparagraph e) of the same article adds that the Board shall participate in the meetings of the Commission, unless the latter deems it advisable to hold closed sessions. However, the Board has the right to take part in any discussion of its own proposals made to the Commission, particularly those under subparagraphs c) and d), the latter of which refers to proposals related to the special regime for Bolivia and Ecuador. The Commission, for its part, must "approve, veto or amend proposals of the Board" (Art. 7, f); and furthermore it "must consider Board proposals in all cases" and decide on them (Art. 12). The voting system applicable to the proposals is that established in Article 11 b) of the Agreement, reproduced in subparagraph 1 a) as well as in Article 23, 3) of the Regulations of the Commission, which adds that to amend Board proposals the qualified rule of the two-thirds majority shall be applied, that is, with no negative vote. According to its Regulations, the Board may modify its proposals while they are being discussed in the Commission (Art. 10); likewise, the Regulations of the latter authorize the Board to take part in the discussion of all its proposals (Art. 3).

Along with the above, one should bear in mind that concerning the objectives and mechanisms provided in the Cartagena Agreement, the Commission, with rare exceptions, makes its decisions "at the proposal of the Board", which means that in substantive matters both organs exercise a type of concurrent competence. Therefore, ever since the final text of the subregional agreement was agreed upon it has been possible to say that "both organs contribute to the formation of decisions, producing a synthesis of national and community interest; such a synthesis is assured through the mechanism of proposals, which is the cornerstone of the institutional equilibrium. This mechanism permits community criteria to be present in all decisions of the Joint Commission /as the present Commission was formerly called/, which controls the basic decision-making power: such mechanism in many cases determines the competence of the Commission, which cannot act without a prior proposal from the Board..." 11/ These relations between the two principal subregional organs reveal in turn their reciprocal autonomy, in addition to that of the Board vis-à-vis the governments of the member states.

The above does not conflict with the fact that, apart from the mechanism of the proposals the Commission may "issue instructions to the Board", nor that the latter must "comply with Commission assignments", as provided in Articles 7 d) and 15 b), respectively, of the Cartagena Agreement. This aspect of the relations between the two organs is perfectly explicable in light of the nature of each one, and furthermore, of the variety and diversity of the functions which the Agreement assigns them. In Article 15 g) itself a specific type of assignment is considered: that of carrying out technical studies requested by the Commission. An interesting example of these instructions or assignments--among the many which could be mentioned--

---

11. Cf. Instituto Interamericano, op. cit., p. 823. Regarding the Board's "power to project and propose", see O. Padrón Amaré, "Interés Nacional y Control de las Decisiones en un Proceso de Integración (con especial referencia al Grupo Andino)", doc. INTAL, Reunión 25/dt. 1, 4-9-75, pp. 2-4.

is the one received by the Board to issue an opinion on the interpretation which should be given to Article 28 of Decision 24. 12/

   Although of a different content and scope, a relationship which offers a certain analogy to the one between the Commission and the Board is that created by the Board's exercise, as expressly delegated by the Commission, of the powers of the latter, as provided in Articles 7 e) and 15 h) of the Agreement. 13/ In this connection, it should be noted how liberally this delegation was authorized. In effect, the first of the articles mentioned reads thus: "to delegate its powers to the Board, when deemed desirable". On the one hand, the Commission may delegate any of its powers; on the other, it may do so under any circumstances that it determines at its discretion. The Commission appealed to this very broad authorization ever since its first meeting. At that time, through Decision 2, it delegated to the Board "the power to conclude acts and contracts, to acquire the rights and contract the obligations indispensable for the normal expansion of its activities; to administer the budgeted funds and to maintain them in any currency as well as to dispose of them in conformity with the provisions of the budget; and, in general, to carry out all acts conducive to the fulfillment of the aims of the Agreement, as expressed by that instrument and the Commission".

   Unfortunately, in the Final Act of the Meeting there appears no reference to this Decision that would permit one to know the true scope of this delegation of the competence to "carry out all acts conducive to the fulfillment of

---

12. See infra, note 45, of Chapter IV.
13. With respect to these provisions of the Agreement, it would be worthwhile to consider an analogous provision of the General Treaty of Central American Integration, according to which SIECA (a nongovernmental technical organ endowed with certain powers assigned to organs of another nature) "shall also exercise the functions that are delegated to it by the Executive Council". (Art. XXIV). Cf. Instituto Interamericano, Derecho Comunitario Centroamericano (San José, 1968), p. 196.

the aims of the Agreement, as expressed by that instrument and the Commission". 14/ However, according to the principles which govern the delegation of competencies, the Commission may at any time reassume the delegated competence or revise an act instituted by the Board in the exercise of such competence; likewise, when exercising these delegated competencies, the Board must do so, as stated in Decision 2 itself, within the limits which the Agreement establishes for the Commission. 15/

As an illustration of this other relationship between the two principal subregional organs, mention should be made of Article 12 of Resolution 70, by virtue of which the Board could include new products not produced in the Subregion in the schedule of products which the Commission was to approve before December 31, 1973, in accordance with the provisions of Article 10 of the same decision, whenever the Board confirms, in the course of its duties or at the request of a member state, that such production is not occuring in the Subregion. Note that here we are dealing with, in addition to a case of delegating competence, a case in which the competence delegated is one for which there is no explicit provision in the Cartagena Agreement. 16/

Before concluding this brief examination of the functional relationships between the Commission and the Board,

---

14. See the Acta Final de la Primera Reunión del Acuerdo sobre la Integración Subregional (Cartagena Agreement, Noviembre 21-25, 1969.

15. Cf. Villagrán Kramer, C. "Sistematización de la Estructura Jurídica del Acuerdo de Cartagena", INTAL, Derecho de la Integración, No. 12, marzo, 1973, pp. 33-34.

16. As will be remembered, the only competence explicitly delegated by Article 65 of the Agreement to the Commission in this matter results from the adoption of "those measures necessary to balance the need for protection of the subregional product with the need to insure a normal supply". For other competences assigned by the Commission to itself or to the Board, see infra, section 5 of Chapter IV.

mention should be made of Article 15 1) of the Agreement, according to which the Board should present to the Commission an annual report on its activities. In its reports the Board relates to the Commission the work accomplished, during the period in question, in the discharge of its functions and in compliance with the assignments received from the Commission, as well as the relations maintained with third countries and international organizations. 17/

2. The Auxiliary Organs: the Advisory Committee and the Economic and Social Advisory Committee

The two "auxiliary organs" mentioned in Article 5 of the Cartagena Agreement are the Advisory Committee and the Economic and Social Advisory Committee. The former is the organ through which the member states maintain close ties with the Board, and it must be composed of representatives of all member states, who may attend the meetings accompanied by their advisers (Art. 19). The Advisory Committee meets at Board headquarters whenever convened by the Board or by the president of the Commission, at the request of any member state (Art. 20). The Advisory Committee is responsible for a) advising the Board and collaborating in the fulfillment of its tasks whenever so requested; and b) analyzing the Board's proposals upon request, prior to their submission for consideration by the Commission. The opinions of the Committee members are incorporated in the form of reports for transmission to the Commission and the Board for their consideration (Art. 21). Through Decision 19 the Commission approved the Regulations of the Committee, which, besides reiterating these provisions of the Agreement, regulates other matters related to the meetings, the presidency, and the acts of the Committee. Up to the present the Committee has had only one meeting, which the

_____

17. As an illustration, see Informe de las Actividades de la Junta (Período: mayo 1973 - mayo 1974), COM. XV/di 2 rev. 1, 12 de septiembre de 1974.

Commission convened to deal with the proposed regulation of Decision 24. 18/

As for the second of the committees or auxiliary organs mentioned in Article 5 of the Agreement--the Economic and Social Advisory Committee (ESAC)--is composed of representatives of the management and labor sectors of the member states; the Commission, within the first year that the Agreement is in force, must determine the composition, the procedure for filling the posts, and the functions of this Committee (Art. 22). The Commission complied with this mandate by adopting Regulations to govern the Committee, which were adopted and amended by successive decisions. 19/ The Regulations establish the purpose of the Committee as that of linking the economic activity sectors of the member states to the principal organs of the Agreement and promoting active participation of the sectors that it represents in the subregional integration process (Art. 1). In view of this, it is the duty of the Committee to: a) advise the principal organs of the Agreement in matters in which its opinion is required; b) present, on its own initiative, its opinions, in the form of recommendations, to the principal organs of the Agreement on general or special aspects relating to the subregional integration process; c) analyze the basis of the proposals of the Board, as appropriate, prior to their consideration by the Commission, in those matters in which the latter considers it desirable to do so (Art. 2).

Concerning its composition, the Committee must be composed, equally, of three representatives of the workers and three representatives of the employers from each member state, in order to seek adequate representation of the new legal forms of socio-economic organization that the member states may have or may adopt (Art. 3). In an analogous train of thought another article requires that the

---

18. Cf. Acta Final de la Primera Reunión del Comité Consultivo de la Decision 24, 12 a 14 de noviembre de 1975.

19. See Decisions 17, 17-a, 55, 72 and 74.

members of the Committee act in the interest of the sectors that they represent and those of the Subregion, and that they not receive instructions from the governments of the member states (Art. 4). Likewise, the members of the Committee must be elected by direct vote of workers' and employers' organizations, respectively, and the member states decide upon the national practices and procedures leading to maximum representation and authenticity in the election of Committee members (Art. 5). The Committee meets in regular sessions twice a year and in special sessions whenever convoked by any of the principal organs of the Agreement or by the chairman of the Committee upon the request of at least three countries (Art. 8).

Concerning the relationship of these auxiliary organs to the two principal ones, there is little to add to the provisions cited in the previous subsection. In the Regulations of the Advisory Committee (AC) practically nothing is added to that contained in Articles 19 through 21 of the Agreement; a brief mention may be made of the provision that the official designated by the Board shall act as Secretary of the AC (Art. 15) and that the Board shall be the depository for the acts and documents of the Committee (Art. 18). Regarding ESAC, besides the provisions of its Regulations, which complement considerably Article 22 of the Agreement, a provision contained in Article 16 of the Regulations should be mentioned here, according to which the principal organs of the Agreement must consider the reports of this Committee, although the acceptance of its statements is optional for them.

3. The Councils and the Meetings of Ministers; Other Institutions

The Cartagena Agreement provides in its Article 29 procedures and mechanisms of a permanent character to achieve the coordination and harmonization referred to in Article 26, i. e., for the coordination of the development plans of the member states in specific sectors and the harmonization of their economic and social policies, directed toward the future creation of a central planning system for the integral development of the area; Article 29 itself gave the Commission until December 31, 1970, to establish, at the proposal of the Board, the procedures and mechanisms it deemed necessary. The Commission began to fulfill this mandate in its Decision 22, entitled "Mechanisms and procedures for the harmonization of policies and the coordination of development plans", whose preamble states that "it is necessary to maintain close ties between the national bodies charged with formulating and executing economic and social policies and the organs of the Agreement".

In the same Decision the Commission created the following five Councils:

a) Planning Council, for the coordination of development plans and strategies and the harmonization of planning methods and techniques;

b) Monetary and Exchange Council, for the harmonization of monetary, exchange and international payment policies;

c) Finance Council, for the harmonization of financial policies for the promotion of investment and the mobilization of resources earmarked for financing the productive sectors, especially those of importance to the Subregion;

d) Fiscal Policy Council, for the harmonization of taxes and other aspects of fiscal policy;

e) Foreign Trade Council, for the harmonization of all aspects of trade policy.

The Commission stated that, at the proposal of the Board, other Councils could be created as required by the process of integration.

The Councils must be composed of high-level representatives from the national institutions charged with formulating and executing development plans and policies in the member states, who will be appointed by the agency designated by each government to maintain direct contact with the Board. The Councils meet whenever convened by the Board, either officially, by petition of the Commission, or by petition of at least three of the member states. By virtue of an amendment introduced by Decision 53, in the latter case the Board will convene the Council only after consulting with the other member states. The Council meetings may request the preparation of reports or studies to be carried out by the respective national institutions, in which case the results obtained shall be forwarded to the principal organs of the Agreement. Likewise, the results of the Council meetings are incorporated into reports and sent to the above-mentioned organs, which must contain the opinions of all the representatives when so requested.

Following the adoption of Decision 22, the Commission created other Councils. Thus, its Decision 36 created the Tourism Council, to advise the principal organs of the Agreement on the harmonization of national tourism policies and on the preparation of corresponding plans. Its Decision 39 created the Social Affairs Council, to advise the principal organs on the harmonization of social policies and on the preparation of corresponding plans and studies. Its Decision 68 created the Health Council, to advise the principal organs on the harmonization and coordination of national policies in the health field. [20/] Decision 71 created by the Physical Integration Council, to advise the principal organs on defining common policies in the areas of transportation, communication, and energy, and on the preparation of corresponding joint programs of investment and action. All these Decisions contain a common clause which provides that, as regards their convening

------

20. In this field, see also Reunión de los Ministros de Salud, prevista en el Convenio "Hipólito Unanue" sobre Cooperación en Salud, suscrito el 18 de diciembre de 1971, en ocasión de la "Primera Reunión de Ministros de Salud de los Países del Area Andina. One of the recommendations of this Convention resulted in the creation of the Health Council, as indicated in the preamble of Decision 68. On other aspects of this Convention, see supra, subsection 7 of Chapter I.

and functioning, the Councils must conform to the rules provided in Decision 22, as amended by Decision 53.

The Andean institutional framework includes organs, institutions or meetings which were not provided for in the Cartagena Agreement nor considered, as in the case of the Councils, by the Commission. These are the meetings of Ministers of Education, Health and Labor, which were considered, respectively, in the three conventions mentioned in Section 7 of Chapter I: the "Andrés Bello" Convention on the Educational, Scientific, and Cultural Integration of the Countries of the Andean Region, the "Hipólito Unanue" Convention on Health Cooperation of the Countries of the Andean Region, and the "Simón Rodríguez" Convention on Social-Labor Integration. Even though it is not an "institutionalized" meeting like those provided for in these three instruments, reference should also be made to the meeting held in May 1971, by the Ministers of Industry and Economy, at which they issued a declaration of industrial development policy, recommending to the Agreement's Commisssion that it develop a mechanism permitting the harmonization of the individual industrial development plans of each country with the requirements of subregional planning; it also proposed the creation of intergovernmental labor groups, which in coordination with the Agreement's Board would develop concrete plans relating to all the activities mentioned in the Declaration. 21/

Although the Cartagena Agreement did not provide for them, meetings of Foreign Ministers of the member states have been held in Lima "for the purpose of closely following the course of economic integration and lending in their political support". 22/ The work accomplished in the course of these meetings is extremely varied in the areas or matters dealt with and very fruitful in producing statements and agreements, some of which are mentioned

---

21. The complete text of the Declaration appears in Historia Documental del Acuerdo de Cartagena, repeatedly referred to in Chapter I, p. 557.
22. Cf. Salazar Santos, F., Una Visión General del Grupo Andino, in doc. J/UC/6, 23 de mayo de 1973, p. 22.

elsewhere in this study. This is evident in reading the Final Act of the meetings held up to the present. 23/

Finally, one should refer to the other organs or entities created by the Commission for the discharge of administrative functions related to some programs or activities. On the one hand, there are committees created for sectoral programs of industrial development, composed of government experts and having the function of advising the Board or Commission on the best way of fulfilling the objectives of these programs; these committees are the Metal-Mechanic Committee (Decision 57, Art. 32) and the Petrochemical Committee (Decision 91, Art. 39). On the other hand, there is the Administrative Commission on International Commercial Highway Transport, created by Decision 56 (Art. 35), which is entrusted with "the administration and control of the norms" established by said Decision. In a third category are the so-called "Contracting Committees" of the Andean technological development projects, provided in Decision 84 (Article 18) to take charge of the "management and administration" of each project. The three existing Committees cover the following areas: copper metallurgy (Decision 86); copper hydrometallurgy (Decision 87); and tropical forest resources (Decision 89).

4. The Financial Organ: the Andean Development Corporation

In Section E of Chapter II of the Cartagena Agreement reference is made to the Andean Development Corporation, which had already been contemplated since the Bogotá Declaration (1966). At that place the Agreement gives attention to the relations that should be established with that organ and, with that objective, provides that "in addition to the functions enumerated in Articles 7 and 15, it shall be incumbent upon the Commission and the Board

---

23. The complete text in Spanish of the Acta Final of the First, Second, Third and Fourth Meetings appears in Historia Documental del Acuerdo de Cartagena, pp. 212, 415, 435 and 475, respectively.

to maintain close contact with the directors and the executive president of the Andean Development Corporation, to the end that adequate coordination with their activities may result and thus facilitate the successful achievement of the goals of the present Agreement" (Art. 24). The Agreement again refers to the Corporation in connection with industrial programming, 24/ the initial programs intended to solve problems of infrastructure, 25/ and the special regime for Bolivia and Ecuador. 26/ As can be seen, it is proper for the Andean Development Corporation to be considered as the "financial organ" of the subregional integration process both because of the relations called for in Article 24 of the Agreement, between the Corporation and the principal organs, as well as because of the commitments acquired by the member states. A broad explanation is presented below of the matters relating to the structure and functioning of the Corporation.

---

24. With respect to this mechanism of the Agreement, according to its Article 40 the Commission must maintain adequate coordination with the Andean Corporation.

25. With respect to physical integration (Chapter XI), the Agreement provides that the problems referred to shall include, insofar as possible, measures for joint action before international credit institutions and, particularly, the Corporation, to insure the provision of financing not available within the Subregion (Art. 87 d).

26. With respect to this regime (Chapter XIII, Section E, on Financial Cooperation and Technical Assistance), the Agreement commits the member states to pledge themselves to act concertedly before the Andean Development Corporation and other national or international subregional organizations for the purpose of obtaining technical assistance and financing for high priority installation in Bolivia and Ecuador of industrial enterprises and complexes, as well as to join efforts to secure the distribution of regular and special resources in such manner as to enable Bolivia and Ecuador to receive substantially greater shares than those which might have resulted were the distribution of such resources to be proportionate to their capital contributions to the Corporation (Art. 16).

Above all, it should be remembered that the Agreement establishing the Corporation, negotiated principally through the same Mixed Commission that prepared the Cartagena Agreement, was signed in Bogotá in February 7, 1968. On account of a prior decision--which was stipulated in the Agreement--the city of Caracas, Venezuela, had been selected as the seat of the Corporation. The Agreement entered into force on January 30, 1970. The purpose of the Corporation, according to Article 3 of its Agreement, is "the furthering of subregional integration". To this end, within a framework of rational specialization and an equitable distribution of investment within the area, taking into consideration the need for effective action to benefit the relatively underdeveloped countries, and in proper coordination with the organization in charge of subregional integration, the Corporation will encourage the utilization of opportunities and resources within its area of operations through the creation of production or service interprises, and the expansion, modernization or conversion of existing enterprises. 27/

Although in principle it was thought that the Corporation would have the character of a private law person in conformity with the laws of the host country, the nature intended in Article 3 is that of "a legal entity of public international law... governed by the articles contained in this instrument" (Art. 1). Along this line of thinking, and

---

27. The complete text of the Agreement appears in INTAL, Boletín de la Integración, marzo de 1968, p. 128 et seq. On the background of the Corporation, consult Roberto Fresard R., Corporación de Fomento de la Producción, Chile, undated. For a detailed analysis of its object, functions, structure, etc., see by the same author "El Tratado que creó la Corporación Andina de Fomento", ibid., INTAL, Derecho de la Integración, No. 3, octubre 1969, pp. 28-35, and Instituto Interamericano, Derecho de la Integración Latinoamericana, pp. 399-404 and 825-839. With respect to Corporation activities, see Corporación Andina de Fomento, 5 Años de Labor - 1970-1975, and the Carta de la CAF, published by its Unidad de Relaciones Públicas.

if it is also borne in mind that the Corporation is organized much like a capital-stock company made up of quotas contributed by its members and represented by shares, this subregional organ is actually a multinational public enterprise. This is corroborated by the fact that it performs its functions in a geographic area or sphere comprising six countries.

The functions of the Corporation are established in Article 4 of the Agreement as follows:

a) To undertake studies in order to pinpoint investment opportunities, and to direct and prepare the corresponding project;

b) To diffuse among the area countries the results of its research and study, in order to guide satisfactorily the investment of available resources;

c) To provide directly or indirectly the technical and financial assistance necessary for the preparation and execution of multinational or complementary projects;

d) To obtain domestic or foreign credit;

e) To issue bonds, debentures and other securities which may be placed within or outside of the Subregion;

f) To encourage the attraction and mobilization of resources. In the performance of the functions referred to in this and preceding paragraphs, the Corporation shall be subject to the legal requirements of the countries in which the said functions are to be performed or in whose national currency the said securities are to be issued;

g) To encourage capital and technological contributions under the most favorable conditions;

h) To grant loans and issue security bonds, pledges and other guarantees;

i) To encourage the underwriting of subscribed shares, and to underwrite them, when the proper requirements have been met;

j) To promote the organization of enterprises, their expansion, modernization or conversion, the Corporation being empowered to this end to subscribe to stocks or shares;

The Corporation may transfer the stock, shares, rights or securities it may acquire, first offering them to public or private entities in the Subregion and, failing their interest, to third parties interested in the area's economic and social development;

k) To undertake under the conditions, which it may fix, any specific tasks or negotiations related to its objectives which may be entrusted to it by shareholders or third parties;

l) To coordinate its action in the development of the Subregion with that of other national and international bodies;

m) To recommend the coordination machinery necessary for the bodies or organizations of the area which provide investment resources;

n) To acquire and alienate personal and real property, to file or defend judicial and administrative actions, and generally, to undertake all kinds of operations, acts, contracts and agreements necessary to the fulfillment of its objectives.

The authorized capital of the Corporation is US$100 000 000 (one hundred million dollars), distributed in shares of the "A" and "B" series, in addition to those of "C" series whose issuance may be authorized by the board of directors. Subscribed capital amounts to US$25 000 000 (twenty-five million dollars), distributed in the following series: series "A", comprising six nominative shares each in the amount of one million dollars; and

series "B", made up of 3 800 nominative shares each for
the amount of five million dollars. In each of the subregional countries one share of the "A" series will be subscribed
by the government or by the institution of the public sector
designated by the government. Shares of the "B" series
will be subscribed within each country by the public sectors,
with 40% of the total number of shares being available for
subscription by natural or corporate persons in their own
right. The nonsubscribed authorized capital (75 million
dollars) may be issued for subscription with the favorable
vote of at least seven directors (Arts. 5 and 6).

Stockholder meetings may be regular or special;
regular meetings take place once a year and special ones
when convened by the Executive president of the Corporation,
the board of directors, or two series "A" stockholders representing at least 25% of paid up capital (Arts. 11 and 12).
In successive articles the functions of the regular and special
meetings are stipulated, including among the latter the function to change the provisions of the Agreement relating to
all administrative and procedural matters required for fulfillment of the proposed objectives (Arts. 13-15).

The board of directors is composed of eleven directors, elected for a period of three years, and they may validly hold a session with a quorum of at least six members.
The functions of the board are explicitly enumerated and
include among them the function to decide, upon request of
the executive president, on any matters not covered under
the Agreement, and to give their sound interpretation, in
the latter case reporting thereon to the stockholders at their
next meeting (Arts. 23-27).

Finally, the executive president, who is called an
international official in the Agreement, is the Corporation's
legal representative and exercises direct management and
administration over it, with the power to decide on and assume charge of any matter not otherwise expressly reserved
to the stockholders' meeting, the board of directors, the Executive Committee, or any other subsidiary organ that may
be created by the board, as well as such other matters as
may be entrusted to him; he is also responsible for the appointment of staff personnel, which also have status of international officials (Arts. 31 and 39).

The Agreement establishes a procedure for compulsory, automatic arbitration before a tribunal composed of three persons in case of any conflict arising between the Corporation and its stockholders. One of the arbitrators is appointed by the board of directors, another by the interested party, and a third by mutual agreement between the other arbitrators. If an agreement cannot be reached, either the Corporation of the interested party may request the Mixed Commission, or any organ that may eventually replace it, that is, the Commission of the Agreement, to appoint the third arbitrator. None of the arbitrators may be of the same nationality as the interested parties to the controversy. If all efforts to reach a unanimous agreement fail, the decision will be taken by majority vote. The third arbitrator may decide all points of procedure and jurisdiction in those cases where the parties cannot agree in these matters.

However, judicial action may be brought against the Corporation only before a court with jurisdiction in the territory of a contracting state where the Corporation has established an office or appointed an agent or attorney with power to accept the summons or notification of judicial action, or where it has issued or guaranteed securities. The contracting states of the Agreement, their representatives or persons whose rights derive therefrom may not file any judicial action against the Corporation. However, stockholders may assert those rights pursuant to the special procedures which may be prescribed, either in this Agreement, in the bylaws of the institution, or in any contracts which they may enter, to settle controversies arising between them and the Corporation (Art. 54).

5. The Jurisdictional Organ: the Proposed Andean Tribunal

During its Sixth Special Meeting (1971) the Commission of the Cartagena Agreement noted in the proceedings thereof its consensus as to the need for creating a jurisdictional organ which would be responsible for "settling controversies that may arise on account of application of the Agreement, the decisions of the Commission and the resolutions of the Board". On that occasion the Commission agreed to recommend to the Board that the necessary studies be undertaken to make available prior to the Regular Meeting of 1972 the guidelines that will make it possible to formulate recommendations to the governments on the creation of that organ. 28/

To that end, the Board requested reports from national specialists and consultants, and with that documentation at hand convoked a Meeting of Experts, which took place in June 1972, and which, in addition to the specialists and consultants, was attended by Prof. Gerard Olivier, the assistant director general of the Legal Service of the European Communities, and Dr. Pierre Pescatore, present judge of the Court of Justice of those Communities. Following this, the Board prepared a draft of the basis for a treaty to form the jurisdictional organ, which was analized at a meeting of government experts held in November 1972. Its report of December 12 of that year contains a revised version of that draft. 29/ The Board then presented, as a proposal, the definitive text of the instrument. 30/

The first chapter of the draft treaty is intended to "complete the normative system of the Agreement by defining its legal structure, the form of incorporation of the decisions of the Commission in national legislation and, finally, the obligations of the member states in terms of

---

28. See the Acta Final of the meeting referred to, dated 9-18 diciembre 1971, p. 6.

29. Cf. Informe de la Junta sobre el Establecimiento de un Organo Jurisdiccional del Acuerdo de Cartagena, COM/X-E/di 5, 12 de diciembre de 1972. The mentioned draft of the basis was circulated as Doc. J/AS 12, 2 de agosto de 1972.

30. Cf. Proyecto de Tratado para la Creación del Tribunal del Acuerdo de Cartagena, JUN/PROPUESTA 43, 18 de enero de 1974.

the norms that make up the legal structure of the Cartagena Agreement". 31/ These provisions of the draft will be examined later on, 32/ as will also the provisions contained in Chapter III of the draft, relating to the "control of legality", that is, to the competencies or jurisdiction of the Tribunal. 33/ The only thing that should be examined in the present chapter is the matter relating to the "Organization of the Tribunal" (Chapter II of the draft).

The Tribunal, which would perform its functions on a permanent basis, would be composed of three justices appointed by common agreement by the governments of the member states, and they must be nationals of a Latin American country, enjoy high moral standing and meet the qualifications required in their country for exercising the highest juridical functions; they would enjoy full independence in the exercise of their functions, would not be able to perform other professional activities whether remunerated or not, except those of a teaching or academic nature, and would have to abstain from any action incompatible with the nature of their position. On the other hand, the member states would be obliged to grant the Tribunal all the facilities necessary to carry out its work, and the Tribunal and its justices would enjoy in the territory of those states the immunities recognized by international custom and, especially, by the Vienna Convention on diplomatic relations.

The justices, the secretary of the Tribunal, and the international officers appointed by him would enjoy in the territory of the host country of the Tribunal the immunities and privileges in accord with their rank; for these purposes, the justices would have the rank equivalent to chief of mission and the other officers would be ranked as established by common agreement between the Tribunal and the government of the host country. The last of the provisions that should be cited relates to the Statutes of the functioning of

---

31. Cf. Report cited, p. 2.
32. See infra, section 5 of Chapter V.
33. See infra, subsection 4 b) of Chapter IV.

the Tribunal, which the Commission would approve at the request of the Board, and whose changes would be approved by the Commission at the request of the Tribunal. These decisions of the Commission would be governed by majority rule of two thirds of the votes cast, provided there is no negative vote.

In the course of the Thirteenth Special Meeting of the Commission (1974) the Board presented a statement on the background and basis of the proposal for the creation of the tribunal or jurisdictional organ. Following a general discussion, in which the representatives presented their initial points of view, it was agreed that the Board should be entrusted to make an additional effort to have the draft treaty which it had prepared made known and discussed in all the member states at the level of the competent, specialized authorities in the matter. 34/ At its Sixteenth Regular Meeting the Commission again considered the topic and agreed on a detailed program of action, which included, among other things, consultations that the Board would carry on with the governments between the months of January and March 1975; the organization, in accordance with those governments, of discussions on the topic on settlement of disputes and others contained in Proposal 43, in which Board members and officials as well as ad hoc consultants, if necessary, would participate; in April 1975 a meeting of high-level government experts within the consultative Committee would be held at Board headquarters, if the Commission so desires, for the purpose of transmitting to it the results of the consultations and so that the Committee might issue an opinion on Proposal 43; following this, the proposal would be included in the Commission's agenda either for the regular meeting beginning July 7 or in a special meeting prior thereto, as the case may be. 35/

---

34. Cf. Acta Final of this meething, held May 27 to to June 5, 1974, p. 5.

35. Cf. Acta Final of this meeting, held 12 to 14 November 1974, p. 4.

6. Institutional Relations with the Outside World

In two recent studies on the law or legal order of Andean economic integration the authors present an interesting institutional question, which relates to the nature that can be attributed to the Cartagena Agreement or Andean Group from the international point of view. Here is a determination made in one of the studies: 36/

> The independence of the Andean Group appears clearly in the institutional sphere. In fact, the Cartagena Agreement created an organic structure much more developed than that of LAFTA and made it capable of expressing its own will, that is to say, different from the will of LAFTA and of the states of the Andean Group.

In the other study the Cartagena Agreement or Andean Group is also conceived as a regional international or intergovernmental organ: 37/

> The Cartagena Agreement is an international organization in the form in which the theory of international institutions considers it, that is to say, not necessarily in a geographic sense but considering other factors such as the interest of presenting a common external front and the necessary functional homogeneity of a group of countries.

This characterization of the Cartagena Agreement or Andean Group explains the multiple and important institutional relations that subregional organs maintain with the

---

36.   Cf. Vendrell, F. J. Le droit de l'integration économique andine (Thèse, Paris, 1975), p. 116. See also, by the same author, "La Organización del Acuerdo de Cartagena", INTAL, Derecho de la Integración, Nos. 18-20, Marzo y Junio, 1975, p. 59.

37.   Cf. Casanova, M., Una Integración Equitativa: Rol del Derecho en el Acuerdo de Cartagena (Santiago, Chile, 1975), p. 83.

outside world. In making reference here to some of these relations, it is proper to begin with those established with the government of the host country, Peru.

First of all, these relations were established by Decree-law 18,092 of December 31, 1969, which appears in document COM/II/di 2 (March 9, 1970) on Personería Jurídica de la Junta (Legal Capacity of the Board), by virtue of which "the Board of the Cartagena Agreement, through its duly accredited officials, may perform all kinds of functions and enter into any contract necessary to the normal development of its activities within the territory of the republic" (Sole Art.). This was followed by the issuance of Supereme Decree 0005 of February 19, 1970, which appears in document COM/II/di 3 (March 9, 1970) on Inmunidades y Privilegios para los Miembros de la Junta y sus Funcionarios (Immunities and Privileges for Board Members and Officials), by virtue of which privileges and immunities would be granted to the members of the Board, the director-secretary and other Board officials while the Agreement on Privileges and Immunities between the organs of the Cartagena Agreement and the Peruvian Government was being subscribed to. Such an agreement, bearing that title, was signed by the Junta and the Peruvian Government on December 29, 1971. 38/ It is curious to note that Article 26 of the Agreement, which is retroactive to January 1, 1970, when Decree-law 18,092 entered into force, states that that law "recognized the legal capacity of the Board of the Cartagena Agreement as an organ of international public law". In any case, in light of the jurisprudence of the International Court of Justice at The Hague on the "objective international personality" of the United Nations

---

38. It was approved by Decree-law 20,175, and its codified text (which includes the notes exchanged on June 21 and July 13, 1973 between the Board of the Agreement and the Ministry of Foreign Affairs, which are an integral part of the Agreement), appears in doc. JUN/di 95 (18 de octubre de 1973).

Organization, 39/ there appears to be no reason for doubt
concerning the international personality of the Cartagena
Agreement or Andean Group, apart from the organ--the
Commission or the Board--through which is exercised the
right or capacity to negotiate and contract internationally.

Institutional relations of the Andean Group with the
outside world generally fall into two major groups. The
first covers those relations which presume to exercise of
a right of delegation, both active as well as passive, each
day more frequently in the life of international organizations. Active delegation is expressly contemplated in Article 8 of the Agreement, to the effect that "The Commission
shall encourage concerted action by the subregional nations
relative to problems arising from international trade which
affects any one of them; and it shall participate in international meetings and organizations of economic character".
As has been indicated, the Andean Group has been represented in international forums such as UNCTAD, GATT,
and CECLA in order to present a common position the procedure for which was established at the First Meeting of
Foreign Ministers of the Group, which dealt with the action
to be taken by LAFTA. This procedure has been extended
to other international forums in which the member states
participate. 40/ With respect to the "common position" of
those countries, one member of the Board has observed
that "the first condition for enabling us to assert our capacity to negotiate is to act with solidarity before others or in
international forums, on the basis of the common interest
of the five /six/ member states". 41/ Aside from this,

---

39. Cf. ICJ, Reports, 1949, p. 185. On this topic,
see F. Seyersted, Objective International Personality of
Intergovernmental Organizations (Copenhagen, 1963), passim.
40. Cf. Casanova, op. cit., p. 83. As for the reference to LAFTA, see, as an illustration, Posición Conjunta
de los Países Miembros del Acuerdo de Cartagena en las
Negociaciones Colectivas de la ALALC", doc. COM/XVIII/
dt. 2, 21 de octubre de 1975.
41. Cf. Informe del Coordinador de la Junta, Ing. S.
Lluch Soler, a la Tercera Reunión de Cancilleres de los
Países Miembros del Acuerdo, in Historia Documental del
Acuerdo de Cartagena, p. 455.

apparently the exercise of the right of active delegation has not as yet been translated into the accreditation of permanent missions but rather into the appointment of special observers or representatives.

Passive delegation, on its part, may also make itself evident in many ways, most of which are regulated in various instruments. Thus, for example, according to Article 4 of the Regulations of the Commission, the latter may invite international organizations and the governments of countries not members of the Agreement to appoint representatives to it as observers or advisers; both may participate in Commissison meetings when invited by the latter. 42/ In turn, the Board is authorized, by Article 7, item 42, of its Regulations "to maintain relations with international organizations and other entities for purposes of information and examination of matters of interest to the subregional integration process". As one can observe, this provision contemplates reciprocal cooperation between that organ of the Agreement and other international organizations and entities. Pursuant to these provisions, representatives or observers have been accredited by the OAS, the IDB, the WHO, and twenty-three American and non-American countries.

The second category of institutional relations of the Agreement results from the capacity to subscribe to agreements with states and international institutions. This contractual capacity, with respect to technical assistance agreements, is also expressly provided for in the Regulations of the Board, wherein the latter has the function "to negotiate for technical assistance with governments, international advisory agencies and other entities and arrange

---

42. The Commission implemented Article 4 through its Decision 11 (Participation of observers in meetings of the Commission) so that permanent observers of countries would not be invited to its meetings, considering the nature of the matters that usually are studied by the Commission and the necessary discretion that must be exercised with respect to them.

the terms under which such assistance can be furnished"
(Art. 7, item 43). By way of illustration, mention may be
made of the technical assistance agreement with Canada of
September 10, 1971, renewed in 1973, and the agreement
on technical and scientific cooperation with Italy of January
18, 1974. There are also agreements on this matter with
international organizations, such as the United Nations and
the IDB. Along another line of thinking, the capacity to
negotiate and contract with states became evident on the
occasion of the accession of Venezuela to the Agreement,
which has been discussed in another chapter of this study. 43/

Considering the close analogy that can be drawn with
relations of this type, mention should be made of the mixed
or joint commissions in which the Andean Group partici-
pates: the Joint Commission with Japan; 44/ the Argentine
Andean Commission; 45/ the Andean-Mexican Mixed Commission; 46/ the Hispano-Andean Mixed Commission. 47/,
47-a/ In connection with the European Communities, at
its Sixth Regular Meeting the Commission, after analyzing

---

43. See subsection 1 d) of Chapter II.
44. See the complete text of the Comunicado Conjun-
to del Japón y del Grupo Andino, signed in Tokyo on October 16, 1971, in Historia Documental del Acuerdo de Cartagena, p. 564.
45. See the complete text of the Declaración Conjunta Constitutiva de la Comisión Andina Argentina, signed in
Lima on November 17, 1972, ibid., p. 567.
46. See Acta Final de la Reunión de Instalación de la
Comisión, signed in Lima on December 15, 1972, ibid.,
p. 575.
47. See the complete text of the Declaración Conjunta Constitutiva de la Comisión Hispano-Andina, signed in
Madrid on June 5, 1973, ibid., p. 582.
47-a. There is also the Andean-Chilean Mixed Commission, created by the Joint Declaration of October 30,
1976, signed by Chile, on the one hand, and the other five
member states of the Andean Group, on the other.

a report of the Board on Andean Group relations with those Communities, expressed its desire to see materialized as soon as possible the constitution of a mixed commission in them and the Andean Group with the aim, as expressed by the Foreign Ministers, "of jointly establishing in a permanent and dynamic manner a global policy for relations between the Communities and the Andean Group". 48/

All these relations still do not exhaust those which the Andean Group maintains with other countries and international organizations, as can be seen in the annual progress reports of the Board, 49/ but they do make it possible to understand the volume and importance of institutional relations under the Cartagena Agreement with the outside world.

---

48. Cf. Acta Final of the meeting referred to (12 a 17 de julio de 1971), p. 4.

49. See, as an illustration, the document cited in note 17, pp. 25-27. See also the reports of the Comission to the Conference of the High Contracting Parties to LAFTA on the functioning of the Agreement, as for example the one cited in note 13 of Chapter II.

Chapter IV

COMPETENCES OF THE SUBREGIONAL
ORGANS

The law emerging from the acts of organs of an economic integration process, especially in the case of processes of a "community" type, plays a role of exceptional importance in the development and strengthening of the juridical order of that integration process. Since this is obviously the case of the Andean legal order, it is natural that
special attention should be given to the acts of the subregional organs by beginning with a thorough examination
of the competences attributed to those organs.

1. The System of Attributing Competences
   According to the Agreement

Notwithstanding the analogies that could be drawn
between the system of attributing competences to the subregional organs adopted by the Cartagena Agreement and
the system adopted by the legal orders of other economic
integration processes, it cannot be denied that the former
presents sufficiently distinctive characteristics that would
block any attempt to show that the systems are parallel in
some way. Actually, this calls for an observation which,
to a greater or lesser degree, may be made practically
with respect to all the other integration processes, except
that in the case of the Andean Group this observation seems
to be justified much more than in others. Therefore, it
becomes necessary to select the method or plan for explaining the different competences that would be proper for
the system to be examined. The one that has been selected
here and which will be explained forthwith would seem at
least to be capable of pointing out the most outstanding
marks and features of the Andean subregional system.

To begin with, an explanation should be made as to
why the title of this section states "attributing" instead of
"distributing" (or "sharing") competences, as is more
customary. Unlike other systems, as for example the

European Communities and LAFTA, 1/ which show a true
distribution or sharing of competences between the integration organs and the member states, in the Andean Pact
this phenomenon is not understood, at least insofar as the
powers ratione materiae are concerned. In fact, the "material" competences as such are, with some exceptions,
reserved for the subregional organs. 2/ This involves
precisely one of the most outstanding characteristics of
the system of the Agreement, through which is revealed
the very broad sphere of action that has been entrusted to
those organs as well as the preponderant role played by
their acts in the subregional integration process.

---

1. See, respectively, P. Pescatore, "Distribución
de competencias y de poderes entre los Estados miembros
y las Comunidades Europeas", in INTAL, Derecho de la
Integración, No. 1, octubre 1967, especially pp. 112-113,
and F. Paolillo, "Repartición de competencias y de poderes entre la ALALC y los Estados Miembros", ibid., No. 2,
abril 1968, p. 20 et seq.

2. These exceptions take on two forms. One permits
a member state to withdraw products from its Schedule of
Exceptions at any time and adjust them to the Liberalization
Program and the External Tariff in force for such products
(Art. 56). The other exceptions take on the form of a power
of the member states to act jointly. In the liberalization
mechanism there are three examples: one in Article 53
authorizes the member states to agree on a selective elimination of products, provided that this be at a more accelerated rate; another in Article 57 calls for negotiations
among the member states for the purpose of finding formulas permitting them to obtain a gradual withdrawal of products from their Exception Schedules within the term expiring on December 31, 1985; and the third example is the
complementarity agreements with the other Contracting
Parties of LAFTA in suitable production sectors, as provided for in Article 59. A final example is the pledge of
the member states to enter into necessary consultations
with the Commission before concluding agreements of a
tariff nature with countries outside the Subregion, as stipulated in Article 68.

From the viewpoint of the so-called "functional" competences or powers, the situation varies only in the form and to the extent that we shall proceed to explain. Apart from a more detailed explanation that will be made in studying the nature and validity of the subregional acts, 3/ at this time it will suffice to point out that only with regard to certain matters is a subregional organ assigned a specific action and the member states another action for the purpose of confirming the validity of the act of the subregional organ in the domestic law of those states. Along this line of thinking one can speak of the "distribution" of powers or of "shared" powers because the powers, from the exercise of which depend the performance of the act and its full validity, are shared between the subregional organ and the member states. Aside from these cases, in which there are, for such purposes, specific statements in the Agreement, 4/ or perhaps whenever it would seem reasonable to presume the need for such domestic complementary action, all the remaining competences assigned to the subregional organs by the Agreement take the form of "exclusive" competences. 5/ Thus, from the viewpoint of "functional" competences, neither would the usual method or plan for explaining the powers seem justifiable.

---

3. See infra, especially subsections 1 (b) and (c) of Chapter V.

4. In Articles 27 and 28 of the Agreement the member states pledge themselves "to adopt all measures necessary to implement" the act of the subregional organ.

5. A competence of an integration organ is "exclusive", either because it is exercised on matters or subjects transferred completely from the jurisdiction of the member states or because the former has been given certain exclusive faculties or powers capable, therefore, of generating acts of validity erga omnes in matters which, aside from this, may or may not be reserved to it. Obviously, the "exclusive" competence par excellence would stem from the first of the two hypotheses, inasmuch as, from a purely juridical point of view, it must be presumed that such competence infers other faculties or powers. As will be seen shortly, in this case fall, by an overwhelming majority, the powers assigned by the Andean Pact.

The system of assigning competences of the Andean Pact, in effect, can be understood more fully when they are examined according to their normative (and regulatory) and executive character, as well as other facts thereof, excluding to the extent possible what relates to the specific powers conferred upon the subregional organs for exercising such competences, which will be studied in the next chapter.

With respect to the normative competences, it should be noted, above all, that most of them are conceived as a specific mandate, even with a term within which they must be complied with. Sometimes the terms relate to those stipulated in the Agreement for the fulfillment of obligations of member states. However, regardless of what the purpose of the Agreement may have been in this connection, repeated practice of the organs has demonstrated that, generally speaking, this type of power does not wear out or terminate after the respective mandate has been complied with. Other competences on the other hand, are conceived in the usual way, to the effect that, regardless of whether or not they refer to specific matters, they are not conceived in terms of a mandate, which has to be complied with within a definite term. Apart from these two forms that normative competences may adopt, the nature of the regulatory competence which, as will be seen in due course, plays a very important role in the Andean legal order, should be indicated.

As concerns the executive competences, neither are all these of the same nature and scope. On the one hand, there are those that look at the proper functioning of the mechanisms of the Cartagena Agreement and the correct application of its provisions, as well as the compliance with the Commission's decisions (and, implicitly, with the Board's resolutions). A second category or type of executive competence refers to those which are assigned to subregional organs to authorize or refuse authorization to member states concerning acts or omissions on their part which are explicitly contemplated in the Agreement, relating to several of its mechanisms. Powers to pass on certain acts of member states or other rights or matters constitute a third group. Some of these competences, together with other different ones, are assigned within the special regime established by the Agreement for Bolivia and Ecuador.

In addition to the normative and executive competences, the subregional organs exercise others that can be classified into two groups. In the first of these fall some powers which are extended in connection with industrial programming and which, because of their nature and purpose, depart considerably from the first two categories. The second group is confined to competence in matters relating to the solution of disputes. Under the same section in which these competences will be examined there will also be explained those which are contemplated for the proposed subregional court.

Finally, the Andean juridical order permits the exercise of "implicit" functions or powers. This affirmation could be based both on some provisions of the Cartagena Agreement that would seem to authorize the subregional organs to act in this way and also on the very practice of these organs, as can be seen in the section which concludes this chapter.

2. The Normative Competences

As was indicated in the previous section, the normative competences assigned to subregional organs by the Cartagena Agreement take on two different forms. Perhaps an explanation should be made, first of all, of those which are primarily mandates on specific matters and which should relate as is done below, to the pertinent objectives and mechanisms of the Agreement.

a) Competences on specific matters

Just as in explaining these objectives and mechanisms in Chapter 1 of this study it was necessary to mention many of these powers or mandates, so in the statement which follows unnecessary repetition will be avoided. In turn, the aspects and facets of interest to the purposes of this chapter will be pointed out.

(i) Coordination of economic policies and of development planning

With respect to these matters, the first of the competences assigned by the Cartagena Agreement stems from the approval, by the Commission at the proposal of the Board, prior to December 31, 1970, of a common regime for treatment of foreign capital and, likewise, regimes, for trademarks, patents, licenses and royalties, inter alia. Once approved by the Commission, the latter had to present them for consideration of the member states, which pledged themselves to adopt the measures necessary to implement such regimes within the six months following approval by the Commission (Art. 27). In a similar vein are the provisions relative to the uniform regime to govern multinational enterprises. Prior to December 31, 1971, the Commission, at the proposal of the Board, was to approve and recommend to the member states such a regime also similar are the provisions referring to the directives to serve as a guide for the unification of legislation on industrial incentives in the member states, which, within the same period of time, the Commission was to approve at the proposal of the Board (Art. 28).

None of these two competences seem to have been exhausted or extinguished once the respective mandates are complied with within the time periods provided for in the Agreement. Thus, in addition to the adjustments introduced to Decision 24 (Common Regime of Treatment of Foreign Capital...) through its Decisions 37 and 37-a, adopted in June and July 1971, respectively, the Commission introduced new provisions in articles 7 and 13 of the original decision adopted in December 1970 through its Decision 70, which it adopted in February 1973 on the occasion of the adherence of Venezuela, on which date all the other member states had already taken the necessary steps for the entry into force of that decision. 6/ More

---

6. As for the competences assigned by Article 28 of the Agreement, by the same Decision 70 the Commission introduced amendments to Article 3 of its Decision 46 (Uniform Regime on Multinational Enterprises...).

recently, by Decisions 103 and 109 introduced further amendments to Decision 24.

In the same fields the Agreement assigns to the subregional organs other competences. As will be recalled, its Article 26 refers to coordination of the development plans in specific sectors and harmonization of the economic and social policies of the member states, which are contemplated in the Agreement with a view to arriving at a system of joint planning for the integrated development of the area. To achieve both goals the Commission, at the proposal of the Board, and by not later than December 31, 1970, was to establish the permanent procedures and machinery necessary therefore (Art. 29). With respect to this other specific mandate, which the Commission implemented through its Decision 22 (amended in its Article 5 by Decision 53), a competence should be mentioned which appears in another place in the Agreement and was conceived there as one of the permanent competences of the Commission: to approve the rules indispensable for coordination of development plans, and harmonization of the economic policies of the member states (Art. 7 (b)).

Returning to the mandates and competences of Chapter III of the Agreement, the Commission, at the proposal of the Board, was to adopt a program of common instrumentation and machinery to govern foreign trade in the member states, to be put into effect by the latter prior to December 31, 1972, except for the Common External Customs Tariff (Art. 30). 7/

(ii) Industrial programming, liberalization program and common external tariff

In the field of industrial programming the Cartagena Agreement assigns to the subregional organs only one

_____

7. As indicated above, in section 3 and note 20 of Chapter I the Commission approved NABANDINA (Decision 51, amended by No. 58).

normative competence: that of approving sectoral program of industrial development, to be jointly implemented by the member states (Art. 33). 8/ Perhaps, as an additional competence complementary to this one, the one assigned to the Board in Article 35 should be considered. According to this other article, the Board should propose to the Commission, in each case, the complementary measures indispensable to facilitate compliance with the pertinent Program and, in particular, those necessary to insure installation of the plants that may be assigned according to the provisions of paragraph (c) of Article 34 and the actual use of the subregional market by such plants. As can be seen, in both cases normative competences of a permanent nature are involved. Aside from this, the Liberalization Program is mentioned in this article due to the fact that the competence assigned in Article 47 of the Agreement is analogous to the one assigned in the referred Article 33, and it is certainly the only normative one which appears under that Program.

Regarding the third of the mechanisms which is discussed in this section, the Andean Pact assigns important normative competences to the subregional organs: the Common External Tariff, which the member states are bound to implement by not later than December 31, 1980 (Art. 61), and the Common Minimum External Tariff, which was to have been implemented by December 31, 1975 (Art. 64). With a view toward the implementation of these two obligations, the subregional organs have been assigned important competences. The first relates to the Draft Common External Tariff, which the Board was to prepare prior to December 31, 1973 for consideration of the Commission, which would approve it within two years thereafter (Art. 62).

---

8. As will be recalled, up to now the Commission has approved the PSDI of the Metalworking Sector (Decisions 57 and 57-a), of the Petrochemical Industry Sector (Decision 91), and of the Sectorial Development Program of the Automotive Industry (Decision 120).

The second competence or mandate relates to the Common Minimum External Tariff, which the Commission was to approve, at the proposal of the Board, prior to December 31, 1970 (Art. 63). As was indicated in the proper place, the Commission implemented this mandate by its Decision 30, which was amended within the same term by Decision 33. 9/ This latter decision was adopted within the term contemplated in Article 63, but the Commission is explicitly authorized, at the proposal of the Board, to modify the levels of common tariffs according to, and at the time this is considered desirable in order to satisfy the needs of the Subregion, to consider the special status of Bolivia and Ecuador, and to adjust these levels to those fixed in LAFTA's Common External Tariff (Art. 66). Evidently, another normative competence of a permanent nature is involved here.

(iii) Measures on agriculture and livestock, commercial competition, origin, physical integration and financial matters 10/

Within Chapter VII (agricultural and livestock measures) of the Cartagena Agreement it is hardly worthwhile to speak of normative competences in connection with some of the measures which, according to Article 70, the Commission, at the proposal of the Board, should take in order to arrive at the goals mentioned in Article 69. The measures referred to are, among others, joint programs of agro-livestock development by products or group of

_____

9. As was indicated in describing this mechanism in Chapter I, at the end of Article 65 (b) of the Agreement, prior to Decision 30, the Commission approved the Common Minimum External Tariff for the products of the first section of the Common List, by Decision 12.

10. The omission of Chapter IV (Safeguarding Clauses) of the Agreement is due to the fact that none of the powers assigned to the subregional organs in that chapter are normative in nature.

products, and common measures and programs on plant and animal sanitation. 11/

The situation is entirely different with respect to the competence assigned to the subregional organs in the case of commercial competition. In effect, prior to December 31, 1971, the Commission, at the proposal of the Board, was to adopt the rules indispensable to forestall or remedy any practices which might constitute unfair competition within the Subregion, such as "dumping", undue price manipulation, maneuvers intended to impede the normal supply of raw materials, and others of similar effect. (Art. 75). 12/ Regarding this competence, the fact should be noted that Article 75 contemplates the need to coordinate the rules referred to with the resolutions that complement or replace Resolution 65 (II) of the Conference of the Contracting Parties of LAFTA, which clearly indicates that there is present here once again not only a specific mandate but also a power to modify the rules in question whenever necessary.

With regard to the origin of merchandise, the Agreement begins by assigning to the Commission the competence to adopt any special measures necessary to classify such origin (Art. 82). The Commission has not yet exercised this competence. However, the Board has the competence to fix the specific requirements of origin for products so requiring it (Art. 83). 13/ According to another provision of the same article, within the year following the fixing of

---

11. The first measures to increase trade in agricultural products, which appear in Decision 43 of the Commission, do not appear to be normative, at least in the sense in which are those approved by that Decision in connection with the previous mechanisms of the Agreement.

12. As indicated above, the Commission complied with this mandate by its Decision 45, "Standards on Competition".

13. As indicated above, the Board has exercised this competence through its Resolutions 1 and 18.

specific requirements, the member states may request a
review by the Board, which must give its summary opinion.
Likewise, upon request of a member state, the Commission should examine these requirements and render a final
decision, within a term of more than six and less than
twelve months, as computed from the date of the establishment of these by the Board. In turn, the Board may at any
time upon its own initiative or at the request of a party
amend any requirements established pursuant to this article, in order to adapt them to the economic and technological progress of the Subregion. 14/ Although some of
these competences would seem to be executive in nature or
to have a stamp that is characteristic of another type of
power, they are esentially normative competences.

    With respect to physical integration, prior to Decem-
ber 31, 1972, the Board was to draft initial programs in
the fields of energy, transportation and communications,
especially in terms of border transit, and present them to
the Commission (Art. 87). The Commission has partially
complied with this mandate by adopting its Decision 56,
which regulates in detail international highway transport.

    As for financial matters, the Board will present to
the Commission proposals on various aspects which are
enumerated in Article 89 of the Agreement, which provides
norms for the solution of the programs that may arise from
double taxation, and to complement Decision 40, which approved the agreement to avoid double taxation between
member states and arrangements to holding agreements on
the same subject between member states and other states
not in the Subregion.

---

14. Acceding to a request of Ecuador, the Board
exercised this other competence, first by its Resolution 9
and then by its Resolutions 10 and 16, both delaying the effects of No. 9. See also other later resolutions in Note 42
of Chapter I.

(iv) Special regime for Bolivia and Ecuador

Regarding this regime, the Cartagena Agreement begins by assigning the subregional organs a general competence by allowing them to propose and adopt the necessary measures in conformity with its rules, in order to achieve the aim of the special regime (Art. 91). Apart from the normative competence exercised by the organs in applying this broad provision, the other competences of this type which are assigned to them in this chapter of the Agreement would seem to be reduced to two: one relating to the complementary measures required to facilitate the fulfillment of the Sectoral Programs of Industrial Development, to the extent that the Board, in proposing such measures to the Commission, should consider exclusive advantages and preferential treatment to Bolivia and Ecuador in the cases in which this may be necessary (Art. 95); and another relating to the application of the Common External Tariff, stating that the Commission, at the proposal of the Board, should determine when Bolivia and Ecuador should adopt minimum tariff levels relative to products of interest to the other member states under certain circumstances (Art. 104).

b) Other normative competences; the regulatory ones

Apart from the powers embodied in specific mandates or dealing with specific matters, the Andean Pact assigns few normative competences to the subregional organs. Insofar as the Commission is concerned, the one in Article 7(a), above all, should be mentioned: "to formulate the general policies of the Agreement and to adopt any measures necessary to achieve its objectives". Surely one would not pass unnoticed which is assigned frequently to the organ which, in other international organizations, including those of the traditional type, is on a high level and performs the outstanding role that the Agreement confers on the Commission. But what is of greater interest to emphasize is the fact that, considering the broad and imprecise terms in which it is conceived, this is a competence whose very nature and scope cannot be known until practice throws light on it, even if it is a power exclusively normative or if it permits the production of acts of the

126

Commission that have taken on a rather executive nature. To date, this competence has not been exercised in an express manner, so that there are no decisions in which the Commission may have referred specifically to Article 7 (a), although, on the other hand, there are initiatives and actions that would seem to imply that this competence has been exercised, as can be seen in section 5 of Chapter III, especially in the joint position of the member states of the Agreement indicated in the document cited in footnote 40 of that same chapter.

At the end of Article 7 of the Agreement the same organ is assigned another competence whose very nature and scope cannot be known either so long as practice does not make it possible to judge. In fact, by stating that the Commission has the power "to hear and deal with any other business of common interest" (item k), the Agreement assigned the Commission a very broad competence which is also totally imprecise to the extent that, by specifying the power to "deal with", one has strong reason for thinking that this refers basically to an executive competence. However, there is evidence to indicate that it is possible that the competence in question is exercised in a frankly normative way. As example of this is Decision 50, by which the Commission, under item k, approved a subregional regime for the temporary impoundment of vehicles of private use. Another example to use of the competence in a normative way would be when the Commission approved Proposal 64 of the Board (November 10, 1975), relating to an Andean instrument of labor migration.

In a different sense, one might also consider as a normative competence, certainly of great importance, the one which the Agreement assigns to the Commission regarding the proposal of the member states to any reform to the present Agreement (Art. 7 j). After conferring this initiative, another competence of approving modifications to the present Agreement is included in Appendix I (which contains the list of matters by which the Commission will adopt its decisions by a two-thirds affirmative vote, assuming there is no negative vote). In connection with this competence, which is a clearly normative one, it is curious to note that the Agreement is silent as to how the modifications which the Commission approved will enter into force and, especially, whether some action will be required or not on the part of each member state. But, as has already been seen, these gaps were filled with the Additional Instrument to the Agreement that was signed when Venezuela became a part of it. 15/

Some of the normative competences of the subregional organs are by nature regulatory. In this connection, it would be proper to begin by referring to the provision of the Agreement which authorizes the Commission "to enact its own internal rules of procedure, and those to govern the Committees, and to approve the Board's rules and any amendments thereto" (Art. 7 i). 16/ But from the viewpoint of this chapter those which are truly of interest are the regulatory competences on substantive subjects or matters, which may be grouped into two major categories: those that the Agreement itself assigns to the organs and those that have generated some of the Commission's decisions.

As a specifically assigned competence, it is only necessary to mention the one in Chapter VIII (competitive commercial practices) which states that "The Commission shall issue procedural rules for the application of the rules of the present Chapter" (Art. 77). The final words of this article would seem also to refer, and perhaps principally, to the rules that the Commission would adopt by virtue of the mandate given in Article 75, and to the one that the Commission complied with through the already cited Decision 45.

Among the competences that have generated decisions of the Commission, mention may be made, first of all, to the regulations for implementing the rules on industrial

---

15. See supra, subsection 1 (d) of Chapter II.
16. On its part, the Board must "draft its internal rules and submit same to the Commission for approval or modifications" (Art. 15 j). Decisions of the Commission approving the respective regulations are N° 6 (Regulations of the Commission) and N° 9 (Regulations of the Board).

property, provided for in Article G of the Temporary Provisions of Decision 24, and which the Commission itself, at the proposal of the Board, was to approve within six months following the date on which the common regime established by that Decision entered into force. 17/ In approving the Directives for unification of legislation on industrial development provided for in Article 28 of the Agreement, the Commission also gave itself the mandate of approving, at the proposal of the Board, the regulations which are necessary for the application of Decision 49. 18/ Finally, in a transitory article of the recently cited Decision 50, the Commission stated that within a brief period it would approve, at the proposal of the Board, a regulation of the regime established in that Decision. 19/

3.   The Executive Competences

Bearing in mind the different types or categories of competences that could be called "executive", perhaps reference should first be made to those that confer a power --at par with a responsibility-- to see to the proper operation of the mechanisms of the Cartagena Agreement and the correct application of its provisions.

The first of these competences is the one assigned to the Commission in Article 7 (g) of the Agreement: "To supervise the coordinated compliance with obligations assumed under this Agreement and under the Montevideo Treaty". Now then, it can be seen that this is a very specific or concrete function: to supervise--not the observance of the stipulations of the Agreement exactly--but the "coordinated compliance" with obligations emanating from

---

17.   This regulation was approved by Decision 85 of the Commission.

18.   Up to now the Commission has not approved any regulations of those mentioned in Decision 49.

19.   The regulation for the temporary impoundment of vehicles for private use was approved by the Commission by its Decision 69.

two conventional instruments or different treaties--the
Treaty constituting LAFTA and the Andean Pact. 20/
Given the problem of the compatibility of the subregional
agreements with that Treaty and, in general, with the
juridical structure of the Association, and that as was seen
in Chapter II, some aspects were later declared compatible
to those agreements by the competent organ of LAFTA,
fully explains the necessity of some regional organ to
supervise the compliance with obligations assumed under
one instrument or another to see that it is "coordinated",
that is, so that incompatible situations with the ties and
relations established between the two juridical orders do
not arise. 21/

The same type of competence, but conceived in terms
which are usually assigned to certain organs within the
institutional framework of an economic integration process,
is the one which is assigned to the Board in Article 15 (a)
of the Agreement; that is, the power "To supervise the

---

20. Notwithstanding the apparent clarity of Article
7 (g) and of the even more explicit provision contained in
Article 15 (a), to which reference is made in the following
paragraph, in one of the whereas of the Declaration of the
Governments of Bolivia, Colombia, Ecuador, Peru and
Venezuela on the Commission, in which Decree-law 600 of
the Government of Chile was declared incompatible with
the Common Regime established by Decision 24, it expressly states "That in conformity with Article 7 of the Cartagena
Agreement, it is an attribute of the Commission to supervise the coordinated compliance with the obligations assumed under this Agreement". Cf. Acta Final del Decimo-
quinto Período de Sesiones Ordinarias de la Comisión,
September 10-14 and 19-20, 1974, p. 4. On other aspects
of this Declaration, see infra, section 6 of Chapter V.

21. Only in this connection it should be realized that
the Commission of the Agreement shares with the Standing
Executive Committee of LAFTA the responsibility that the
Montevideo Treaty assigns to this organ "for supervising
the implementation of the provisions of the present Treaty
..." (Art. 39 of the Treaty).

implementation of the present Agreement and of the Commission Decisions". Hence, the following observations of the then Coordinator of the Board, to the effect that the Board, 22/

> .... to use the expression of Mr. Denian, a member of the Commission of European Communities with respect to that organ, ... is the watchdog of the Cartagena Agreement. It must zealously supervise the progress of the process so that it is carried out with exact submission to the juridical rules established in the Agreement and emanating from the Commission. In this line of thinking, it is incumbent on the Board to see that the Commission Decisions are put into force in due time in each of the member states, that the interchange of commodities is carried out in accordance with the rules of the liberalization program...

All of this truly presumes a responsibility and a competence to supervise the integrity of the communitarian order, according to the expression used with respect to Central American integration. 23/ Aside from other action that has been taken in the matter, the Board presented to the Twelfth Regular Meeting of the Commission a report that "it has been supervising the fulfillment by the member states of the obligations imposed on them by the Agreement and the Commission Decisions", and noted that it had begun "a task of systematic evaluation of the progress of the integration process with the purpose, among others, of checking the level of fulfillment of the diverse obligations assumed by the countries and the way that each

---

22. Cf. F. Salazar Santos, "Aspectos jurídicos de la integración andina", in INTAL, Derecho de la Integración, No. 13, julio 1973, p. 155.
    23. Cf. Instituto Interamericano, Derecho Comunitario Centroamericano (San José, 1968), p. 374.

one of the governments interprets those obligations". 24/
This is very closely related to the Junta's specific mandate
to evaluate annually the results of the subregional integration process, since it assumes a responsibility complementary to the one conferred by Article 15 (a) referred to. 25/

In addition to these competences, the Agreement
assigns to the organs others of the same type on specific
subjects or matters. Thus, in matters of commercial
competition, the Board is entrusted with "surveillance
over the application" of the rules to forestall or to remedy
any practices which might constitute unfair competition
within the Subregion, as noted in Article 75 of the Agreement, in the particular cases which are denounced. With
respect to the origin of the merchandise, the Board "shall
implement compliance measures for the norms and requirements of origin within the subregional trade. Likewise, it

---

24. The same document reflects on the forms a-
dopted by nonfulfillment of the obligations stipulated in the
Agreement. Cf. Informe de la Junta sobre el Cumplimiento del Acuerdo y las Decisiones, doc. CDM/XXII/di 3, 14
de julio de 1973, pp. 3-4.

25. According to Article 15 (f) of the Cartagena
Agreement, it is a function of the Board "To assess annually the accomplishments of the implementation of this Agreement, and the progress in the achievement of its goals,
giving special attention to compliance with the principle of
equitable distribution of integration benefits; and to propose to the Commission any corrective measures of positive character that may be pertinent". Although the Board
has not formally presented any annual assessment to date,
it has done work of this nature on various aspects of the
integration process and the Commission has referred to
this work in its reports to the Conference of the High Contracting Parties of the Montevideo Treaty. See, for example, the reports presented in 1974 and 1975 doc. COM/
XVI/dt 5/Rev. 1 (15 de noviembre), p. 8 and COM/XV-E/
dt. 1 Rev. 1 (24 de noviembre), p. 2, respectively.

shall propose any measures considered necessary to settle conflicts of origin which might hinder the achievement of the goals of this Agreement" (Art. 85).

The second category or type of executive competences consists of those by which the subregional organs can authorize or refuse authorization to the member states concerning acts or omissions on their part explicitly contemplated in the Agreement. One of these powers is the one assigned to the Board, concerning the mechanism of the Common External Tariff. According to Article 67, "In order to cover temporary deficiencies in supply which may affect it, any member state may raise this question with the Board, which shall verify the situation within a time period compatible with the urgency of the matter. Once the Board has verified that the problem does exist and so informs the affected country, the latter may adopt such measures as a provisional reduction or a suspension of charges of the External Tariff, within the limits indispensable to correct its problematic situation". The Board has exercised this competence on several occasions, as has already been indicated. 26/

The Agreement assigns this same type of competence in connection with three other mechanisms. Within the agro-livestock sector saving clauses are contemplated (the ones provided for in Article 28 of the Montevideo Treaty), but the country that imposes these measures must send notice to the Board immediately, and any member state that considers itself injured by virtue of these measures may appeal to the Board, which will analyze the case and propose to the Commission the measures of a positive nature that would be appropriate, in view of the objectives stipulated in Article 69. The Commission would then render a decision on the applied restrictions and on the measures proposed by the Board (Art. 73). In matters of

---

26. See note 34 of Chapter 1, in which are enumerated the Resolutions of the Board referred to.

commercial competition, the member states may not adopt the corrective measures proposed in Article 75 of the Agreement unless authorized in advance by the Board (Art. 77).

The third mechanism referred to relates to the saving clauses. As will be recalled, the Agreement authorizes the adoption of the safeguards provided for in Chapter VI of the Montevideo Treaty in the situations covered therein, but if, as a result of the imposition of the Liberalization Program of the Agreement, serious disadvantages are caused or threaten the economy of a member state, or a significant sector of its economic activity, that state may, with advance authorization of the Board, apply corrective measures of an emergency nature in a nondiscriminatory manner. The Board should analyze periodically the evolution of the situation in order to avoid prolonging the restrictive measures beyond what is strictly necessary or to consider new measures of coordination that should be taken (Art. 79). 27/ Also, if monetary devaluation effected by one member state should alter the normal competitive conditions, another state which considers itself prejudiced may bring the case to the Board, which must render a brief summary opinion. If the disadvantage is verified by the Board, the injured state may adopt corrective measures of a provisional nature for the duration of the prejudicial situation, as limited by the Board recommendations. Without prejudice to the application of the said provisional measures, any member state may request the Commission to render a final decision on the matter. The member state which has ordered the devaluation may request the Board at any time to review the situation in order to attenuate or suppress the above-mentioned corrective measures. The decision of the Board may be overruled by the Commission (Art. 80).

---

27. As will be recalled, through its Resolution 20 the Board declared that it could not accede to the request of Peru on application of measures of this type.

134

Other types or categories of powers appear in the
Liberalization Program of the Agreement. One consists
in the authority of the Board to determine, at its own
initiative or upon request of a party, in the necessary
instances whether a measure that is unilaterally imposed
by a member state constitutes a "charge" or a "restraint",
in the sense that these terms are employed in Article 42 of
the Agreement (Art. 43). 28/ Under the same Program
the subregional organs are assigned competences that are
emphatically executive in nature. With respect to the
Sectoral Programs of Industrial Development, and considering the normative competences assigned by the Agreement
on the subject, prior to December 31, 1970, the Commission, at the proposal of the Board, was to determine which
goods would be reserved for such Programs. 29/ Within
the same period the Commission, at the proposal of the
Board, would prepare a schedule of goods not being produced within any of the subregional countries, nor reserved
for any Sector Program of Industrial Development, and
would select those to be reserved for production in Bolivia
and Ecuador (Art. 50). In this Article and in Articles 51
and 53 the Agreement confers on those two subregional
organs other powers of an analogous or similar nature on
the same subject. 30/

---

28. An analogous competence or power is the one
conferred on the Board by Article 58 of the Agreement to
determine when substantial trade has existed, or whether
there is a definite expectancy that it will exist, in both
cases for the purposes consigned in that article. Not so
analogous as this one, but similar, other powers of judgment are provided for, as will be indicated later.
29. As indicated in Chapter I, the Commission,
through its Decision 25, approved the list of these products.
30. As indicated in Chapter I, the Commission approved, first of all, the list contained in the Annex of Decision 26 (replaced by the Annex of Decision 60), and then
the one contained in Annexes I and II of Decision 28, which
is the list of the products reserved for production in Bolivia and Ecuador. See section 4 of that chapter.

As for the obligation of the member states to abstain
from altering their tariffs and the exceptions contemplated
for Bolivia and Ecuador, these exceptions must be certified by the Board and authorized by the Commission (Art.
54). Up to November 30, 1970 the Commission, at the
proposal of the Board, could modify the number of items
referred to in the first paragraph of Article 55 and the
Board, on its part, could authorize the maintenance of
some exceptions beyond the time period proposed in paragraph four of that article. Finally, in duly qualified cases,
the Board may authorize a member state to incorporate on
its Schedule of Exceptions those products which, although
reserved for Sectoral Programs of Industrial Development,
had not been so programmed (Art. 56).

Under the special regime for Bolivia and Ecuador
new executive competences appear. The first of the provisions of this regime cover the adoption by the organs of
the Agreement of measures necessary to achieve the aim
to which the regime purports (Art. 91). Some of the measures or acts contemplated specifically entail executive
competences. Thus, the Commission, at the proposal of
the Board and prior to December 31, 1970, was to approve
schedules of goods to be liberated for the benefit of Bolivia
and Ecuador on January 1, 1971 (Art. 97 b). As for fulfillment of the Liberalization Program, the Commission,
at the proposal of the Board, would determine the manner
and the time limits within which Bolivia and Ecuador would
liberalize the products which, although reserved for Sectoral Programs of Industrial Development, were not in
fact included in them (Art. 100 b). Furthermore, the
Commission could modify the number of items on the
Schedule of Exceptions of the two countries in the terms of
the second paragraph of Article 55 (Art. 102). Finally, as
regards the Common External Tariff, the Agreement assigns powers to the subregional organs concerning the
adoption by the two countries of minimum tariff levels and
the establishment of exceptions by them. 31/

---

31. Regarding the applications of these provisions of
the special regime, see note 45 of Chapter I.

4. Other Competences of the Organs; Competences of the Proposed Tribunal

The remaining competences assigned by the Cartagena Agreement to the subregional organs can be classified into two groups, in the first of which fall those which are conferred in connection with industrial programming. One of them consists in the authority, and even the mandate, of the Commission to promote programs tending to rationalize the production of merchandise in those cases in which, in its discretion, it is possible and desirable to do so pursuant to the aims of the Agreement (Art. 36). Also, the Commission, at the proposal of the Board, may recommend the creation of multinational enterprises for installation, expansion or complementarity of specific industries (Art. 38). When the Board deems it desirable, but in any event in its annual assessment of accomplishments, it must propose to the Commission those measures it considers indispensable to insure equitable participation by the member states in common Sectoral Programs of Industrial Development, in the implementation of them, and in their promotion of the goals (Art. 39). Finally, the Commission is empowered to coordinate its work adequately with that of the Andean Development Corporation and to negotiate the collaboration of any other national and international institutions whose technical and financial contributions may be deemed desirable (Art. 40).

a) Competences relating to the solution of disputes

The second group of competences concerns the solution of disputes, as provided for in Article 23 of the Cartagena Agreement. This article initially provides that the Commission has the power to execute any procedures of negotiations, good offices, mediation and conciliation that may be necessary in cases of disputes arising from the interpretation or implementation of the Agreement or of the Commission Decisions. The true content or scope of this provision has been clarified sufficiently in the Regulations of the Commission (Decision 6, Ch. VII), as can be seen below.

As for negotiation, the affected countries must seek a solution of their differences by this direct method. In any case, they must inform the Commission of the results of such negotiations. If a solution by direct negotiation is not forthcoming, or if disputes are only partially solved, the Commission must interpose its good offices and if the Commission feels that these are insufficient or that the matter in dispute requires more direct intervention on its part, it must offer to mediate and seek an agreement by proposing formulas that it considers appropriate within a time period that it will establish for this purpose. If the efforts indicated above should fail, the Commission must undertake the procedure of conciliation. For this purpose it must appoint a conciliation committee composed of one national from each of the countries in disagreement and one national from each of the other member states. This committee must investigate the facts and hear the parties in dispute. Following this procedure the committee, with the majority vote of its members, must issue a report containing proposals that it believes will lead to a final solution. This report must be placed in the hands of the Commission within a period of three months from the date of constitution of the conciliation committee.

According to a second provision of Article 23 of the Agreement, if settlement is not obtained after following the procedures indicated above, the member states must observe the procedure established in the "Protocol for the Settlement of Disputes", signed in Asunción, Paraguay, on September 2, 1967 by the Foreign Ministers of the Con-tracting Parties of the Montevideo Treaty. The procedures established in that Protocol are direct negotiation, good offices or proposal of formulas by the Standing Executive Committee of LAFTA, and arbitration, which takes into consideration a Court of Arbitration, whose constitution and functioning are regulated in detail. [32]/ Apart from

_____

32. The complete text of the Protocol appears in Inter-American Institute, "Instruments of Economic Inte-gration in Latin America and in the Caribbean (Oceana, 1975), vol. I, p. 127.

the provisions in the Agreement, the Regulations of the Commission provide that if all procedures of direct negotiation, good offices, mediation and conciliation should fail, the countries in dispute must submit to the arbitration procedure established in the Protocol of Asunción.

Article 23 of the Agreement contains another important provision, relating to matters to which compulsory arbitration procedures will apply as established in the Protocol. The third paragraph of Article 16 of the latter provides as follows: "If as a consequence of the process of integration provided for in the Montevideo Treaty and supplementary provisions the contracting parties shall sign new agreements, they must specify therein the subjects to which the compulsory arbitration procedures of the present Protocol shall apply". For the purposes contemplated in Section 3 of Article 16, in the Protocol the member states declare that all matters covered under the Agreement and the Commission Decisions are included thereunder. With respect to both this declaration and the general obligation to resort to the methods and procedures mentioned, one wonders why the Resolutions of the Board are excluded. Considering the nature and content of these other subregional acts, it is evident that it would be difficult to consider the raison d'être for such exclusion. 33/

b) Competences of the proposed tribunal

It is also pertinent to explain at this time the competences provided for in the proposed Andean tribunal, to which reference has already been made in relation to the structure and functioning of the subregional organs. 34/ As will be recalled, just as the Commission understood the matter in taking the initiative to create a jurisdictional

---

33. In the last section of Article 23 the member states pledge themselves to try to ratify the Protocol at the earliest date possible. Up to the present none of them have done so.

34. See supra, section 5 of Chapter III.

organ, this would be charged with reconciling any disputes arising concerning the application of the Agreement, the Decisions of the Commission, and the Resolutions of the Board". 35/ The proposed treaty for the creation of the jurisdictional organ or tribunal prepared by the Board considers another type of competence for the new subregional organ. In fact, what the Board has recommended is "a system of control over legality and uniform interpretation in lieu of a procedure for the pure and simple solution of disputes between member states." In the document which it presented to the Commission, the Board indicates the reasons why it considered it necessary to recommend such a system. 36/

In order to exercise control over legality an action of nullity of the Decisions of the Commission and the Resolutions of the Board is contemplated, first of all. As has been seen, this competence has been conceived in broad terms since the possibility of impugning any act emanating from the Commission or from the Board is provided for, by means of an action of nullity based on any one of the following grounds: (a) violation of the rules that form the juridical structure of the Agreement; or (b) deviation of power. The broad nature of these grounds makes it possible to include within them the defects of incompetence and of violation of substantial forms on the part of the

---

35. Cf. Acta Final del Sexto Período de Sesiones Extraordinarias de la Comisión, 9-18 de diciembre de 1971, p. 6.

36. The Board especially noted that "a system such as the one established in the Cartagena Agreement requires a procedure for control of legality much stricter than that necessary for an organization whose decisions are taken only by the unanimity of its components or which have only the faculty of recommending". Cf. Informe de la Junta sobre el Establecimiento de un Organo Jurisdiccional del Acuerdo de Cartagena, COM/X-E/di 5, 12 de diciembre de 1972, pp. 2 and 13 et seq. The final text of the proposal appears in doc. JUN/PROPUESTA 43, 18 de enero de 1974.

140

organs. 37/ The member states could promote this action
unless they have expressed their approval at the time of
approval of the act, if it concerns Decisions; the Commission could do so concerning Board Resolutions; the Board,
concerning Commission Decisions; any natural or juridical
person in the member states, concerning Commission Decisions or Board Resolutions that are applicable to such
person.

For the same purposes of legality control, an "action
of noncompliance with the legal order of the Cartagena
Agreement" is also contemplated. What is concerned here
is the competence that the proposed court would have to
hear cases of noncompliance with the obligations emanating
from the Andean legal order for member states. Consistent with the basic concept of the Report itself, it states
that "under the legal structure of the Agreement conflicts
arising from common rules are not disputes between member states that can be resolved through direct negotiations...
They Are, basically, conflicts between a party that does
not fulfill its obligations and the legal structure of the
Cartagena Agreement. For that reason, the procedure
recommended by the Board excludes the traditional phases
of direct negotiations, mediation, or good offices between
the member states...". Now then, since the action relates
to acts of member states, in the opinion of the Board the
tribunal should not be competent to nullify them, since this
would represent an invasion of competences reserved to
the national jurisdictions; the decision of the tribunal would
be limited to verifying the situation of noncompliance.
Furthermore, only the member states and the Board could
interpose this action of noncompliance by understanding
that the right of natural and juridical persons is protected
by the possibility of recourse to the national courts of the
country in which the noncompliance situation has arisen,

---

37. Cf. F. Orrego Vicuña, "La creación de un Tribunal de Justicia en el Grupo Andino", in INTAL, Derecho
de la Integración, N° 15, Marzo 1974, p. 40.

in which case the procedure of pre-judicial interpretation, to which reference is made below, would apply. 38/

The third and last of the competences that the proposed subregional court would exercise is the power of interpretation, by pre-judicial procedure, in form and purposes similar to that assigned to the European Court of Justice by Article 177 of the Treaty of Rome. 39/ Departing, perchance, from the premise that none of the two competences and actions above make it possible to overcome the differences of interpretation that could arise as a result of the application of subregional rules by the national courts, in the Report it is recommended that when litigation is interposed before those jurisdictions the national judges should request of that court a judgment on the interpretation of the common subregional rule. The national judge would be competent to resolve the matter under litigation, based on the interpretation of the rules derived from the legal structure of the Agreement that the subregional tribunal has made. The latter would not act as a kind of court of cassation, inasmuch as it would not be competent to resolve matters under litigation in the

---

38. Report cited in note 36, pp. 21-23.

39. This article provides for the following: "The Court of Justice shall be competent to hear cases on a pre-judicial basis: (a) affecting interpretation of the present Treaty; (b) concerning the validity and interpretation of acts performed by the Institutions of the Community; (c) affecting interpretation of the Statutes of the organs created by an act of the Council, when this is provided for in the Statutes. Whenever a question of this kind is submitted to a jurisdiction in one of the Member States, this jurisdiction may request, in case it considers it necessary to issue its judgments, a ruling on this point by the Court of Justice. Whenever a question of this kind is submitted to a national jurisdiction against whose decisions jurisdictional recourse in internal law may not be presented, that jurisdiction shall be obliged to resort to the Court of Justice".

national courts; however, it would be competent--because it deals with a matter excluded from domestic jurisdiction-- to interpret the subregional rules or acts involved. 40/

5. Implied Competences or Powers

As has been seen concerning competences of the organs of Central American integration, whatever the system of distribution of competences may be (that of the federal state, international organizations of the traditional type or institutional structures of the economic integration processes) the federal organs, the international organs and the communitarian institutions cannot always, in the performance of their functions, limit themselves to the exercise of the competences or powers that have specifically and expressly been conferred on them for the purpose. Even in the exercise of these same competences or powers the problem sometimes arises due to the fact that they are not conceived in sufficiently explicit and clear terms. Therefore, it is necessary to resort, by way of exception naturally, to the exercise of so-called "implied" or "inherent" functions or powers. This fully explains that the legitimacy of the exercise of such functions, competences or powers has been recognized repeatedly, both by the International Court of Justice at The Hague and by the Court of Justice of the European Communities. 41/

As concerns Andean economic integration, there are provisions in the Pact itself that would seem to authorize the exercise of powers not explicitly delegated. Thus, for example, the authorization to formulate general policy of the Agreement and to adopt whatever measures the Commission may feel are necessary to achieve its ends evidently embodies a capacity to act which permits the subregional organ to perform acts which are not explicitly provided for in the Agreement (Art. 7 a). Another example is offered by item (k) of that same article, to the effect

---

40. Report cited, pp. 23-24.
41. Cf. Instituto Interamericano, op. cit., in note 23, pp. 342-347.

that the Commission is authorized "To hear and deal with any other business of common interest", which is equivalent to a truly "residual" power. 42/ This involves, therefore, at least apparently, provisions of the Agreement that constitute sources of functions or powers that are "implied"; a sort of a "residual" competence or power.

The practice of the subregional organs, especially the Commission's, reveals the exercise of the type of power to which reference is being made. At times there are acts by which the Commission assigns to the Board or to itself powers not expressly delegated to those organs by the Agreement. An example of the second case is Decision 24 (Common Regime of Treatment of Foreign Capital ...), concerning which the Commission gives itself the mandate, not provided for in the Agreement, of approving, at the proposal of the Board, a regulation for the application of rules on industrial property. 43/ In Article 52 of the Decision the Commission is assigned powers that are quite executive in nature, such as the power to "adopt other measures which tend to facilitate the attainment of its objectives". This same Decision offers an example of the first case, in which the Board is conferred, in Article 52, the power to "supervise the implementation and fulfillment of the regime and of the regulations approved by the

---

42. As indicated in subsection 2 (b) of this chapter, in application of section (k) and invoking it, the Commission approved a Régimen subregional para la internación temporal de vehículos de uso privado (Decision 50), in attending to a recommendation of the First Meeting of the Tourism Council, even though dealing with a subject or matter not expressly contemplated in the Agreement. The Andean instrument on labor migration, contained in the mentioned Proposal 64 of the Board, is a second example.

43. As indicated in the same subsection 2(b), in compliance with this self-mandate the Commission adopted in June 1974 Decision 85 (Reglamento para las normas sobre propiedad industrial) in application of transitory article (g) of Decision 24.

Commission on this subject". 44/ A second and significant example is the function of interpreter of legal texts
and provisions which the Commission has conferred on
the Board. 45/

Perhaps the most unequivocal--and at the same time
most important--expressions of the competences   functions or power to which this section refers to are those
which the subregional organs have been exercising concerning the matters or subjects on which they had a specific
mandate after having complied with it.   Thus, for example,
after having approved the Common Regime of Treatment
of Foreign Capital, and even after the entry into force of
that regime, the Commission introduced new provisions
in the original Decision 24. 46/

---

44. See also the power provided for in Articles 10
and 12 of Decision 70, in supra, section 1 of Ch. III.
    45. In relation to point 12 of the agenda of the Thir-
teenth Special Meeting (May-June 1974), the Commission
requested the Board to issue its opinion on the interpretation that should be given to Article 28 of Decision 24. The
opinion of the Board appears in the Acta Final of this
meeting, pp. 7-8.
    46. See subsection 2 (a) (i) of this chapter.

Chapter V

NATURE AND VALIDITY OF THE SUBREGIONAL ACTS

It can already be noted by now that the Cartagena Agreement does not define the various acts of the subregional organs, neither as to the various forms they adopt nor the effects they cause; that is to say, their validity. At least up to now, the practice of the organs and the internal, domestic practice of the member states have contributed relatively little to overcome this gap in the Andean legal order. Perhaps the best way of becoming aware of this situation is to approach the topic first of all from the strictly formal point of view, that is, by examining it to the letter and, if so desired, also under the spirit of the Agreement and other relevant instruments, to examine it later in the light of the reception that the subregional acts receive in the legal order of the member states.

1.   Form, Effects and Entry into Force of the Acts

This first section concerns the strictly formal approach referred to and should obviously begin with an examination of the way in which the various acts of the major organs of the Cartagena Agreement, the Commission and the Board (Junta), are adopted.

a)   The "decisions" of the Commission and the "resolutions" of the Board

As concerns the Commission, according to the Cartagena Agreement it "shall express its will through Decisions" (Art. 6). Except for that brief reference, the Agreement no longer mentions the word but employs verbs such as "approve", "adopt", "promote", etc., in referring to the various acts that this organ must carry out in the exercise of its competences. Thus, the word "Decisions", in itself, does not have any given basic connotation, but is simply the generic term given to all of the acts of that subregional organ. The Regulations that the Commission gave to itself (Decision 6) would appear to confirm this observation. Indeed, after dealing with the purely formal aspects, the Regulations established that "in those cases where its provisions (those of the "Decisions") involve obligations for the member states or for the organs of the Agreement, the date of their entry into effect shall be indicated in the final article. Otherwise, shall be understood that the effective date is the date of the approval of the final act of that particular meeting. " (Art. 21). Thus, at least the obligatory or non-obligatory nature of the acts has no effect at all on the form that they adopt: they are always called "Decisions". 1/

Despite what has just been stated, it has been noted that the decisions do not constitute the only mechanism by means of which the Commission expresses its will, since in actual practice the so-called accords inscrits have been resorted to. 2/ These acts, which appear in the final acts of the meetings of the Commission under the heading "conclusiones y constancias" presumably have the same binding character as the decisions. Although, as a general rule, these acts refer to topics or matters that belong to the internal domain of the organs of the Agreement--such as for example, the instructions or mandates that are issued to the Board--sometimes they go beyond this scope and bind the member states. Examples of this are the following: when the Commission "has made it known that the rights established by Decision 24 for foreign and mixed enterprises are the greatest that can be granted by the member states and consequently any of them could apply more restrictive measures whenever considered appropriate", and when the Commission performed several additional acts as concerns Annex I of

---

1. Articles 20 and 21 of the Regulations indicate the terms and expressions that should be used for drawing up the preamble and the operative part of the decisions, as well as the text of the operative part will be divided into articles, all of which obviously is to fulfill the purpose of making this body of instruments uniform.

2. Cf. Vendrell, Francisco J. , Le droit de l'intégration économique andine (Thèse, 1975), vol. I, pages 94-95.

Decision 28. 3/ These cases obviously reveal a high degree of flexibility in the Andean institutional system, which
strengthens the regulatory competence, and when appropriate the executive competence of one of the principal organs
of the Cartagena Agreement. Even though in their purpose
and in their scopes they do not have the hierarchy of the
decisions, these other acts undoubtedly constitute a mechanism to which the Commission can resort on circumstances
in which it considers this form of expressing its will to be
the most appropriate.

As concerns the Board, the Agreement does not
contain an equal or similar provision to that of Article 6
thereof. Only its joint functioning with the Commission is
contemplated; hence, only those proposals that are to be
made by the Board to the Commission pursuant to relevant
provisions are provided for (Art. 17). In contrast, its
Regulations, approved by the Commission through Decision
9, devote a chapter to the "Resolutions of the Board", and
in the first article it is established that "in those matters
in which the Board has its own decision-making powers,
as contained in the text of the Agreement or delegated by
the Commission, it shall express its will in the form of
Resolutions, which shall be numbered consecutively".
(Art. 11).

In addition to the decision-making nature attributed
to these acts of the Board, the Regulations states, for
purposes of authentication by the Director-Secretary of
"other acts", as well as the entry into effect of the resolutions, that both will be on the date in which they are
adopted (Arts. 11 and 13). As can be noted, in contrast
to the generic nature of the "decisions" of the Commission,
the "resolutions" of the Board are reserved to a specific

---

3. Acta Final del Tercer Período de Sesiones Extraordinarias, December 14, 1970, p. 4 and 4-5,
respectively.

category of acts: those that make up the exercise of "its own decision-making powers". 4/

The above makes it possible to clear up the doubts that necessarily arise, at least from initial reading, in some terms or expressions of the Agreement referring to certain actions of the subregional organs. Thus, for example, at the proposal of the Board, the Commission "shall introduce" those programs that presuppose the joint planning stipulated with a view to the industrial development of the subregion (Art. 36), which involves the idea of the act of recommending. The "recommendations" are furthermore specifically contemplated in other provisions: those that the Commission can make, also at the proposal of the Board, concerning the establishment of multinational firms for the installation, expansion or complementarity of specific industries (Art. 38), and those that the Board itself can make after verifying the problems caused by a monetary devaluation made by one of the member states (Art. 80). Despite the use of these other terms or expressions, in the case of the Commission, the act will adopt a form of a "decision" and in the case of the Board the act will adopt the form of a "resolution".

The use of the term "directive" can also bring about some doubts if the above considerations are not taken into account. As will be recalled, the Cartagena Agreement uses that term in regard to the harmonization of legislation on industrial incentives of the member states (Art. 28). Far from being an instrument or act similar to the European "directive", as will be noted in the definition to be cited at the beginning of the next subsection b), it would appear to make up a type of guideline. Indeed, the Agreement, in referring to the "directives that shall serve as a basis for

---

4. The formalities to be met in the resolutions of the Board are also established in the remaining provisions of Chapter V of the Regulations, as well as in the provisions contained in Articles 20 and 21 of the Regulations of the Commission.

the harmonization", apparently proposes to distinguish those directives from the type of instrument constituting the regimes that it provides in Article 28 and in Article 27, that is to say, instead of providing a third common or uniform regime for this matter, apparently what is being provided are guidelines that help to harmonize the national legislations on industrial development. 5/ Hence, it has been observed accurately, in view of the opinion of those who find similarities with the European "directive", that the "notion of directive" employed in the Agreement does not have a specific legal content. The term should be understood in its grammatical sense and consequently as an "orientation", "trend", "indication". 6/

b) Effects of the various acts; those that require supplementary national action

The Treaty of Rome that established the European Economic Community is quite explicit in regard to the effects arising from the various acts of the organs of that community. To facilitate examination of the topic with reference to the Andean institutional system, the complete text of Article 189 of that Treaty is given:

> Article 189. In order to carry out their task the Council and the Commission shall, in accordance with the provisions of this Treaty, make regulations, issue directives, take decisions, make recommendations or deliver opinions.

---

5. This nature of the directives contemplated in Article 28 of the Cartagena Agreement is confirmed by the terms in which Decision 49 is conceived, by means of which the Commission accomplished the mandate contained in the second paragraph of that article.

6. Cf. Casanova, Manuel, Una Integración Equitativa: Rol del Derecho en el Acuerdo de Cartagena (Santiago, Chile, 1975, page 204).

A regulation shall have general application. It shall be binding in its entirety and directly applicable in all Member States.

A directive shall be binding, as to the result to be achieved, upon each Member State to which it is addressed, but shall leave to the national authorities the choice of form and methods.

A decision shall be binding in its entirety upon those to whom it is addressed.

Recommendations and opinions shall have no binding force.

As can be noted, the foregoing provisions characterize the various acts and, above all, specify or make it possible to know the effect exerted by each of the categories mentioned in the Article.

The situation in the Cartagena Agreement is completely different. This instrument only mentions the acts as such a single time (the "decisions" of the Commission in Art. 6), and even then without characterizing them or specifying their effects or validity from the standpoint of the internal legal order of the member states. It is true that, as has been seen, the Regulations of the Commission distinguish between the decisions whose "provisions involve obligations for the member states or for the organs of the Agreement" and those that are "otherwise" (Art. 21), and that the Regulations of the Board limit the scope of its resolutions to the matters in which this organ "has its own decision-making powers" (Art. 11). This is not enough, however, since the first distinction is made in regard to something else (the date of entry into effect of the two types of decisions) and the second distinction is made to give a name (that of "resolutions") to the acts of the Board which are not the proposals that it is to submit to the Commission in the exercise of the competences attributes by the Agreement to the two organs.

Despite the fact that the Agreement makes no reference to the effects of the subregional acts, it is not difficult to identify or to define them within the context of the Agreement itself. This task is made still easier when starting out from the premise that, except for the case of mere recommendations or steps that are only proposed to promote the action of the member states, the acts of the subregional organs are legally binding and therefore the rules they issue are mandatory for and/or in those states. This is actually a corollary of the principle pacta sunt servanda, in the sense that since the rules of the basic instruments are mandatory and above all since the Agreement has the nature of a "traité-cadre", those generated by the exercise of the competences attributed by the Agreement to the organs are also binding, naturally, on the conditions stipulated in the Agreement in attributing each competence. If these conditions are taken into account, the validity or effects of the subregional acts can be inferred in each case.

The conditions that have just been referred to can be understood better when taking into account the two large categories of acts which, from this point of view, can be distinguished in the Cartagena Agreement. The first category of acts contemplates, in addition to the competence and specific action of the subregional organ or organs, a supplementary action on the part of the member states, upon which depends the full validity and force of the act. As will be recalled, Articles 27 and 28 of the Agreement specifically envisage the "measures /on the part of the member states/ necessary to implement" the common and uniform regimes that the Commission would have to approve upon the proposal of the Board. 7/ Although this

---

7. The respective decisions of the Commission, 24 and 46, provide that "the present regime shall enter into effect when all of the Member states have deposited in the Office of the Secretariat of the Board the instruments by which they put it into practice... " This provision, besides repeating what had been stipulated in the articles mentioned of the Agreement, establishes the date of entry into force at the subregional level of the regime as such. As will be seen in footnote 17, the Commission introduced the system provided for in Articles 27 and 28 of the Agreement in one of

distribution of competences and powers among the subregional organs and the member states is a situation apparently similar to the "ratification" of international
treaties and conventions, those in which such regimes appear should not be assimilated into the latter instruments. 8/
In contrast to such international instruments, the nature
of which is essentially contractual, the regimes provided
for in Articles 27 and 28 arise from the exercise of competences and powers attributed to subregional organs, except that their full validity and force have been made to

---

7. (Cont.) the two conventions on double taxation
it approved by means of its Decision 40.

8. Pursuant to article 2 of the Vienna Convention on
Treaties, "ratification, acceptance, approval, and accession, means in each case the international act so name
whereby a state establishes on the international plane its
consent to be bound by a treaty". Thus, in the second of
the conventions on double taxation mentioned in footnote 7,
involving a standard convention to be held between member states and other states outside of the Subregion, the
Commission adopted the traditional system of ratification.
Although that word is not used, the instruments contemplated in Article 41 of Decision 56 for the entry into effect of that decision, the text of which is transcribed in
subsection 1, (d), infra, also appear to be instruments of
this type. Perhaps it should be asked why. Because, in
contrast to the regimes provided for in articles 27 and 28
of the Agreement, in which the commitment of "implementing" them is stipulated, the acceptance of the regime
on international highway transportation established by the
decision is optional, which explains why article 41 refers
to "putting into effect" (italics added) that decision.

depend upon an additional internal action. 9/

In addition to the foregoing considerations it is obvious that the terms in which Articles 27 and 28 of the Agreement have been drawn up justify certain doubts on what they actually provide for. In effect, it should be pointed out that in regard to a regime which shall be submitted "for consideration of the member states" the adoption of measures is required to implement it and the member states are also compelled to do so within a certain period of time. In the absence of legislative background to shed light on this matter or, in any event, in the absence of such background in written form, it would be logical to interpret these provisions of the Agreement in the sense that what predominates is the commitment or obligation of implementing the regimes within the specified period of time. If they (Arts. 27 and 28) are not interpreted in this way, this could lead to the idea that the member states had an option to accept or reject such regimes, which would assume the existence of a juridical and institutional

---

9. Although the situation is not entirely similar, the acts contemplated in Articles 27 and 28 of the Agreement are much more similar to the European "directive", the definition of which appears in the Article of the Treaty of Rome transcribed at the beginning of this subsection. As noted, "the directives attribute to the Communities a power substantially similar to the formal regulatory power that they exercise in view of the adoption of general decisions or regulations. Reserved, in contrast, to the competent national authorities, including if necessary the parliaments, is the task of application and execution to be exercised in view of the adoption of the form and means that are most opportune..." Cf. Catalano, N., Manual de Derecho de las Comunidades Europeas (INTAL, Buenos Aires, 1966), p. 162. Therefore, there does not appear to be any foundation for the opinion according to which the national instruments provided for in Articles 27 and 28 are equivalent to a "ratification, an approval or an acceptance of the decisions in question". Cf. Vendrel, op. cit., p. 100.

inconsistency which the subregional pact does not have and which should not be attributed to it. 10/ If this is a commitment or obligation and not an option, then it must be admitted that this is a _sui generis_ situation since it is undeniable that without national measures the regimes approved by the subregional organ could not enter into effect.

Added to these doubts are the ones arising on the true nature of the "measures" or legal instruments by means of which the regimes are to be "implemented", as well as the exact meaning or scope of this second term. Subject to returning to this matter in section 2 of this chapter, for the present time it would be sufficient to reiterate that in regard to the power attributed to the member states with a view to perfecting the acts resulting from the exercise of the competences attributed to the subregional organs with regard to the category of acts referred to, this can only constitute a merely supplementary action to the subregional action; this does not underestimate in any way the national action, since in its absence that of the subregional organs would lack full validity or binding legal force for and/or in the member states.

The acts provided for in Articles 27 and 28 of the Cartagena Agreement are not the only ones that come into the category of those in which the full validity and legal force depends upon a supplementary national action. Pursuant to Article 30, the Commission, at the proposal of the Board shall agree on a program of common instrumentation and machinery to govern foreign trade in the member states, "which shall be implemented by them before December 31, 1972". National action is also contemplated vis-à-vis the Common External Tariff, in the

---

10. The option would assume not only a marked contradiction with the commitment expressly entered into to put the regimes into effect. It would assume a right to change them at the national level whenever they were subject to "consideration" by the competent organs of the member states.

process of approaching such tariff that the member states must begin starting with December 31, 1976 (Art. 62), and in regard to the Minimum Common External Tariff starting with December 31, 1971 (Art. 64). One should add to these acts those for which it is the subregional organ and not the Agreement which subordinates their full validity or legal force to a supplementary national action. Thus, for example, pursuant to Article 41 of Decision 56 (international highway transportation) it "shall enter into force when three states have deposited in the Office of the Secretariat of the Board the instruments by means of which the decision is put into effect in their respective territories". A second example is Article 86 of Decision 85 (regulations for the implementation of the rules on industrial property): "The Governments of the member states agreed to adopt all of the measures necessary to incorporate the present regulations into their respective internal legal orders, within six months following the approval of this decision". It should be noted in regard to this provision, that the same type of commitment is established by an act of a subregional organ as the one that the member states enter into in Articles 27 and 28 of the Cartagena Agreement.

c) Validity erga omnes of the other acts

The second category of acts referred to is composed of those acts concerning which the Cartagena Agreement does not envisage, at least in a specific manner, in addition to the competence and specific action of the subregional organ or organs, any additional action on the part of the member states to supplement and perfect these other acts. In contrast to the other category, it is reasonable to assume that these are acts which ab initio are fully binding upon and/or in the member states. It is appropriate to refer further to this matter not only because most of the acts provided for by the Agreement fall under this situation, but also and above all because this is the situation that has the greatest effects on the traditional concept and practices of national sovereignty, in particular in regard to the competences reserved by constitutional provisions to the legislature. In this frame of ideas, and without the fear of exaggerating as to similarities, this is the situation that brings the Andean institutional system closer to that of the European Communities.

In defining one of the acts or instruments (the "regulations") listed in Article 189 reproduced earlier, the Treaty of Rome establishes that "it shall be binding in its entirety and directly applicable in all Member States". In referring to the equivalent acts or instruments of the European Coal and Steel Community (the "decisions"), the Court of Justice of the Communities took the occasion to indicate that "these are quasi-legislative acts emanating from a public authority and have a regulatory effect erga omnes". 11/ In commenting on this statement of the Court, it has been said that the "direct applicability" of the regulations of the European Economic Community constitutes their basic characteristic and therefore in order for a regulation to become applicable it is not necessary for the legislator to "incorporate" it into its national law by a particular act that "transforms" it. 12/ Consequently, it would appear that the acts belonging to the second category are just as the European acts or instruments mentioned, binding and directly applicable for and/or in the member states. This feature, which is attributed by the Treaty of Rome in an explicit manner, is implicit in the provisions of the Cartagena Agreement referring to this category of subregional acts.

The regulatory provisions governing the Commission and the Board which were examined in subsection a), despite the fact that they refer to the "binding" nature of some of the decisions of the former and to the "decision-

---

11. Cf. Affaire 8/55, cited by E. Wohfarth and B. Sehloh in Les Novelles, Droit des Communautés Européennes, (published under the direction of W. J. Ganshof Van Der Meersch), 1969, Chapt. Pre. Les Actes des Institutions, p. 416.
12. Ibid.

making" nature of some of the resolutions of the latter, shed very little light on the essential aspect of the question, as could be noted. Perhaps an exception should be made vis-à-vis Article 13 of the Regulations of the Board, which establishes that the resolutions of that organ "shall enter into force on the date in which they are approved", as well as Article 15 of the regulations, in which reference is made to cases in which the provisions of a resolution "involve obligations for the member states". In any event, the observation of the Board would appear to have greater and more direct relation in the essential aspect of the matter referred to, in the sense that the decisions of the Commission "are binding for the member states from the very moment they are approved."[13]

The rationale should not be shared, however, which led the Board to formulate its correct observation. Here is the pertinent passage of the report:

A description has already been given in the preceding point on the way in which the process of adopting decisions is carried out. The persons voting on these decisions are plenipotentiary representatives of the Government. They are provided with full powers and act by virtue of instructions from their Government, and reach the decisions after debates in which the possible alternative solutions are discussed in each case. In casting their vote or providing their consent to the decisions, they exercise these full powers and therefore obligate the countries that they represent. In accordance with any theory that is adopted on this form of mandate, there is no doubt that the properly accredited plenipotentiary obligates the country that he represents. [14]

---

13. Cf. Informe de la Junta sobre Cumplimiento del Acuerdo y las Decisiones, doc. COM/XII/di 3, July 14, 1973, p. 2.

14. We had the opportunity to hear the same reasoning from one of the members of the Board, Dr. F. Salazar Santos, in the course of a speech given at the meeting on

The preceding reasoning is the one that would be appropriate if the decisions were to involve agreements of a contractual or conventional nature, the validity and mandatory nature of which resides, for each contracting country, in the granting of its consent. But decisions are acts of a completely different legal nature, since they stem from the exercise of competences and powers that the Agreement attributes to the Commission on certain matters. The situation did not change in the case of decisions requiring unanimity. Institutionally this is still an act of an international organ competent to obligate the member states and not an agreement or a merely contractual relationship between them, as occurs in those cases in which the Commission is a vehicle for the entering into of agreements properly so called. 15/

Notwithstanding the observations that have just been made, the declaration of the Commission, which appears in Article 37 of its Decision 70, in the sense that the "adherence of Venezuela to the Cartagena Agreement signifies its acceptance of the Decisions approved by the Commission until this date...", and that, "Likewise, the Resolutions of the Board shall be fully applicable to it", seems to be an indirect but unequivocal assertion of the

---

14. (Cont.) Promotion of Latin American Investments and Joint Enterprises organized by INTAL (Buenos Aires, November 21 and 22, 1975).

15. Thus, for example, to meet the objectives of the agriculture and livestock system of the Cartagena Agreement, the Commission will periodically take the following measures, among others, upon the proposal of the Board: a) the entering into of agreements on the supply of agriculture and livestock products among the pertinent state organisms, and b) the promotion of agreements between the national organisms involved in the planning and execution of agriculture and livestock policy (Art. 70). Other provisions contemplate contractual relations between the member states, for which the commission can also serve as liaison (Arts. 53, 57 and 68). Regarding these other provisions, see supra, section 4 of Chapter II.

intrinsic validity of the acts of these two subregional organs. 16/

From a strict legal point of view, there does not appear to be any justification whatever on the reasoning behind that assertion. Both the spirit and the letter of the provisions of the Cartagena Agreement concerning the competences and powers of the subregional organs clearly reveal the binding nature of the acts being referred to. This is explicitly established in the institutional system of the European Communities, but the absence of an explicit statement to this regard does not prevent attributing in another system the same legal validity to the acts of its organs. What is important is the intention of the states, parties to the basic instrument, and in this regard there would not seem to be any reason for serious doubts. As will be seen in the next sections, the situation is not as clear when it is examined in the light of the reception of the subregional acts in the internal, domestic legal order of the member states.

d) Entry into force of the acts

The Cartagena Agreement makes no mention of the entry into force of the subregional acts in general. It only contains provisions on this matter in relation to the regimes provided for in Articles 27 and 28, but only in the sense of indicating a deadline within which each member state "shall implement" those regimes, which is not necessarily equivalent to their entry into force, not even at the national level. The provisions relative to the Common External Tariff are also not precise. Indeed, by virtue of

---

16. It should be clarified in regard to the provisions of Article 37 of Decision 70 that the Venezuelan law approving the Cartagena Agreement, which will be examined in subsection 4, b), infra, "approved", in addition to the Agreement, not all but only certain decisions of the Commission.

one of them, the member states agree "to implement" that tariff "no later than December 31, 1980" (Art. 61). By virtue of the provision relative to the Minimum Common External Tariff, the member states will take certain measures "so that it becomes fully applicable by December 31, 1975" (Art. 64).

The Commission has sought to fill in this gap in the Agreement through its own Regulations and the Regulations that it approved for the Board. As will be recalled, according to Article 21 of the regulations of the Commission, when the provisions of a decision involve obligations for the member states or for the organs of the Agreement, "the date of their entry into effect shall be indicated in the final article. Otherwise, it shall be understood that the effective date is the date of the approval of the final act of that particular meeting" (Art. 21). Two possible dates of entry into effect are provided for in these Regulations: the date that the Commission is required to indicate and the date which, in the absence of such indication by the Commission, will goven suppletorily. The observation of the Board that was cited in the preceding subsection could also not be disregarded, in the sense that the decisions of the Commission "are binding for the member states from the very moment they are approved". Now, should the binding character of a decision be admitted whose entry into effect occurs on a date subsequent to the date of its approval, as is possible by virtue of the provisions in Article 21 of the Regulations of the Commission?

The Regulations of the Board, in turn, are considerably more elaborate on this matter, as can be noted in Articles 13 and 15 thereof:

Article 13. The Resolutions of the Board shall enter into effect on the date they are approved. They shall be communicated to the member states through the national organs referred to in Article 15, i) of the Agreement, by letter sent by the Director-Secretary.

Furthermore, within 24 hours following the approval of a Resolution, the Director-Secretary shall cable an extract of its text to the national organ referred to without disregarding other additional forms of publicity that may be considered oportune.

The Director-Secretary shall leave a record of his compliance with the above formalities and the date of the communications.

. . . .

Article 15. The operative part /of the resolution/ will be divided into articles. In cases where its provisions involve obligations for the member states, the date of compliance will be indicated.

In contrast to the provisions of the Regulations of the Commission, Article 13 of the Regulations of the Board establishes a single and definite date for the entry into force of the Resolutions. The form and time of communicating those Resolutions to the member states are also established. The Regulations become somewhat obscure or, in any event, inconsistent at least in appearance with what is provided for in Article 15 which refers to "date for complying with them", allegedly the compliance with the obligations deriving from provisions of the Resolutions and not the provisions themselves. The problem is the following: if the resolutions of the Board will enter into force on the date they are adopted (Art. 13) whether or not they imply obligations for the member states, how should the Board be authorized, in the affirmative, to establish or indicate a date for compliance with said obligations?

It should be pointed out that, in actual practice, the decisions of the Commission, in contrast to the resolutions of the Board, generally do not contain provisions on notification of the member states and on the form and date of entry into force. Regarding the latter date it should be understood that, as an additional date, there is the date of the approval of the final act of the meeting at which the decision was approved, as provided for in Article 21 of the Regulations. As an example of exception to this practice there is Article A Transitional of Decision 24 (and the one pertaining to Decision 46), by virtue of which

"this regime shall enter into force when all of the member
states have deposited in the Office of the Secretariat of the
Board the instruments by which they put it into practice in
their respective territories, in accordance with the provisions of the second paragraph of Article 27 of the
Cartagena Agreement. 17/ A propo, Decision 37 (through
which the Commission made adjustments in the Common
Regime established by Decision 24) mentions June 30,
1971 as "date of entry into force of said common regime"
implicitly nullifying the provision contained in Article A

---

17.   The Commission extended this system of entry
into force to one of the two conventions on double taxation
it approved by means of its Decision 40. Article 3 of the
decision itself states that "the member states shall adopt,
prior to June 30, 1972, the necessary measures to implement (italics added) the convention for avoiding double
taxation among the member states so that it may enter
into force as established in Article 21 of that convention.
This article of the Convention provides that the countries
mentioned "shall deposit in the Office of the Secretariat of
the Board of the Cartagena Agreement the instruments by
which they "put in application" (which is equivalent to the
expression used in Decisions 24 and 46) the present Convention", and that "it shall enter into force..." on different
dates, according to whether natural persons or enterprises
are concerned or in regard to the taxes on net worth, but
in the three cases always established in relation to "the
date of deposit of the instruments referred to by all of the
member states". When dealing with the English version
of the different terms and expressions the discussion may
well be considered one of pure semantics. It is only when
one looks at the original Spanish texts that the distinctions
made are clearly seen. The equivocal Spanish expression
poner en práctica is the one that creates the problem.

Transitional that provided another date of entry into
force. 18/

The Commission once again deviated from the practice referred to in its Decision 50, by which it approved
the Subregional regime for the temporary importation of
vehicles for private use. Pursuant to a Transitional article,
the Decision "shall enter into force 30 days after the date
of approval of the regulations" to that regime, which the
Commission committed itself to do before July 31, 1972.
A third example of these exceptions is given by Decision 56,
on international highway transportation. According to its
Article 41, "the present Decision shall enter into force
when the countries have deposited in the Secretariat of the
Board the instruments by which they put the Decision into
force in their respective territories. For the other countries, the date of entry into force shall be date of deposit
of the respective instruments".

---

18. Decision 37 was approved at the Fourth Period of
Special Sessions of the Commission, held on June 23 and 24,
1971. As indicated in the Final Act (p. 2), "the Commission
reiterated that the respective governments shall put into
force the common regime... by the corresponding legal
instruments on June 30 of the present year". With this, the
Commission apparently wished to comply with the deadline
stipulated in Art. 27 of the Cartagena Agreement. In any
case, the Commission was consistent with a decision of the
Second Meeting of Ministers of Foreign Affairs of the member states of the Cartagena Agreement, to the effect that
there would be carried out on June 30, 1971 in the respective capitals, "acts solemnizing the simultaneous announce-
ment of the entry into force of the regime mentioned". Cf.
Acta Final de la Reunión in Historia Documental del Acuerdo de Cartagena, p. 423. For the pertinent provisions of
the national instruments by which the Common regime should
be put "into force", see infra, subsection 3 b). It should be
pointed out, lastly, that pursuant to Art. A Transitional, the
regime had to enter into effect on July 13, 1971, the date of
deposit in the Secretariat of the Board of the last of those
national instruments, the Ecuadorian Decree which will be
mentioned in that subsection.

In regard to this third type of exception, two questions obviously arise. The first resides in the fact that the Commission has subjected the entry into force of the decision to the occurrence of circumstances that are not consistent with the provisions of Article 21 of its Regulations. This is certainly a system similar to the one used in the transitional articles of Decisions 24 and 46, but in these two cases the system used is justifiable, owing to the requirements stipulated by Articles 27 and 28 of the Cartagena Agreement, for the respective regimes to have full validity and force. The second question also involves a question of principle or legal technique and consists in knowing how the expression "put into force in their respective territories" can be used, since these are subregional acts, assumed to be fully valid from the very moment that the pertinent decision is approved, as sustained by the Board, and effective starting from the dates stipulated in Article 21 of the Regulations of the Commission. Although this is a case of exception, there is no doubt that it would excuse, to a certain extent, the member states owing to the "approbatory" character or effect that most of the national instruments incorporating the subregional acts into the internal legal order at least appear to have. 19/

As concerns the resolutions of the Board, a certain lack of uniformity has also been observed. Obviously, the specific and categorical nature of the provision of the Regulations, in the sense that they "shall enter into force on the date they are adopted", does not leave the margin that the Commission has for establishing the date of entry into force of its decisions. Thus, the resolutions generally are silent on this matter. Sometimes, however, this does not occur, as in Resolutions 3 and 4. In Resolution 3 it is stated that "this Resolution shall enter into force on the date of its enactment". Resolution 4 adds that "and this shall be communicated..." Resolution 8, despite being an

---

19. On the character or effect of these national instruments, see infra, subsection 4, c).

166

application of Article 67 of the Cartagena Agreement, as in the case of the two that have just been mentioned, refers only to the communication thereof to the national organs. Now, these and other differences noted in the resolutions of the Board are only modalities which, although they denote a certain lack of uniformity, absolutely do not involve any great discrepancies. In contrast to what occurs in the case of the decisions of the Commission, whatever the forms or expressions used in the resolutions of the Board, all of them enter into force on the date established by Article 13 of the Regulations.

2.   Reception of Subregional Law in Domestic Law; Experience Relative to the Approval of the Agreement Itself

After examining the nature and validity of the subregional acts under the context of the Cartagena Agreement and other pertinent instruments, it is appropriate now to examine the topic in the light of how these acts are incorporated in the internal, domestic law of the member states. To facilitate this other task, however, it would appear suitable first of all to examine the experience on the approval or reception of the Agreement itself.

a)   The original approbatory instruments

As will be recalled, it is provided, for purposes of entry into force in Article 110 of the Agreement, that besides the declaration of compatibility on the part of the Permanent Executive Committee of LAFTA, that "each Member State shall approve it in conformity with its respective legislative procedures and forward the corresponding act of approval to the Executive Secretariat of LAFTA". In due time, the instruments that comprised the act of approval by the respective member states, were mentioned, five of which are the original approbatory instruments. [20]

Certain observations should be made concerning these instruments. First of all, in two of the first five member

---

20.   See supra, footnote 12 of Chapter I.

states, there was no Congress or legislative body, so that actually there is no reason for the problem to arise of how the Cartagena Agreement "would be approved". Surely due to the fact that the Executive Branch had assumed, as is customary, the legislative functions and powers, among which in general there is the power to approve or ratify international treaties or conventions, the approbatory instruments of the Agreement assumed the nature of a law, not that of a merely executive instrument. 21/ In the case of Ecuador the problem also did not appear to arise, but not for the same reason: after being submitted for approval by the Senate of the Republic on October 24, 1969,

---

21.　Thus, in the case of Peru, on October 14, 1969 the Revolutionary Government approved the Agreement by Decree Law No. 17851 and on October 15 the respective instrument of "ratification" was issued "with which the Agreement was incorporated into the national legal order in the form of a law of the Republic". Cf. Primera Reunión de Expertos, Organo Jurisdiccional, Respuestas al cuestionario presentado por la Junta del Acuerdo de Cartagena a los consultores nacionales, (Perú), (Dr. Héctor Cornejo Chávez), doc. JUN/Re.OJ/I/di 9, June 23, 1972, p. 2. In the case of Bolivia, Decree Law No. 08985 was approved on November 6, 1969. As declared by the Supreme Court of Justice, in Bolivia the Decree Laws fall into the "Category of laws..." Ibid., (Bolivia), (Dr. Renato Crespo Paniagua), doc. JUN/RE. OJ/I/di r, June 23, 1972, p. 2. It should be noted that the Peruvian instrument and the Bolivian instrument employ the term "ratification", in contrast to the others, and that the Bolivian one calls itself "instrument of ratification". See the complete text of the five instruments in Historia Documental del Acuerdo de Cartagena, p. 184 et seq.

Executive Decree No. 1932 was enacted, which is the instrument approving the Agreement and which was declared to be a "Law of the Republic". 22/

In the case of the Chilean instrument, although it did not cause any difficulties or problems, it did result in an opinion being issued by the Office of the Comptroller General of the Republic, which is an independent entity with the power to render decisions on the constitutionality and legality of supreme decrees. The instrument in question is Supreme Decree No. 428 of July 30, 1969. The Executive explains the failure to submit the Agreement to legislative approval in the whereas clauses of the decree, through arguments essentially put together and developed in the opinion issued by the Office of the Comptroller General through its Legal Department. Here are the principal passages of that opinion: 23/

> In regard to the decree of reference, this office is of the opinion that it is essential to take into account the legal nature of the Montevideo Treaty. In effect, this international instrument constitutes what is

---

22. See the series of documents cited in the preceeding footnote, (Ecuador),(Dr. Ramiro Borja y Borja), doc. JUNE/RE.OJ/I/di 8 June 23, 1972, p. 14-15. Regarding these three countries, Bolivia, Ecuador and Perú) the statement by the respective delegations in signing the Cartagena Agreement should be recalled, in the sense that they signed ad referendum. Cf. Acta Final de la Segunda Segunda Sesión de la Sexta Reunión de la Comisión Mixta de la Declaración de Bogotá, De. Bol. Co. Mix./VI-2/Acta Final, p. 4 - 5.

23. See other passages of the opinion as well as the whereas clauses of the Supreme Decree, in F. Orrego Vicuña, "La incorporación del ordenamiento jurídico subregional al derecho interno. Análisis de la práctica chilena", in INTAL, Derecho de la Integración, No. 7, Oct. 1970, pages 49-50. Also see the document pertaining to Chile of the series of documents cited in the two preceeding footnotes prepared by Dr. Jacobo Schawlsohn N, doc. JUN/RE.OJ/I/di 7, June 23, 1972, p. 13-14.

called a "traité-cadre", that is to say, a treaty that only sets general principles, creates mechanisms and establishes organs for the execution of the purposes of the treaty, which with their actions fill out the entire structure of the Treaty.

. . .

Thus, the Treaty of Montevideo did not spell out the manner of accomplishing its purposes, but granted powers to do so to its organs, which, in essence, in accomplishing their powers determined that the subregional agreements were a feasible means of integration, through which they indicated and regulated this so that the countries entering into such agreements would come under the system of the Treaty of Montevideo and accomplish its purposes. In this form, legislative approval of the subregional integration agreement would not be necessary, from the time that the provisions of the Treaty are being executed through implementation of the resolutions of the organs established by it. Those resolutions were issued within the spheres of their competence, clearly set forth in that Treaty.

As noted elsewhere, the "derivative" nature of the Andean Pact and its very close connections and relations with the legal and institutional framework of LAFTA are not the only factors or circumstances that should be resorted to for avoiding legislative approval. In effect, Article 110 is drawn up in terms that permit the member states, which so desire and can, to implement the "act of approval" of the Pact, through a merely executive action. 24/ In the case of the Chilean instrument, not only was the authorization set forth in this provision of the Pact resorted to, but reasons were put forth in favor of the action observed, which are consistent with the connections and relations existing between the legal framework of LAFTA and the subregional legal framework.

_____

24. See supra, section 4, of Chapter II.

170

The same observations are appropriate with regard
to the fifth original approbatory instrument: Decree No.
1245 of August 8, 1969 through which the Colombian Government approved the Cartagena Agreement. This other instrument, however, did encounter serious difficulties and un-
chained a process which in the end terminated in the adoption four years later of a new "Act of Approval" of the
Agreement on the part of Colombia. The problem resided
primarily in the fact that the Government, based on the
law approving the Treaty of Montevideo, which authorized
it "to adopt all measures aimed at... that it considers appropriate for the development of the present Treaty", 25/
ignored altogether the legislative process and proceeded to
the approval of the Agreement by means of Decree 1245. 26/
In this regard, the question raised consisted in determining
whether or not the Cartagena Agreement was a "development"
of the Treaty of Montevideo. The problem also resided in
finding out whether the Agreement was an international
treaty or an instrument of another nature. For both of
these reasons, two proceedings challenging the constitutionality of the Decree were filed in the Supreme Court of
Justice. 27/

---

25. See the complete text of Law No. 88, of September 29, 1961 in the Diario Oficial of October 9, 1961.

26. One of the whereas clauses of the Decree itself
states: "whereas the Government is authorized by Law 88
of 1961 to implement all of the commitments that Colombia
has as a Contracting Party of the Montevideo Treaty". The
text of the Decree, as well as the text of the documents to
which reference will be made ahead, appears in Jurispru-
dencia y Práctica Nacional Relativa a la Entrada en Vigor
del Acuerdo de Integración Subregional y otros Instrumentos Emanados del Acuerdo de Cartagena, I, Colombia OAS
doc. OEA/Ser.Q/II.5, July 1972, p. 3.

27. The first of these recourses is reproduced in
the document cited in the preceeding footnote, p. 5.

b) Decision of the Supreme Court of Colombia

The opinion put forth by the Attorney General of the Nation was in agreement, essentially, with the opinion issued by the Office of the Comptroller General of Chile referred to above, in the sense that "under the modern concept of international law and in the light of community and integration law, the Cartagena Agreement is not a treaty in the classical sense of the term, and its true legal nature is that of an agreement of complementation, development and execution, at the subregional level and for the Andean Group, of the outline Treaty of Montevideo, and of the legal structure of the Latin American Free Trade Association (LAFTA)". 28/ The Supreme Court, in contrast, put forth, among others, the following reasons: 29/

> In comparing, even in a summary fashion, the two regulations contained in the Montevideo and Cartagena agreements, it turns out that they comprise two different acts from many points of view. For example, the contracting parties, the subjects of the rights and obligations stemming from each agreement, are different, since all of the members of LAFTA are not in the Andean Pact, and are outside of the legal connections engendered by it. Furthermore, the organs governed by the Treaty of Montevideo and those of the Andean Agreement are different, and also have different powers as well as different matters with which they are concerned.
>
> In view of such evident disparity, the Andean Pact cannot be considered as a development and execution of the Montevideo Treaty.

---

28. Ibid., p. 46, in the document from the OAS (Organization of AmericanStates), the opinion put forth by the Attorney General to the Supreme Court is reproduced in full starting with p. 13.

29. Ibid., p. 62. The full text of the opinion issued by the Supreme Court on July 26, 1971 is reproduced in the OAS document starting with p. 51.

These and other reasons led the Colombian Court to conclude that "the decree approving the Andean Agreement, owing to a shortcoming of formation, runs counter to the constitutional framework" and "the Government did not adhere to the Constitution since it abstained from submitting the Andean Pact for necessary study by Congress and, in contrast, exercised an authorization contained in Article 2 of Law 88 of 1961, concerning the carrying out of executive measures aimed at the development of the Montevideo Treaty, a power that could not be converted into the right to review international acts and to approve an agreement entered into with other governments... " 30/ In view of these reasons and conclusions of the majority, five judges of the Court cast a dissident vote who espoused the opinion of the Attorney General as well as other reasons. 31/

Despite the reasons and conclusions of the Supreme Court, the deep-rooted internationalist tradition of that organ prevented the declaration of unconstitutionality of Decree No. 1245. After making some references concerning that tradition, the Court reiterated its lack of competence for "declaring the inefficacy of the law approving a treaty, after having received the ratification of the other contracting party". In the opinion of the Court: 32/

> The Government and the people of the Nation would find themselves in an unsolvable conflict; on the one hand, in the obligation of fulfilling the provisions of a perfect international pact in which they would be solemnly committed under public faith; and, on the other hand, in the duty of observing the decision of the highest judicial body of the country, which in declaring the Treaty unconstitutional would implicitly instruct that it not be obeyed. It should in no way be assumed that such an absurdity, which would arise

---

30. Ibid., p. 64.
31. See the full text of the Salvamento de Voto, as well as the comment made by Judge Luis Sarmiento Buitrago, in ibid., ps. 73 and 99, respectively.
32. Ibid. p. 68-69.

from the literal application of Article 214 of the Charter /the Constitution/, was in the mind of those who issued that constitutional act.

Decree No. 1245 was then replaced, in its capacity of "act of approval" of the Cartagena Agreement, by a legislative instrument, Law 8, of March 21, 1973, published in the Anales del Congreso on June 8 of the same year. 33/

Only a few months after the promulgation of the Colombian law, Venezuela adhered to the Andean Pact, followed by the instrument approving it, the Law of September 3, 1973, published in the Gaceta Oficial of November 1, 1973. 34/

Before going on to examine the reception achieved in the domestic law by the various subregional acts, some brief observation should be made on this initial experience of reception for incorporation of Andean law. To start out, there is no doubt, as admitted on repeated occasions, about the "derivative" character of the Cartagena Agreement and its very close linkage and relationship with the legal and institutional framework of LAFTA and that, consequently, that said Agreement can very well be considered as a "development" of the Montevideo Treaty. There is also no doubt that the subregional instrument contains substantive commitments (rights and obligations vis-à-vis the states that are parties of the Agreement) of considerable scope and that, furthermore, these states are subjected to a new institutional structure, considerably more autonomous and dynamic than that of LAFTA, so that, despite the fact that this is a "development" of that Treaty, the Andean Pact has the essential characteristics and elements of a new Treaty or conventional instrument, which is therefore subject to the act of approval considered necessary in each

---

33. The complete text of the law also appears in INTAL, Derecho de la Integración, No. 13, July 1973, p. 226.
34. Also reproduced in INTAL, ibid., No. 15, March 1974, p. 405.

State to be bound by such Pact. The circumstance that Article 110 thereof authorizes, under the terms in which it is drawn up and the purposes for which it is intended, a merely executive "approval", does not imply in any way that the traditional process or system of ratification, which involves legislative intervention and approval, had been excluded. 35/

3. Experience Relative to the Regimes Provided for in Articles 27 and 28 of the Agreement

As has been seen in subsection 1, b) the common and uniform regimes provided for in Articles 27 and 28 of the Cartagena Agreement fall under the category of subregional acts that specifically require, in order to be fully valid and binding, a supplementary national action. The Agreement, however, fails to spell out exactly what that action is, since it only refers to the "measures necessary to implement" those regimes. This phrase, as also indicated on the same occasion, raises not only the problem relative to the nature of the "measures" or legal instruments by means of which such action would be taken but also, and to some extent primarily, the question of what significance or scope the expression "to implement" (poner en práctica, in the original Spanish text) those regimes actually has in that sentence. Both things, therefore, must be taken into account in examining the various instruments through which the common and uniform regime was received in the domestic law of the member states.

a) Reception of Decisions 24 and 46

The experience relative to the reception of the Common regime for treatment of foreign capital, etc. (Decision 24) is the one that sheds the most light for purposes of this section. As concerns Bolivia and Peru, the same procedure was followed as for the approval of the Agreement, that is, the procedure of the decree-law which, as indicated in due time, is the instrument that assumes the nature or category

---

35. For further information on this matter see supra, section 4 and footnote 34 of Chapter II.

of law in both countries. 36/ Now, in contrast to the respective instruments approving the Agreement, they were not called "instruments of ratification". The Bolivian Decree Law simply states: "Let the common regime of treatment... be approved". 37/ The Peruvian Decree Law, in turn, reads as follows: "Let Decisions Nos. 24 and 37 of the Commission be given the force of law starting with July 1, 1971... " 38/ The difference surely arose in both countries from the fact that whereas the Cartagena Agreement was given the treatment of an international treaty or instrument subject to an "act of approval", which could assume, if so preferred, the nature of an act of ratification, Decision 24 was given a different treatment: that of an act of a subregional organ, which required, through specific provision of the Agreement, a supplementary national measure of action, presumably of an executive nature.

Ecuador also deviated from the procedure followed in approving the Agreement, but in another way: legislative intervention and approval were omitted and the Common regime was declared "in force" by means of a supreme decree, that is to say a merely executive act. 39/ Concerning Venezuela, as already indicated, the Law of September

---

36. See footnote 21. These and other instruments relative to the reception and application of Decision 24, issued by each of the then six member states, have been compiled in Pico Mantilla, Galo, Legislación Andina de Inversiones Extranjeras y Tecnología (Universidad Central de Venezuela, Caracas, 1975).

37. Decree Law No. 09798 of June 30, 1971. The complete text appears in Instrumentos para los cuales se pone en vigor en los países miembros el régimen común de tratamiento a los capitales extranjeros, etc. , Doc. JUN/di 14, September 7, 1971, p. 16.

38. Decree Law No. 18900 of June 30, 1971. The complete text appears in ibid, p. 22.

39. Supreme Decree No. 974 of June 30, 1971. The complete text appears in ibid, p. 28.

3, 1973, approving the Cartagena Agreement, also "approved", among others, Decision 24. When the statement of reasons (exposé de motives) of the Law is examined in subsection 4 b), this will explain the reasoning behind submitting several decisions of the Commission for legislative process and approval.

In Colombia, in decreeing the "entry into force" of the Common regime, without legislative consultation and approval, a process arose which was similar to the one that brought about the approval of the Cartagena Agreement, the major aspects of which are described in Section 2 a), supra. The instrument in question, Decree No. 1299 of June 30, 1971, also invoked Law 88 of 1961, as well as Article 15 of the Montevideo Treaty, which provides for harmonization of treatment applicable to investment from outside of the region, based on the power once again exercised by the Executive Branch. 40/ In contesting the constitutionality of the Decree, in addition to alleging that Decision No. 24 was an "international treaty" and that, as such, it had to be submitted for approval by the Congress, it was also alleged that the Common System was going to modify Colombian legislation in the fields of banking, insurance, corporations, taxation, foreign exchange, contracts, custom system and others. 41/

Thus, the question was once again raised relative to the nature of the international instrument, in this case a "decision" of the Commission of the Cartagena Agreement. Pursuant to his previous position, the Attorney General of the Nation felt that "the Decisions of the Commission of the Cartagena Agreement are the technical and legal instruments by means of which, in specific application of the basic principles of that Agreement, gradual compliance is

---

40. See the complete text of Decree No. 1299 in the Board document cited in footnote 37, p. 10. It is also reproduced in the OAS document cited in footnote 26, p. 119.
41. See the complete text of the petition itself in the OAS document, p. 121.

being given to its objectives... The legal nature of these decisions is similar, thus, to that of the resolutions of the Council of Ministers of LAFTA and of the Conference of Contracting Parties..." Then, after indicating the competence of the Commission for adopting decisions such as those stipulated in Article 27 of the Agreement in harmony with Article 15 of the Montevideo Treaty, he concluded that "...this itself is indicating that, for purposes of Article 76-18 and 120-20 of the Constitution, such decisions do not have the nature of treaties or agreements that must be submitted for approval by the Congress." 42/

In its turn, the Supreme Court of Justice was also consistent with the position that it maintained vis-à-vis the approval of the Agreement. Here are the pertinent passages of its decision. 43/

> Pursuant to the precise words of Article 27 of the Cartagena Agreement, Decisions 24 and 27 can only be understood as a bill submitted "for the consideration" of the Government of Colombia, never as a text of an obligatory nature. Given that Decree 1299, equivocally, gives the latter scope to those decisions, it deprives of value the invocation arising from Article 27, a circumstance that makes it unnecessary to evaluate it from any other aspect.

> The second part of the procedure remained without fulfillment, according to which the signatories of the Cartagena Agreement committed themselves to "adopt such measures as are necessary to put this system into practice", a purpose which, under Colombian law cannot be met except by means of the law (issued by the Congress or delivered by virtue of special powers of the Government). As long as legislative provisions do not adopt the rules proposed to Colombia in resolutions 24 and 37 of the

---

42. The opinion of the Attorney General also appears in ibid. p. 133.

43. See the complete text of the Court's decision of December 13, 1971 in ibid., p. 149.

Commission of the Cartagena Agreement relative to various matters of existing legislation, altering it in many points, these proposals do not acquire an obligatory nature, since they are inconsistent in their enactment with Article 76, attributes 1 and 12 of the Charter /the Constitution/.

Based on these and other reasons, the Court decided that Decree No. 1299 "could not be executed" (inexequible). 44/ In casting a dissident vote, seven of the judges expressed, among other things, that "in accordance with doctrine, positive Colombian law and its practice, the Common Regime, put into force by Decree 1299, cannot be referred to as an international treaty which, in order to be valid, must, from its preparation to its conclusion, cover the successive stages of negotiation, signature, approval, exchange and deposit of the instruments of ratification and promulgation, under the terms of Article 2 of Law 7 a) of 1944", and that "consequently, defined by two international agreements or treaties (the Montevideo Treaty, Article 15, and the Cartagena Agreement, Article 27), the duty of Colombia to adopt for its domestic legal order a special statute for foreign capital or investment could well be regulated by the President of the Republic in its details or forms and declared in force, as he did by means of Decree 1299 of 1971". 45/

---

44. For this purpose it became necessary to adopt a new instrument: Decree No. 1900 of September 15, 1973 (Diario Oficial of October 10, 1973), promulgated in accordance with the authorization given to the Executive Branch by Article 3 of Law 8 of the same year, which will be referred in subsection 4, b). Subsequently, by means of Decrees Nos. 2819, of December 28, 1973 (Diario Oficial of February 15, 1974) and 2788 of December 31, 1977 (Diario Oficial of February 15, 1974), the application in Colombia of some provisions of Decree No. 1900 was exempted.

45. The "Salvamento de Voto" appears in the OAS document, page 157.

Concerning the declaration of "inexecutability" (inexequibilidad, that is, that Decree No. 1299 was of no effect, that could not be executed), it should be pointed out that some of the other reasons referred to were not consistent with the deep-rooted internationalist tradition of the Colombian Supreme Court of Justice, which became evident also on the occasion of the proceedings against the Executive instrument approving the Cartagena Agreement (Decree No. 1245), with the Court refusing to declare it unconstitutional although it was of the opinion that the Agreement should have been submitted to legislative approval. 46/ In any event, as will be seen further on, the Court deviated completely from the position adopted in declaring Decree No. 1299 inexecutable, to adopt another in which it exceeded even its "internationalist" tradition, since it adhered fully to the "community law" concept of the Cartagena Agreement and its system of attributing competences. 47/

In Chile, in contrast to the experience of this country relative to the approval of the Agreement, objections were also raised to the instrument which was resorted to for implementing ("putting into practice") Decision 24, although, as will be seen further on, that instrument did not experience the same fate as the Colombian decree. The process began with the consultation by the Government, even before the adoption of that decision by the Commission, to the Council of Defense of the State, a legal entity in charge of fiscal matters. In the opinion of that entity, it was necessary to follow the way of the supreme decree, since with the existence of a law-treaty, which was the Montevideo Treaty "the problem shifted from domestic legislation to that of international political relations in the framework of dynamic multilateral agreements which require, for

---

46. See supra, subsection 2 b), on this aspect of the decision of the Court to which reference is made.

47. See the new decision of the Supreme Court of Colombia in infra, subsection 4 b).

their fulfillment, secondary national rules, which are incumbent upon the Executive... by means of Supreme Decree". 48/

The Government also consulted the Office of the Comptroller General of the Republic, which, this time, did not share the opinion that a merely executive procedure sufficed. The major reasons of the Office of the Comptroller were the following two: 49/

... That the execution of the agreements or application of mechanisms proper to a derivative law, of a "traité-cadre" to the extent that they involve modification of legal systems fully in force, must receive the approval or ratification of the National Congress, the only approval which under our institutional system could give them the force necessary for their proper acceptance as law of the Republic.

. . . . .

... It is necessary to stress the consequences in all of their magnitude that would arise from sustaining at any cost a doctrine which based on a community law emanating or deriving from "traités-cadres" is always incorporated into domestic law, taking supremacy over this law, and without observing the hierarchical structure of its rules, on the basis that these are mechanisms or systems suitable for accomplishing the purposes or objectives of such treaty. This could create a situation in which the generation of the rules of law would entirely escape the margin of the institutional channels provided for in the Fundamental Charter.

Despite the opinion of the Office of the Comptroller General, in the sense that Decision 24 required legislative

---

48. Cf. Orrego Vicuña, in INTAL, Derecho de la Integración, No. 11, October 1972, p. 56.
   49. Ibid., p. 56-57.

approval, since it involved modifying legal systems in force and since it affected institutional channels provided for in the Constitution, 50/ the Government proceeded to enact Supreme Decree No. 482 of June 25, 1971. 51/ The Office of the Comptroller General refused to accept the decree and returned it to the Executive, which caused the Executive to issue a "decree of insistence" (Decree No. 488 of June 29, 1971), which required the Office of the Comptroller General to implement Decree No. 482. 52/

Notwithstanding examining further on these national instruments, as well as those relative to Decision 46 (Uniform Regime on multinational enterprises) from another point of view, a brief observation should now be made on the objections that were put forth in two member states, Chile and Colombia, to the instruments with which the respective Executives Branches implemented Decision 24. As to the nature of the national instrument, there was obviously no opposition of any type to resorting to a legislative act or instrument, but it is also obvious that this was not necessary, and even less so if the need to resort to such act or instrument resided on the belief that the decision in question involved the nature of an international treaty or convention. In the same way that this opinion is valid, as has been admitted, in regard to the Cartagena Agreement, it is not valid nor could it be so with respect to this or any

---

50. This second reason apparently coincides with the reservation that the President of the Council of Defense had made, in the sense that if it would come to the point of "altering the domestic legal order in matters requiring a law, the right of the inhabitants of the Republic arises to not have their legal order altered by a new supreme decree" Ibid., p. 56. For other passages of the opinion of the Office of the Comptroller, as well as of the Council of Defense, see the document pertaining to Chile in the series cited in footnote 23 (JUN/Re. OJ/I/di 7) p. 24 and 17, respectively.

51. The complete text of this Decree appears in the document of the Board cited in footnote 37, p. 4.

52. Cf. Orrego Vicuña, loc. cit., p. 57.

of the decisions of the Commission. As was indicated at
the proper time, such decisions or acts have a completely
different legal nature since they result from the exercise
of competences and powers attributed by the Agreement to
the Commission on certain matters or topics. [53]

The argument also did not seem valid that Decision
24 required legislative approval because it involved modification of existing legal systems and because it affected
institutional channels provided for in the national Fundamental Charter. Regarding this last argument or opinion,
the following question should be raised: Is it not precisely
the purpose of international treaties of the type of the
Cartagena Agreement to produce such consequences? In
this order of ideas, given the system of attributing competences under the Agreement, what is actually of importance,
as has just been reiterated in the preceding paragraph, is
the scope of those competences attributed to the subregional
organs and not the type of national approval, legislative or
executive, through which the acts of those organs are
incorporated into the domestic legal order. After these
competences have been conferred by virtue of the acceptance
of the Agreement, would this not amount to de facto and
de jure, claiming them back in admitting the argument that
the subregional act modifies existing national legislation
and affects "institutional channels" of a constitutional type?

The experience relative to the "Uniform Regime on
the multinational enterprises and regulations applicable to
the treatment of subregional capital" (Decision 46) does
not differ, as to the nature of the national instrument by
means of which that regime was implemented, from the
experience relative to the Common regime (Decision 24),
even though apparently in no case did difficulties arise of
the nature of those that brought about the Colombian and
Chilean Decrees by which the other regimen was implemented. This surely stemmed from two different reasons,
which will be indicated further on.

---

53. See supra, subsection 1, c).

Decree No. 281 was issued in the case of Chile. 54/
The reason why this other Chilean instrument did not cause
any difficulties, despite the fact that it was of the same
nature as the one enacted with regard to Decision 24, would
appear to reside in the different content and scope of the
two systems in effect. The arguments put forth at that
time by the Office of the Comptroller General of the Republic concerning the Common regime were not applicable,
at least not to the same extent, to the Uniform regime.
As concerns Colombia, the reason appears to be more in
the fact that Decree No. 1897 of September 15, 1973 had
been issued by virtue of the powers expressly granted to
the Government by Law 8 a), a second Colombian instrument approving the Cartagena Agreement which has been
referred to earlier. 55/

Following the chronological order, the Venezuelan
law of September 3, 1973 should be referred to, which approved the Cartagena Agreement and through which, as
indicated above, Decision 46, among others, was "approved". 56/ The remaining instruments are similar in
nature to those pertaining to Decision 24: Bolivian Decree
No. 11.835 of September 27, 1974, 57/ and Ecuadorean
Supreme Decree No. 457 of June 30, 1975, 58/ and Peruvian Decree Law No. 21516 of June 8, 1976. 59/

---

54. Diario Oficial of July 21, 1972. The complete
text of the Decree also appears in doc. JUN/di 40, of
August 16, 1972.

55. Diario Oficial of October 15, 1973. The complete text of the Decree also appears in doc. JUN/di 99 of
November 24, 1973. See infra, subsection 4 b), on the
provision of Law 8 that specifically authorized the Colombian Government to "put into force", among others, Decision 46.

56. See infra, subsection 4 b) on the provision of the
Venezuelan law by means of which various decisions were
approved, including Decision 46.

57. The complete text of the Decree appears in doc.
JUN/di 145, of November 12, 1974.

58. Registro Oficial of June 10, 1975. The complete text of the decree also appears in doc. JUN/di 176 of
June 30, 1975.

59. El Peruano of June 15, 1976.

b) Provisions of the national instruments regarding entry into force of the two regimes

Subsection 1, d) of this chapter shows a certain lack of uniformity in the practice of the subregional organs, particularly in the case of the Commission, concerning the establishment of the date of the entry into force of these acts. Now, and notwithstanding the observations made at that time on some of the forms shown by this practice, there is no doubt that, owing to the provisions introduced in the regulations of the organs mentioned, the gap from the silence in this regard in the Cartagena Agreement was satisfactorily filled. At least in the beginning there was no problem in learning of the date of entry into force at the subregional level of the acts of the pertinent organs.

Nevertheless, the problem once again arises in regard to the pertinent provisions of the national instruments by means of which the subregional acts are entered into the domestic legal order of the various member states. Although this does not exhaust the situations referred to, perhaps the most prominent ones were created by the pertinent provisions of the national instruments by means of which Decisions 24 and 46 were "put into practice", or implemented. As will be recalled, pursuant to Transitional Article A of Decision 24 (and the one pertaining to Decision 46), "the present regime shall enter into force when all of the member states have deposited in the Office of the Secretariat of the Board the instruments by means of which they put the regime into practice in their respective territories, in accordance with the provisions of the second paragraph of Article 27 of the Cartagena Agreement".

In reference to Decision 24, Chilean Decree 482 established expressly that "this decree shall enter into force as provided for in Article 27, paragraph 2 of the Cartagena Agreement, and Transitional Article A of Decision 24..." [60] As will be noted, Article 27, paragraph

---

60. In the preceeding subsection see the complete reference relative to this and the other national instruments cited further on.

2, leaves no doubt as to the date of entry into force of the common regime. Thus, the entry into force and validity at the national level were made consistent with the entry into force or validity at the subregional level, as provided for in the Decision approving that regime. In contrast, Colombian Decree No. 1299 established, on the one hand, that "starting with July 1, 1971 the following common regime shall enter into force..." and, on the other hand, that "this decree is in force starting with July 1, 1971", that is to say, that it indicated a definite date which could coincide or not coincide with the date contemplated in Decision 24. 61/ Bolivian Decree Law No. 09798 presented another approach: that of absolute silence on the entry into force of both the common regime and the decree law itself. Peruvian Decree Law No. 18900 limited itself to giving "force of law, starting with July 1, 1971, to Decision 24...." In similar terms, Ecuadorean Supreme Decree No. 974 declared "the regime... is in force in the national territory starting with this date". 62/

The situation is essentially the same in regard to Decision 46, which contains a provision on its entry into force identical to Transitional Article A of Decision 24 (Article c. of the Transitional Provisions). Whereas Chilean Decree No. 281 contained a clause of the same type as the decree relative to Decision 24, the remaining ones adopted other systems, some consistent with those

------

61. The second Colombian decree mentioned in the preceeding subsection, Decree No. 1887 of 1973 uses equivalent expressions, which are now explained in view of the circumstance that the common regime had already entered into effect at the subregional level on the date of its promulgation. In this regard see supra, subsection 1, d).

62. No reference should be made here to the Venezuelan instrument, the Law of September 3, 1973, since it came after the entry into force of Decision 24 and obviously does not involve the question raised in the present subsection.

of the instrument cited in the preceding paragraph. Thus, Colombian Decree No. 1897 established that "The uniform regime shall be applied starting from the enactment of the present decree...." Bolivian Supreme Decree No. 11,835 similar to the one relative to Decision 24, made absolutely no indication to the entry into effect of either the Uniform regime or the Supreme Decree itself. Ecuadorean Supreme Decree No. 457, in turn, under a specific provision in it, would enter into force from the time of its publication in the Registro Oficial. Lastly, Peruvian Decree Law No. 21516 made no reference as to the entry into force of the regime; it only ordered publication and implementation of the Decree Law.

As can be noted, with the exception of the system adopted by the Chilean instruments, which is entirely consistent with the transitional provisions of Decisions 24 and 46, the systems adopted by the other instruments, with the exception perhaps of the Bolivian instruments which keeps silence in this regard, obviously introduce or are capable of introducing at least certain confusion as to the true date of entry into force of those decisions, both at the subregional and the national level. In regard to the latter, would it be necessary to distinguish among these two levels of entry into effect? From a purely legal standpoint, one should only think in terms of a single and only date of entry into full force and validity of the subregional act, that which is stipulated by the organ which has been given power by the Cartagena Agreement to implement the act concerned. Thus, the systems adopted by the instruments referred constitute, strictly speaking, acts that are incompatible with the respective subregional acts. 63/ They are not always consistent with the

---

63. Without wishing to justify the procedures of reference, it should be noted that they are perfectly explainable in the light of the apparently "approbatory" nature of the national instruments that adopt said procedures. In effect, given this "approbatory" nature, how could the subregional act, which enters into force and is valid owing to those instruments or acts of national approval, come into force or become effective starting from a date different than the one established by the pertinent national instrument

provisions of the Commission on this matter in its Decision 37, as might have been noted. 64/ Furthermore and as indicated at the same opportunity, pursuant to Transitional Article A of the Common Regime, it was supposed to enter into force on July 13, 1971, the date of deposit in Office of the Secretariat of the Board of the last of the national instruments.

4. Reception of the Other Subregional Acts

As was seen in subsection 1, b), except for the cases in which the Cartagena Agreement contemplates a national action aimed at supplementing and perfecting the subregional act, it will be valid erga omnes for and/or in the member states. This does not prevent naturally that one of them enacts the legal provisions with a view towards facilitating, and if appropriate rendering viable, the execution or application of the act concerned. As has been noted, notwithstanding the directly binding (vinculante) nature of the subregional legal order, the practice of enacting decrees or other measures for the purposes indicated is considered appropriate. 65/ It is in the light of these

---

63. (Cont.) or act? As indicated in a preceeding footnote, see infra subsection 4, c) on the "approbatory" nature which, at least formally, most of the national instruments have.

64. See footnote 18.

65. Cf. Roundtable of Caracas referred to in footnote 20 of Chapter II. The complete text of the observation or conclusion of that roundtable is the following: "Notwithstanding the directly binding (vinculante) nature of this subregional legal order, the current practice was considered appropriate of translating the subregional rules into decrees or other measures of the national legal order for purposes of facilitating their application and compliance on the part of the various national authorities; in any case, these internal measures recognize their direct and immediate source in the subregional binding rule and must conform to this in the strictest manner".

considerations that the reception of that category of acts in the various member states will be examined.

a) Nature of the action required by the domestic law of each member state

To understand completely how the subregional acts that are valid erga omnes have been received, it would perhaps be appropriate to know first of all the nature of the national action that must be followed according to the domestic law of each member state. To this end, one should resort, as the authorized source of information, to the responses provided by the national consultants to the questionnaire submitted to them by the Board of the Cartagena Agreement for the purpose of the meeting of experts on the creation of a jurisdictional organ. 66/ The responses that are now of interest are those that were given by the consultants to point 6 of the questionnaire, the text of which is as follows: 67/

6. Based on the categories given below, how would you classify the decisions or other acts of the Commission from the point of view of the requirements necessary for them to enter into force in your country?

a) Those that do not require any subsequent act by the Government.
b) Those that require a subsequent act by the Government.
c) Those that require prior approval of organs of the State other than the Government.

As can be noticed, the inquiry was not drawn up following the terms in which the question is actually raised. In effect, what is sought to be known is not always what is

---

66. Concerning this meeting, see supra, section 5 of Chapter III.
67. Cf. Questionnaire presented by the Board of the Cartagena Agreement to the National Consultants, doc. JUN/RE.OJ/di 4, June 23, 1972.

required in order for the subregional acts to "enter into force". In a purely legal sense, this is only of interest with respect to the acts whose full validity and force depend upon a supplementary national action. With regard to the other acts, what is of interest is something else: the national action or instrument required merely to facilitate or make viable the execution of such acts. In this way of thinking, the obligatory nature or the validity erga omnes of this last category of subregional acts amounts to their "entry into force", notwithstanding, it should be repeated, the internal requirements needed for these acts to also become "executable" or "applicable". 68/

---

68. Except for the probable case that the Board wished to say something else in using the expression "enter into force" (entrar en vigencia), it is evident that such an expression is not consistent with the statement of the Board itself, cited in subsection 1 c), in the sense that "the decisions of the Commission are binding for the member states from the very moment they are approved". Furthermore, on that same opportunity the Board made the following observations: "what has been stated in the preceeding point does not signify that in the opinion of the Board all of the decisions of the Commission are automatically and immediately applicable in the territory of each one of the member states starting from the date of their approval. The difference is known between the so-called self executing obligations, that is, those that are immediately applicable, and others that require certain procedures, varying according to the constitutions, to be incorporated into the legal order of the states. Those of the first type will be applied immediately. The others must be received in that legal order, but whatever the branch of the state called upon to accomplish the necessary procedures, it must put them into effect by virtue of the principle already stated: "Pacta sunt servanda". From these observations it would appear to clearly follow that, also in the opinion of the Board, what is in question is not always the binding nature or validity of the decisions, but the time, conditions and form in which they are "applicable". Cf. Document cited in footnote 13, p. 2.

In any event, the replies from the national consultants shed considerable light on the domestic law requirements which have just been referred to. 69/ In the case of Bolivia, the reply by the consultant, Dr. Renato Crespo Paniagua, was the following: 70/

> VI. Since both the Montevideo Treaty and the Cartagena Agreement have been approved by means of Decree Laws, which under de facto governments are equivalent to laws, the decisions or other acts of the Commission require approval only by means of a Supreme Decree by the Executive Branch, since in our opinion the decisions and the acts of the Commission implement the Montevideo Treaty and the Cartagena Agreement, which can be compared to the constitutional rules of the community.

It should be observed that reference is made to the "approval" of the decisions and that under the context in which this term is employed it would appear that it is being used in the same sense in which it is used with regard to the Montevideo Treaty and the Cartagena Agreement, except that with respect to the decisions it is indicated that merely executive action will be sufficient.

In the other replies, in contrast to the preceding one, various requirements or procedures are indicated, according to the nature, content or scope of the subregional act. Here is the reply from the Peruvian consultant, Dr. Héctor Cornejo Chávez: 71/

> Since the Cartagena Agreement was incorporated into the Peruvian legal order in the capacity and

---

69. A comparative summary of the replies from the national consultants to the questionnaire of the Board has been published in Spanish, doc. JUN/RE. OJ/di 10, June 23, 1972.

70. Cf. doc. cited in footnote 21, p. 4.

71. Cf. doc. cited in footnote 21, p. 3.

with the hierarchy of a Treaty, that is to say by
means of a specific law, and since that agreement
empowered the Commission to take valid decisions
under its own authority, these decisions should be
considered as having equal force as the Agreement
itself, provided that they involve matters included
in the Agreement or pertinent to its execution. If
by their nature these decisions require a subsequent
act of the government to be executed, that act must
occur without objections, as was provided for in the
Agreement. Under the assumption that some of
these decisions normally require, according to the
Peruvian legal order, prior approval of some other
organ of the State than the Government, that circumstance would have become known in the form of a
reservation, prior to the legal approval of the agreement.

It is noted, on the one hand, that decisions are contemplated which, by their nature, require a subsequent
act of the government for their "execution", which implicitly admits that others do not require any national action to this end, and, on the other hand, it would appear
that in the last sentence of the reply the idea of the "approval" is once again admitted, although now this action
is specifically limited, when appropriate, to the Executive
Branch.

One of the most elaborate replies was from the
Chilean consultant, Dr. Jacobo Schaulsohn H. The most
pertinent parts of his reply are given ahead: 72/

16. a) The decisions and acts of the Commission that assume a merely instrumental domestic or
administrative nature for the development at the
international level of the Agreement do not require
"any subsequent act of the government" to come into force.

---

72. Cf. doc. cited in footnote 23, p. 15 and 17.

Nor will any acceptance be necessary by domestic administrative or governmental act of those decisions or determinations of the Commission relating to directives or guidelines among states with respect to programs, direct measures or recommendations which, in their form and substance, are not intended for producing by themselves legal effects capable of making liable /sic/ for responsibility by action or omission in their acceptance either by means of compulsory execution or indemnifying equivalence or by any other sanctioning means.

b) In contrast, "subsequent act of the government" is necessary if the decisions or other acts involved assume forms and contents of rules necessary or obligatory in regard to conduct, that is to say, with precise and determined legal effects in their purpose and intended parties.

In view of the scope of the legislative treaty, which by its nature and content encompasses the multilateral Treaty of Montevideo, confirmed by the legislative history of its approval and doctrine of the Office of the Comptroller G neral of the Republic, the incorporation of said determinations for implementation and entry into force in Chile will require solemn certified promulgation and publication by means of a Supreme Decree.

c) Those decisions or acts of the Commission which require the proceeding of prior approval by Parliament in compliance with the constitutional provisions set forth in No. 2 of this document will not govern or obligate Chile if they are not "ratified" in advance and with the authorizing agreement of the National Congress.

18. If the decisions or acts of the Commission concern matters that, by constitutional mandate, must be governed in Chile by law, or if they run counter to existing laws, there is no easy solution to the problem and there are contradictory criteria in competent Chilean organs.

Although in the abstract it would appear, prima facie, that within the objectives and terms spelled out in the Treaty, the "complementary legislation" of the Commission, as it is special and has the nature of "law", would not require prior national legislative approval, but only a Supreme Decree, it is not possible to affirm this precisely. (The underlined and in quotation marks is in the original text).

Regarding Section 16 c) of the reply, the provisions referred to are those of Article 43 and 72 of the Chilean Constitution concerning the respective powers of the President and the Congress in the entering into, signing, approval or rejection of treaties. This section is only applicable, therefore, in the case that the decisions adopt the form of an international treaty or agreement, as is the case of Decision 40, mentioned in subsection 1, c). [73]/

As concerned Section 16 b), which has to do with decisions of the Commission requiring "subsequent act of the government", the second paragraph of the reply clarifies the nature of this national action: [74]/

The Supreme Decree, the situation of letter b), will not be equivalent in any way to a decree with force of law, since this will not involve a power that is delegated for the Chief of State to "issue provisions with force of law," the assumptions in Article 44 Section 15 of the Constitution copies on page 5 could not occur. The legal rules will be created and produced by the "Commission organ" and not in an immediate and direct manner by the Chilean public branches. The President will attest to its force and nothing more.

---

73. As indicated in footnote 17, Decision 40 did not constitute in itself a normative instrument, it only approved texts comprising two agreements, both subject to approval procedures (one of them involving ratification).

74. Cf. doc. cited in footnote 23, p. 16.

Notwithstanding Section 16 b) and the clarifying comment just transcribed, which would appear to deny "approbatory" nature to the executive action, new doubts arose in Section 18 on the same type of action, legislative or executive, that will be required under the two assumptions referred to in that section.

In regard to Ecuador, the national consultant, Dr. Ramiro Borja y Borja, classifies the decisions of the Commission of the Agreement into three large groups, "according to the degree of force", but before this he formulates the observations that appear in the first two paragraphs of the next transcription: 75/

> 38. By virtue of the provisions of the Montevideo Treaty in the first section and in section a) of Article 34 and the Cartagena Agreement in section b) of Article 7 and in Article 112, the "resolutions of the Conference of the Contracting Parties of LAFTA and the decisions of the Commission of the Cartagena Agreement" are valid as international pacts, being the work of their signatories, and thus occupy in the Ecuadorean legal order, that is to say, that of the laws, as indicated in sections 27 and 29.
>
> The need for domestic rules to apply some of these "resolutions" and "decisions" does not stand in the way of the conclusion. This need does not signify that the existence of these domestic rules are a condition of their entry into force.
>
> If a pact among nations presupposes an internal rule of a signatory country in order to be implemented, this means that this sets forth the duty or grants the power to issue a given rule by whoever is capable of acting in the name of such State; in imposing the former or establishing the latter, it governs over the person who has the authority or on the respective people, imposing the obligation of not opposing the power granted.

---

75. Cf. doc. cited in footnote 22, p. 20 and 25.

The Treaty that imposes this duty, while it is not fulfilled, does not directly govern the people of the State on behalf of which the complementary rule is to be issued, but it does govern whoever has to issue it.

43. From this it follows that the decisions of the Commission of the Cartagena Agreement are classified according to their degree of force in Ecuador into the following:

a) Decisions that do not require any rule: Decisions 1, 2, 3, 4, 7, 8, 9, 10, 11, 12, 13, 14, 15, 16, 18, 21, 23, 27, 29, 30, 32, 33, 34, 37, 37-a, 38, 42, 45, 47 and 48.

b) Decisions requiring a rule from the President of the Republic: Decisions 6, 17-a, 19, 22, 24, 25, 26, 28, 31, 35, 36, 39, 41, 43, 46, 49, 50 and 51.

c) Decisions that presupposed a rule from the Congress and rule from the President of the Republic preceeded by the former, or cooperation by both: Decisions 5, 17, 20, 40 and 44.

The above classification agrees, in general terms, with the distinctions made by the Chilean consultant. Never the less, it is not easy to understand why there are included in the same group b) decisions such as numbers 24 and 46 (Common and Uniform regimes), which by virtue of the specific provisions of the Cartagena Agreement required complementary national action in order to become fully effective and valid, with other decisions for which such action is not required, including some, as Decision 6, which, owing to its regulatory nature, only governs the functioning of the Commission.

Concerning Colombia, the reply from the national consultant, Dr. Jaime Vidal Perdomo, also distinguishes the national action that must be followed in accordance with the specific act of the Commission involved. Here are the pertinent passages of the reply: 76/

> It is evident that some acts of the Commission do not require any subsequent action by the Colombian government. This statement is valid in view of two assumptions: that what is involved are purely internal acts of the Pact or administrative matters in which it is to be assumed that the member states having entrusted decision-making /power/ on those matters to the common authorities, or also in the case of purely declaratory acts or involving recommendations that are not given binding legal force, as the case of Decisions 13 and 43.

> Acts may also exist which, because it is so required in the Cartagena Agreement or because they involve domestic Colombian rules, must be adopted by national authorities. This statement, which covers possibilities b) and c) /of point 6 of the above-transcribed questionnaire/, exists for the former when the measure in question pertains, internally, to the exercise of an ordinary power of the government deriving from the Constitution directly or from the law, that is, stated in terms of Colombian legal rules, when the act mentioned can be adopted by regulatory decree or by constitutional regulation.

> For example, the measures involving modification in the Customs Schedule can be adopted by regulatory decree, since Law 6 of 1971 provided that, pursuant to Article 205 of the National Constitution, they must be issued by decree subject to such general rules as set forth by the law. This constitutional authorization of the so-called "leyes-cuadros" (laws-tables), provided for in Colombia through the reform of 1968, had its first development in Law 6 (through which general rules are issued which must be followed by the government in modifying customs schedules, tariffs and

---

76. Cf. JUN/RE. OJ/di 6, of the same series and date cited, p. 5.

other provisions relating to the customs systems) and can be very much applicable in the field of the Cartagena Agreement.

Lastly, the need has already been felt in Colombian law to accept decisions by the authorities of the Andean Group specifically by means of law. This criterion was made known by the Supreme Court of Justice in the Decision of January 20, 1972 that declared unconstitutional the Decree 1299 of 1971 "by means of which there is put into force the Common regime of treatment of foreign capital and trademarks, patents, licenses and royalties of the Cartagena Agreement".

In regard to the last reply, the question should be raised of the true meaning of the phrase "must be adopted by national authorities", which is used in the second paragraph of the transcription. The problem obviously does not arise vis-à-vis that acts provided for under letter c) of point 6 of the questionnaire from the Board but vis-à-vis the acts provided for under letter b), that is to say the acts of the Commission "that require subsequent action by the government". Should the word "adopted" be understood as equivalent to the action of "approving" or "putting into force"? The answer would appear to be yes, particularly in regard to what is stated further on in the same paragraph and the next paragraph. In any case, the reply as a whole should be revised in the light of the provisions set forth on this matter by the Colombian law of 1973, which should be examined now, together with the Venezuelan law of the same year, both of which involve special legislation on the matter. 77/

    b)   <u>The special legislation of Colombia and Venezuela; the new decisions of the Colombian Supreme Court</u>

The Colombian legislative instrument just referred

---

77. Since Venezuela did not adhere to the Cartagena Agreement until after the Meeting of Experts, a reply from a Venezuelan consultant was not available.

to is Law 8 of March 21, 1973, published in the <u>Anales del Congreso</u> of June 8, 1973. Here are the pertinent provisions of that second Colombian instrument approving the Cartagena Agreement, referred to earlier. <u>78/</u>

Article 2.

. . . .

The National Government can put into force the decisions of the Commission and of the Board or of the agencies carrying out the Andean Subregional Agreement which do not modify the legislation or are incumbent upon the legislator.

In contrast, such decisions, to be approved and to enter into force, must be submitted to the Congress by the government when they involve matters incumbent upon the legislator or when they amend existing legislation or when the government has not been invested with prior legal powers.

By Article 3 of the Law the President of the Republic was given "extraordinary powers up to December 31, 1973 to put into effect the rules he considers appropriate in those contained in Decisions 24, 37, 37-a, 46, 47, 48, 49, 50 and 56 of the Commission of the Cartagena Agreement and to enter into an agreement with the other contracting parties on the amendments to Decision 24". Article 4 also has to do with the "approval" and entry into force of the Decisions of the Commission.

The legislative history of the second Colombian "approbatory act" of the Cartagena Agreement begins with the bill proposed by the Executive on August 1, 1972. In the Statement of Reasons /Exposición de Motivos/ signed by the Ministers of Foreign Affairs and of Economic Development reference is made first of all to the reasons that lead the Government to approve the Agreement by means of a decree (Decree 1245, of August 8, 1969), as well as the reasons that the Supreme Court of Justice had to consider necessary approval by the Congress. The Statement

_____

78. See <u>supra,</u> footnote 33.

of Reasons indicates that the decisions of the Court had created a problem, consisting in "the lack of powers for the government for the purpose of putting into force the decisions emanating from this economic integration agreement, which must be accomplished in a continuous and permanent matter, and to prevent that situation we submit the present bill based on sections 18 and 11 of article 76 of the Constitution". Pursuant to that bill, the government will be authorized to enact such measures as are necessary for the implementation of the decisions of the Commission of the Cartagena Agreement on the basis of equality and reciprocity with the other contracting states. The Government, in turn, would request, prior to approving those decisions and whenever it has not been invested with prior legal powers, the opinion of an interparlamentary commission. [79]

The reasons and arguments put forth to reject the bill appear in particular in the following passages of the report, unanimously approved, of the Second Permanent Constitutional Commission of the Colombian Senate: [80]

---

79. See Anales del Congreso of August 24, 1972, pp. 710 and 711. One of the passages of the Statement of Reasons is given ahead, in which the Government provides the reasons and the foundation for its draft law: "the legal capacity of the organs of the Andean Community should not be exaggerated, in particular that pertaining to the Commission which is composed of representatives of the five member states. There is furthermore no doubt that the Agreement presupposes the desire to reach more coherent and harmonic stages in the Andean economy obtaining concrete results in the course of integration and reaching the goals indicated in the Agreement itself. There consequently follows the need of giving the President of the Republic, as supreme director of the external relations of the country, pursuant to Section 20 of Article 120 of the national constitution, the capacity to participate in the work of the Andean Group and to accept its decisions". Ibid p. 711.

80. Anales of November 14, 1972, pp. 1335-1336.

This Treaty of Economic Integration /Cartagena
Agreement/, it suffices to read it, is related in such
a close manner with our positive law that tax legislation, labor legislation, foreign exchange legislation,
the legislation in regard to commerce, petroleum,
planning, agriculture, finance, customs, international trade, transportation, monetary policy and industry are all affected by the provisions of the treaty or
by its developments. Most of the important decisions
of the Commission of the Agreement, such as the
case of Decision 24 on Common Regime of Treatment
of Foreign capital, either change our domestic law
or regulate matters that were not contemplated under
the law.

The Commission of the Agreement pretends to be a
supranational institution. The rules of the Agreement
seek to create community law. The regulations of
the Commission and the regulations of the Board of
the Agreement confirm this. Even the wording of
the articles of the Treaty is imperative in tone...

We then ask: How do these obligations of the Treaty
that are converted into Decisions of the Commission
of the Agreement enter into our law? How are they
inserted into our legal order? Many of them contradict and will contradict our laws. Will approval of
the Treaty by the Congress be sufficient for all of
its developments and consequences to enter our law
automatically and become mandatory within the
territorial limit of Colombia?

The above considerations are given abundant attention
in other passages and the constitutional question is specifically raised in the sense that "a constitutional reform is
needed that expresses the idea that the decisions of supranational entities will enter into force and will obligate
Colombian citizens by means of simple promulgation on
the part of the national government. As long as an article
like this does not exist in the Colombian Constitution it
will not be possible to do away with the promulgation of
the law putting into force the decisions of the Commission
of the Agreement".

The Venezuelan instrument that approved the Cartagena Agreement, Law 3 of September 1973, and that also approved Decisions 24, 37, 37-a, 40, 46, 50, 56 and 70 of the Commission, contained provisions similar to those of the Colombian Law: 81/

> Paragraph one. The decisions of the Commission of the "Cartagena Agreement" that alter Venezuelan legislation or involve matters which are the competence of the Legislative Branch require approval, by law, of the Congress of the Republic.
>
> Paragraph two. The decisions of the Commission the contents of which do not affect matters under the competence of the legislator shall be put into effect by the National Executive at such time as considered appropriate pursuant to the provisions of the Agreement, as well as the provisions contained in decisions concerning entry into force, if appropriate, and the internal legal provisions governing its activity.

Paragraphs three and four of the Law authorize the Executive to issue such regulations as are necessary for the application of the decisions of the Commission as required by the decisions, as well as the regulation or establishment of a special regime in those cases in which some decision of the Commission contemplates such possibility, with the exception of those cases in which legislative approval is required by means of a law.

The Statement of Reasons of the Law referred to is based on "some of the Decisions of the Commission having a regulatory nature and general content and that when they are incorporated into the domestic law of the countries constitute rules of a legal scope and are therefore of mandatory observance by all of the citizens and organs of the state. Others, in contrast, do not have such nature and therefore are limited to standardizing policies or

---

81. See supra, footnote 34.

criteria at the administrative level among the Governments of the member countries". This distinction between two categories of decisions raises a constitutional question, as explained in the following passage of the Statement of Reasons: 82/

> This necessarily raises the problem of the immediate validity of the community acts since, although these are acts provided for in the Agreement itself and therefore authorized by the Legislative Branch at least in principle, when the Treaty is ratified there is no doubt that in the Venezuelan constitutional system the power of legislation is incumbent upon the Legislative Branch and, consequently, the Congress of the Republic should ratify those decisions containing rules referring to matters which the Constitution defines as being part of the "Legal Reserve", whether or not they are consistent with provisions of the domestic law.

The constitutional question referred to in the above passage of the Statement of Reasons is the one mentioned in the first paragraph of the Law transcribed above. In effect, although the "immediate validity" of the subregional acts is admitted, "at least in principle", since they are provided for in a conventional instrument that has been ratified, approval of the Legislative Branch shall be required in the areas reserved by the Constitution to the Legislative Branch. 83/ Thus, what appears to be stated is that, despite the intrinsic validity of the subregional acts, a process equivalent to approval or ratification of

---

82. The complete text of the Statement of Reasons is also reproduced in INTAL loc. cit. in footnote 34. The passage transcribed appears on p. 404.

83. The expression "immediate validity" apparently does not refer to the time in which the decisions become valid, but to the time in which they are "applicable" to their intended parties.

international treaties or agreements will have to be followed so that they can be executable (or so that their provisions can be applicable).

In concluding this brief description of the special legislations of Colombia and Venezuela it should be stressed, above all, that the question is formally raised of the relations between Andean law generated by the acts of the subregional organs and the domestic law of the various member states, in the sense of knowing: a) which will prevail in the event of conflict between the rules of Andean law and domestic law; and b) if the complementary action of the member states could paralyze, hold back or modify the subregional acts. A favorable response to the predominance of the domestic law could be inferred in the two hypotheses, at least by reading the provisions transcribed and from the spirit that seems to have animated the adoption of both laws. 84/ What other sense or purpose could there be in submitting for national approval any subregional act covering matters or topics that the respective legislatures continue to consider of their exclusive competence? 85/

In another order of ideas, a second question should be raised: should a distinction be made, as is done by the Colombian and Venezuelan legislations, owing to the legislative or executive nature of the matter involved in the acts of the subregional organs, when the Cartagena Agreement does not do this nor permits doing so? Far from this, certain matters are reserved to the subregional

----

84. See _infra_, section 6 on the hierarchical relation between the Andean legal order and the municipal orders.

85. It should be taken into account in this regard that Article 3 of the Colombian law cited above authorized the Executive Branch to put into force "the provisions it considers appropriate" of the ones contained in Decisions 24, 37, 37-a, 46... ".

organs in the system of distribution of competences of the
Agreement, independently of the nature of those matters
in the domestic legal order of the member states. As can
be noted in this and the preceding chapter, this is indeed
an attribution of competences to the subregional organs not
conditioned by reason of the legislative or executive nature
of the matter involved in the subregional act. Even in the
case of the Common and Uniform regimes provided for in
Articles 27 and 28 of the Agreement, the complementary
national action contemplated to "put them into practice"
does not constitute a requirement that justifies the distinction that is made by the legislations referred to. Such
complementary national action may indeed very well consist
in a merely executive act, despite the markedly "legislative"
nature of the matters involved in those regimes. 86/

It is evident, thus, that in not admitting the validity
or effects of all of the acts resulting from the exercise of
the competences attributed by the Cartagena Agreement to
the subregional organs, the Colombian and Venezuelan
laws constitute a revival of a traditional position. In this
way of thinking, these laws constitute, formally, legislative
acts that are incompatible with the spirit and the letter of
the rules attributing competences of the Agreement. They
are equivalent to a "reservation", given the effects that
they can cause, although this has not been established in
such form and name in the instruments that approve the
Agreement and therefore thus not constitute an actual reservation from the point of view of international law. 87/

---

86. See, in particular, the observations made on
this matter at the end of subsection 3, a).

87. According to the Vienna Convention on the Law
of Treaties, reservation means "a unilateral statement,
however phrased or named, made by a State, when signing,
ratifying, accepting, approving or acceding to a treaty,
whereby it purports to exclude or to modify the legal effect
of certain provisions of the treaty in their application to
that State" (Article 2 (1) (d).

To sum up, the two laws, in principle, affect by their very essence the subregional legal order created by the Andean Pact, since they rendered potentially inoperative the system of distribution of competences and powers among the subregional organs and the member states adopted by that Pact.

In relation to the observations that have just been made, one should refer, on the one hand, to the opinion that seems inclined to justify the attitude assumed by the Colombian and Venezuelan legislatures. For example, for Morales Paúl, "... as a result of both laws of incorporation, the rules of direct application are limited to a small number, especially the rules contemplating obligations not to act." To which the Venezuelan professor immediately added this comment: "It should be recalled, however, that integration is a process and not an end in itself. It is preferable to overcome stages, gradually but boldly, and not confront a reality that resists very radical changes". 88/ In contrast to this opinion, there is the one that feels the attitude assumed by those legislatures is inacceptable and unjustifiable. Thus, for Caicedo Perdomo, "A true economic integration is impossible at the present time without accepting supranationality. The law approving the Cartagena Agreement (Law 8), in establishing the forms of incorporation of the decisions, leaves the organs of the Agreement without any regulatory power." Based on this premise and other similar considerations, the Colombian professor concludes with this observation: "It is now necessary to revise the Cartagena Agreement in a totally supranational sense. If supranationality is inacceptable to Colombia, then we have the obligation to state this clearly to the other member states and to withdraw from the treaty after rejecting it." 89/

---

88. Cf. "La aplicación del derecho comunitario por el juez nacional", in INTAL, Derecho de la Integración, No. 15, March 1974, pp. 26-27.

89. Cf. "La Incorporación de las Decisiones 24 y 37 al Derecho Colombiano", in La Revista de la Cámara de Comercio de Bogotá, June 1973, No. 11, pp. 57 and 58.

The foregoing observations and opinions should be evaluated in the light of the new position that the Supreme Court of Justice of Colombia has taken in recent decisions. As was indicated in examining in Section 3, a) the sentence of that Court relative to the national instrument by which decision 24 was implemented, in those decisions the Court adhered fully to the "community law" concept of the Cartagena Agreement and of its system of attributing competences.

The first of the decisions referred to resolved a petition put forth by two citizens, requesting that Articles 2 and 4 of Law 8 of 1973 be declared inexecutable (inexequible). Along with the two petitioners, the Attorney General of the Nation took part in this suit. The infractions cited were, among others, those of certain provisions contained in Articles 76 and 120 of the Colombian Constitution. These provisions are the following, respectively:

> By means of treaties or agreements approved by the Congress, the State may bind itself in order for supranational institutions to be created, on bases of equality and reciprocity, that have the purpose of promoting or consolidating economic integration with other States. (Art. 76).

> The powers and duties of the President of the Republic as the Chief of the State and supreme administrative authority are:

> . . .

> 20. To direct diplomatic and commercial relations with other states and entities of international law; appoint diplomatic agents; receive the corresponding agents, and conclude treaties and conventions with foreign powers, which shall be submitted to the Congress for approval (Art. 120).

In regard to these matters the Court formulated, among others, the following considerations and pronouncements: <u>90/</u>

The attribution of regulatory powers to the community organs, under the law of economic integration, comes from a transfer of competences that the contracting parties undertake voluntarily and initially in the constitutive treaty. Thus, according to current terminology, a change is made, a cession, a transfer of prerrogatives from the national to the supranational level. Whatever the appropriate names are, in the economic integration of several countries there is a relevant and differential note that they lose legislative powers that they had exercised exclusively by means of provisions of internal law on certain matters and that the regional organizations inherit them in their favor.

Under the cover of this phenomenon, new figures appear in contemporary law, figures which have required constitutional reforms for insertion into the domestic legal orders. This has thus taken place in Colombia with the institutional amendment of 1968 which introduced, with article 11 of the legislative act of that year, the current text of section two of article 78-18 of the Constitution, which gives a natural role to external institutions having a supranational nature, that is, with powers to regulate connections of internal law with value sometimes greater than the national law itself. After this reform, there is no need for discussion on the capacity that certain international organizations can enjoy to legislate, with jurisdiction in Colombia, matters of their competence on the terms established by the Constitution in Article 76-18, section two.

The decisions of the <u>Commission</u> and the acts of the <u>Board</u> produce results in the framework of the nations that form the group. The question as to whether it is necessary or appropriate to strengthen

---

90. <u>Cf.</u> Foro Colombiano, Vol. XII, No. 69, March 1975, pp. 245, 249-250, 251, 257.

the community determinations by means of provisions of domestic law is a matter that the Colombian Constitution reserves to the Executive, as the entity entrusted with accomplishing and seeing to the accomplishment of the laws (art. 120-2-3) and, above all, through its mission "to direct diplomatic and commercial relations with the other States and entities under international law" (120-20). The Government is empowered in these cases to undertake such conduct as must be followed and to evaluate the reasons that should orient such conduct.

Paragraph two of article 2 of law 8, however, restricts the constitutional power of the President and only permits him to put into effect the acts of regional law which "do not modify legislation or are not under the competence of the legislator", a distinction which is different from the version of the above text which has just been cited. That limitation constitutes a cutting off of competence. When a rule of regional law must be applied it is executed for its own merit, directly, or in the manner provided for by the community charter or the competent regional organ and, as appropriate, lastly, the Colombian Executive. That legal provision, in establishing assumptions to a power of the Government that the Constitution has not stipulated, infringes it. On this point, the disparity between a legislative provision and the constitutional order is noteworthy.

. . .

Consistent with paragraph two, paragraph three of the same article 2 underscores the limiting intent of the legislator and, referring to orders of the Government on compliance with rules emanating from the Andean authorities, states: "In contrast, such decisions, for their approval and entry into force, must be submitted to the Congress by the Government, when they involve matters of competence of the legislator or when the Government has not been invested with prior legal powers".

Here we are faced with another restriction, more defined, on a power granted by the Constitution through article 120-20, without restrictions. The same drawback of inexecutability already indicated reappears: The Government, in charge of diplomatic and commercial relations with other States and with international institutions as the one created by the Cartagena Agreement, enjoys freedom of action to select the most efficient means to accomplish the obligations contracted by virtue of treaties. This is a freedom of the Executive which, since it is constitutional, cannot be restricted by the law. Hence, if a legal text pursues this restrictive end it cannot be executed. That is what occurs with paragraph 3 of article 2 of law 8. The unconstitutionality of that paragraph follows from the study done up to now.

In what follows, the Court issues an opinion on the hierarchical order between international treaties or conventions and the national laws, and the supremacy of the former even with respect to the national laws that approve them.

International conventions are entered into to be complied with strictly and in good faith. It cannot be sustained that the Constitution, after requiring that they be obligatory, permits a subsequent act of the State to disavow them.

If international agreements have the force of law, which the State cannot disavow even by means of another law, it is evident that they have a greater value than that of the legislative act which approves them. Thus, the Constitution considers this in very exceptional cases (Art. 3, in fine, 76-18, 120-20, 210).

These and the previous passages of the decision by the Court are sufficiently explicit to require further comments on the content and scope of the special legislations examined in this subsection. Perhaps what would be most appropriate would be to cite this part of the "Clarification

of Vote" that was signed by four judges: "We the undersigned judges have approved and signed the foregoing decision since, with the other judges, we consider that this
involves a legal and current interpretation of the constitutional provisions on this matter, this being the first time
that the Court accepts, as it could only do, the existence
of a modern international law, the community law and its
supranational organs, with all of the consequences deriving
from this. " 91/

The transcription and analysis of the special legislation of Colombia and Venezuela should not be concluded
without raising the question of what position the Supreme
Court of Venezuela would adopt, in view of the fact that
the Venezuelan Constitution does not contain, in contrast
to the case of Colombia, a provision specifically authorizing the State to "bind itself so that supranational institutions can be created, on bases of equality and reciprocity,
which have the purpose of promoting or consolidating economic integration with other States." In other words, is
the new position of the Colombian Supreme Court conceiva-
ble, uniquely and exclusively, given the presence of this
constitutional provision? The answer to this question
would appear to be found in the conclusions reached by the
Round Table on "The Integration of Latin America and the
Constitutional Question", which was sponsored by the Instituto Interamericano de Estudios Jurídicos Internacionales
(Inter-American Institute of International Legal Studies),
which was held in 1967 under the auspices of the National

---

91. In the second of the decisions mentioned, the
Court reiterated its new position in regard to another
appeal petitioning the Court to declare the "inexecutability"
of Article 2, of Law 88 of 1961 which empowered the
Government to adopt all measures leading to the development of the Montevideo Treaty; subsequently, the Court
declared article 2 "executable". Cf. Foro Colombiano,
volume XII, Number 72 (June 1975), p. 538.

University of Colombia. Here are the pertinent passages
of the Conclusions: 92/

. . .

The study of the "question of constitutionality" led
to the conclusion that the contemporary spirit that
pervades our countries' constitutional and public
law in general is in no way contrary to that law, but
rather is naturally and historically compatible with
it, and is conducive to the accomplishment of the
common aim of Latin American integration. Consequently, although the constitutions do not always
contain provisions authorizing the competent organs
of the state to promote such integration and to bind
the state in community relationships for economic
and social purposes, the interpretation and application of the constitutions must support this desire.
Moreover, it is this line of thought and consequent
action that have made it possible to establish the
Central American Common Market and LAFTA.
The foregoing notwithstanding, the Round Table
recommends that it would be useful and advantageous
for states to incorporate additional provisions into
their constitutions to reflect present-day realities
of and future prospects for the achievement of the
Latin American community.

As a result of the preceding considerations the
Roundtable reached the following conclusions:

1. Those current provisions in Latin American
constitutions which govern the international activity
of the state are not incompatible, in principle, with
the granting to international organs of the competence to take erga omnes decisions in matters

---

92. Round Table on the Integration of Latin America
and the Question of Constitutionality, Universidad Nacional de Colombia, Bogotá, February 6-8, 1967. Report of
the General Secretariat of the Institute (Washington, 1967)
pp. 27-28.

relating to the contemplated Latin American economic and social community order under consideration.

2. The attribution of competences of this kind to such organizations under conditions of equality and reciprocity, far from impairing or affecting in any way the national sovereignty proclaimed by all Latin American constitutions, is in itself a typically sovereign act, inherent in the joint exercise of sovereignty by various states for the common welfare of their peoples.

3. Therefore, no constitutional incompatibility would exist, in principle, in the conclusion of a treaty constituting the proposed Latin American common market-- subject to the approval of the competent organs of the states as provided for in their respective constitutions--which would attribute to the organs of the said common market competence such as those referred to above.

Thus, notwithstanding the feeling that it was useful and beneficial to include specific provisions on the matter in the national Constitutions, the jurists and statesmen who participated in the Round Table of Bogota admitted the feasibility or constitutional compatibility of attributing competences to international organizations to make decisions erga omnes on matters relating to a Latin American community order, independently of the nature or character of those matters. The experience of the European Communities stands out in this regard. Upon the conclusion in 1951 of the treaty that established the first of these communities, the European Iron and Steel Community, only one of those States was authorized specifically by its Constitution to participate in "supranational" organizations, and with the conclusion in 1957 of the treaties that established the European Economic Community and EURATOM, only two other countries had introduced reforms to these in their Constitutions. Nevertheless, the entering into of these treaties per se and their subsequent execution did not present constitutional impediments that cannot be overcome. This fact clearly demonstrated, for the first time in the field of economic integration, that formal constitutional reform was not an unavoidable or irreplaceable condition for the State to be able to participate in organizations of that nature. 93/

c) Diverse effects of the national instruments through which reception is performed

The lack of adequate and uniform domestic provisions governing the reception of the subregional acts in the legal order of the member states just referred to explains to a large extent the marked diversity of the national instruments through which the reception process is performed. This diversity begins to become evident through the fact that the same subregional act is "received" in a different way in the member states. But this would not be of great importance if the differences resided only in the form of the instrument (law, decree law, decree, etc.), and provided that such form did not impinge on the nature or effects of the act of reception, which is the true and only basic question. What is, however, of importance, is that the differences referred to also reside in the latter, that is to say, in the character or effects of the national instrument. A few examples will suffice to demonstrate such differences. 94

First of all, there are few instruments that contain only provisions on the pure and simple application or implementation of the subregional act. Such is the case for

_____

93. See in this regard "The Integration of Latin America and the Question of Constitutionality", Memorandum prepared by the Department of Legal Affairs, General Secretariat of the OAS (1967), reproduced in the Report on the Round Table, p. 61.

94. The Board of the Agreement has published, in addition to the text of each instrument separately, a document mentioning in regard to each decision the national decrees that put into force the decisions adopted by the Commission, J/RI. AT/12/Rev. 3, April 29, 1974.

the Colombian decrees that establish the date starting from which "the rules contained in Decision 48 shall be applied ... ", the text of which will be reproduced in the decrees. 95/ In contrast with this type of reception, which implicitly admits the validity _erga omnes_ of the subregional act, most of the national instruments would appear to assume an "approbatory" nature, or at least this can be ascertained from the terms in which they are drafted. For example, the word "to approve" is even used in a number of those instruments. Thus, pursuant to Peruvian Decree Law No. 19534, "Let Decision 48 be approved... " 96/ mentioned earlier. Chilean Decree No. 1030 of May 25, 1971, also "approved" the Minimum Common External Tariff contained in the Annex of Decision 30 of the Commission. 97/

In other cases, the apparently "approbatory" nature or effect of the national instrument follows from other terms. For example, the Ecuadorian Decree referring to Decisions 57 and 57-a, concerning the Sectoral Industrial Development Program of the Metalworking Sector, uses the expression "Let it be declared in effect in the national territory starting with September 20, 1972... ", which is, as will be recalled, the same expression used in the Ecuadorian instrument relative to Decision 24. The

---

95. _Cf._ Decree No. 1899 of September 15, 1973, published in the _Diario Oficial_ on October 16, 1973 and in the doc. JUN/di 101, November 24, 1973. Having the same tenor is Decree No. 1910, of September 15, 1973, published in the _Diario Oficial_ on October 25, 1973, and in doc. JUN/di 102, November 1973, relative to Decision 56 (International Highway Transportation).

96. The Decree is dated September 19, 1972, published in _El Peruano_ of September 20, 1972 and in doc. JUN/di 50, September 28, 1972. The same term is used, among others, in Supreme Decree No. 0002-72-ONIT, of September 12, 1972, relative to Decision 38, published in _El Peruano_ of September 21, 1972 and in doc. JUN/di 48, September 28, 1972.

97. The decree was published in the _Diario Oficial_ of August 27, 1971 and in doc. JUN/di 26, June 5, 1972.

same instrument orders publication of the decision in the Official Gazette and commissions compliance thereof to the Ministers of Industry, Commerce and Integration and Finance. 98/ Lastly, without exhausting the examples being offered for the lack of uniformity in the national instruments, reference should be made to those that "decree" what is provided for in the decision of the Commission, which once again gives the impression that they substitute, de facto and de jure, the decision concerned. By way of example, reference should be made to the Colombian decree which stipulates the application of the NABANDINA (Brussels nomenclature adapted to the Andean Pact) in the Customs schedule, 99/ and the Ecuadorian Decree by means of which duties and restrictions are eliminated on products originating from Bolivia included in Annex I of Decision 29 of the Commission. 100/

In regard to the foregoing, one should take into account the observation made in the sense that the expression "put into force" does not mean that the national instrument using that term is "approbatory" in nature, to which end the Commission of the Cartagena Agreement is referred to on the occasion when "it felt appropriate that, pursuant to the legal procedures proper to each country, the decrees putting into force the common regime mentioned should be enacted". 101/ This observation cannot be objected to, similarly as the remark that appears in the Final Act of the Fourth Period of Extraordinary Sessions of the Commission, in particular insofar as it intends to deny the

---

98. Cf. Supreme Decree No. 365, of April 4, 1973, published in the Registro Oficial of April 13, 1973 and in doc. JUN/di 8, May 30, 1973.

99. Decree No. 1484 of July 28, 1973, published in doc. JUN/di 87, August 15, 1973.

100. Supreme Decree No. 143 of February 14, 1973, published in doc. JUN/di 62, March 13, 1973.

101. Cf. Caicedo Perdomo, loc. cit., in footnote 89, p. 89.

"approbatory" nature of an instrument (Colombian Decree No. 1129 of 1971), through which Decision 24 only was to be received in the domestic legal order. Since this involves subregional acts for the full validity or force of which the Agreement itself provides national measures that "put them into practice", what is of importance is to prevent the complementary national action from being perverted.

Now, when the question no longer involves this type of subregional acts, but those that have validity erga omnes then what other nature or effect, besides the "approbatory" one, can the expression "put into force" or some expressions analogous or similar to that have in the pertinent national instrument? In order for doubts not to arise vis-à-vis the instrument pertaining to the subregional acts that required complementary national action, it would be appropriate to use expressions that do not confuse or detract in some way from the nature of the instrument of reception. 102/

5.   Initiative by the Board to Surmount the Current
      Problems of the Reception

In the Report mentioned in subsection 1, b), on compliance with the Agreement and the decisions of the Commission, the Board raised the question in the following terms: 103/

... The reasons have already been mentioned at the beginning upon which the prestige of the Andean Group is based in the Subregion and abroad and the grave

---

102. By way of illustration, the following sentence should be cited from Colombian Decree No. 1900 of 1973, mentioned in footnote 44: "DECREES: Article 1, starting from the enactment of the present decree, there shall be applied the Common Regime... approved by the Commission of the Agreement...".
103. See doc. cited in footnote 13, p. 4.

consequences to the stability and seriousness of the process if credibility would begin to deteriorate by virtue of the fact that the decisions of the Commission "are obeyed but are not complied with". An example of a similar situation is the case of LAFTA, whose stagnation is not due to the lack of resolutions on various matters but the fact that those approved by the Conference have remained written in many cases and the contracting parties have begun to fall into what someone has called "legislative cynicism" which consists precisely in making it look like something is being accomplished without the desire to accomplish it.

The Board considers that it is its duty to raise this problem. Document J/SG/12 Rev. 1, updated to July 11th of this year, is attached as an annex to show the many cases in which one or more countries, and sometimes all, are in a situation of noncompliance in the form which is being analyzed. There are decisions that have been adopted quite a long time ago that have not been put into force in the territory of one or more countries and, as already stated, sometimes in none of the countries.

As stated by the Board in one of the ordinary sessions of the Commission of 1972, there is an urgent need to examine the causes of this noncompliance and to adopt measures to remedy it.

The concern shown by the Board in this document is very praiseworthy, since it is caused by the desire to safeguard the prestige of the Andean Group in the Subregion and abroad. In this way of thinking, the Board is fulfilling the responsibility assigned to it by the Cartagena Agreement to watch over the implementation of that Agreement and "the compliance with decisions of the Commission". But this is not the aspect of interest in the passages transcribed from the point of view of the nature and validity of the subregional acts. From that point of view what is of importance is to show how, particularly in the second of those passages, it would once again appear to be allowed, at least implicitly, that compliance with the decisions depends upon the fact that they have been "put into force" in the member states.

If the expressions used in the report from the Board are taken, so to speak, literally, it could be thought that the criterion was continuing to be reflected in that document which is still predominant among those persons who issued an opinion on the matter, as well as in the practice relative to the reception of the subregional acts that have been examined in the preceding section; that is to say, the criterion that those acts require a certain type of specific "transformation" or "incorporation", even though this complementary national action is not provided for in the Cartagena Agreement. It has already being seen, however, in other passages of the report itself, that the Board specifically distinguishes between the acts that require that complementary action and those that are self-executing. 104/ As previous initiative of the Board would precisely appear to obey to this other criterion, as well as the concern manifested in the paragraphs transcribed at the beginning of this section. That initiative was taken on the occasion of the proposal on the creation of the jurisdictional organ.

That initiative consists in proposing "provisions that, in view of the fact that they appear in an international treaty /which the Board has proposed for the creation of the jurisdictional organ/ permit completing the normative system of the Agreement, defining its legal structure, the form of incorporating the decisions of the Commission into the national legal orders and, finally, the obligations of the member states with regard to the rules making up the legal structure of the Cartagena Agreement". 105/ Those provisions are the ones appearing in Chapter I of the draft treaty and are reproduced ahead: 106/

---

104. See footnote 68.

105. Cf. Informe de la Junta sobre el Establecimiento de un Organo Jurisdiccional del Acuerdo de Cartagena, COM/X-E/di 5, December 12, 1972, p. 2.

106. Ibid., p. 29.

ON THE LEGAL STRUCTURE OF THE CARTAGENA AGREEMENT

Article 1. The legal structure of the Cartagena Agreement includes:

a) The Cartagena Agreement;
b) The present Treaty;
c) The Treaty of Montevideo, its Protocols and the Resolutions of the Conference of the Contracting Parties and of the Permanent Executive Committee, which will be applied whenever appropriate under terms established in Article 114 of the Cartagena Agreement;
d) The Decisions of the Commission;
e) The Resolutions of the Board; and
f) Other rules emanating from principal organs of the Agreement.

Article 2. The Decisions obligate the Member States from the date of their approval by the Commission.

Article 3. The Decisions shall be directly applicable in the territory of the Member States starting from the date indicated in their text or else eight days after their publication in the Official Gazette of the Agreement.

Whenever so provided for in their text they shall require a rule of municipal law for their application in the territory of each Member State.

Article 4. The Member States are bound to adopt such measures as are necessary to assure compliance with the rules making up the legal structure of the Cartagena Agreement.

They furthermore commit themselves not to adopt or use any measure that is contrary to those rules or that impedes their application in some way.

The preceding provisions are inspired in the result of the lengthy and very interesting discussion on the topic that took place during the deliberations of the Meeting of Experts convened by the Board for purposes of the projected creation of a jurisdictional organ and in which the very well-founded concern was continuously expressed of assuring the validity as well as the efficacy of the subregional acts in the territory of the member states. 107/

Notwithstanding the foregoing, the provisions in themselves are susceptible to some observations. Thus, the provision contained in Article 1, in systematically listing the instruments and rules establishing the legal structure of the Cartagena Agreement, which is the equivalent to saying the sources of the Andean subregional law, omits the instruments and the rules that the member states adopt to facilitate or to make viable the application of the law emanating from the Agreement or from any other international treaties or conventions entered into by those countries and from the acts of the competent subregional organs. At least in a broad sense, the law or legal structure of an integration process includes, besides the type of instruments and rules that are listed in Article 1, the other category which has just been referred to. 108/ This concept of the law of integration is particularly relevant when what is being sought is to define the legal framework within the competences granted to a jurisdictional organ are to be exercised. In the present case, in Article 24 of the draft treaty proposed by the Board, competence is granted to the subregional tribunal whose exercise may

---

107. Unfortunately, the typed minutes of the deliberations of the Meeting of Experts have not been published; thus the author takes this opportunity to express his gratitude for the access he was given to those minutes in the Permanent Secretariat of the Cartagena Agreement.

108. On this item, see the opinion of the Court of Justice of the European Community in Instituto Interamericano de Estudios Jurídicos Internacionales, Derecho de la Integración Latinoamericana (Buenos Aires, 1968), p. 923.

very well have an effect on the mentioned national instruments and rules of the member states. 109/

Articles 2 and 3 which have been transcribed undoubtedly bring the Cartagena Agreement closer to the system of the Treaty of Rome and consequently would considerably improve the present situation, in the sense that the date from which the decisions will become mandatory and the date when they would be directly applicable in the territory of the member states would be specified

---

109.   Article 24 provides the following:

It is up to the Tribunal to interpret, through the Courts, requiring judicial decision before the final judgements, the norms making up the legal structure of the Agreement, for the purpose of assuring their efficacy and their uniform application in the territory of the Member States.

The national courts having cognizance of a suit on the application of some rule of the legal structure of the Agreement and whose decisions can be appealed in municipal law can request the opinion of the Tribunal of the Agreement on the interpretation and scope of the provisions issued by the principal organs of the Cartagena Agreement.

When the decisions of the court that is trying the case cannot be appealed in municipal law it will be bound to request the opinion of the Tribunal of the Agreement.

After the opinion of the Tribunal has been issued, the interpretation it contains will have to be applied by the court trying the case.

by Treaty. 110/ From a practical standpoint, it would also contribute to overcome the gaps shown by the domestic law of those states on this matter if the Commission would require them to adopt rules for the application of certain decisions in their territories. Concerning the provision contained in Article 4, even though it involves a tacit clause of any international treaty or convention in which obligations to act or to refrain from acting are set forth, it is undeniable that the rendering of such mandatory obligations is facilitated with the presence of an explicit clause of that nature.

In examining further the initiative of the Board it can be noted that the essence of the provisions proposed is implicit in the Cartagena Agreement, as indicated in

---

110. On this matter, in the opinion of the Board "it is essential to fill in the gaps of the Cartagena Agreement as refers to the incorporation of the decisions of the Commission into the national legal orders, by means of specific provisions adopted in a legal instrument of sufficient validity, so that the practice of the Member States can be made uniform in this regard and so that the discrepancies existing at this time which could lead to the dispersion of the legal order derived from the subregional integration process can be removed". Further on it completes this opinion by expressing that "it is necessary to the success of the integration process to incorporate the principle of direct application of the rules derived from the Cartagena Agreement into the national legal order". See doc. cited in footnote 105, pp. 16 and 17. In contrast to the concern of the Meeting of Experts, which is justifiably shared by the Board, it has been sustained that the Cartagena Agreement did not provide in its text "with extreme realism, a mechanism of immediate and direct application of the decisions of the Commission." Cf. O. Padrón Amaré, Interés Nacional y Control de las Decisiones en un Proceso de Integración (con especial referencia al Grupo Andino), doc. INTAL, Reunión 25/dt. 1, 4-9-75, p. 4.

subsection 1, b) of this chapter. What these provisions do is to assign expressly, as occurs in the system of the European Communities, the validity or automatic binding nature of the decisions of the Commission and their direct applicability, that is, their "immediacy". 111/ Hence, without in any way pretending to underestimate the practical importance and usefulness attributed to those provisions in the foregoing paragraph, it is appropriate to insist once again on the need for the pertinent national authorities, when appropriate naturally, to recognize that the acts of the subregional organs are valid by the mere fact of their approval, that the source of their validity resides in the fact of having been approved by organs which have been given the power to do so, and that the national action or measures needed for their execution constitute a merely mechanical element of the process of creation and application of the Andean legal order as a whole. We have already seen the definite inclination on the part of the member states towards specific reception, in the sense of goving the instruments through which the subregional acts are incorporated into the domestic law of these countries an "approbatory" nature, at least apparently. This inclination perhaps does not result as much from the lack of provisions of the type proposed by the Board as from an attitude vis-à-vis an integrationist phenomenon of a genuinely "community" type, which does not easily fit in with deep-rooted legal traditions which have not yet been completely overcome in the Subregion.

6.   Hierarchy of the Andean Legal Order

In the process of reception of the rules stemming from the subregional acts, just as in the case of the rules of the Cartagena Agreement itself, a conflict may arise

---

111. On this concept see Constantinesco, L. , "La Supranacionalidad de las Comunidades Europeas", Anuario Uruguayo de Derecho Internacional, Vol. IV, 1965-66, p. 65.

between one of those rules and a rule of the domestic law of the member states, since the two are of different content and incompatible. Despite the differences of opinions still subsisting in the field of international law on how to resolve this type of conflict, it is evident that the legal order of an economic integration process, especially in the case of a system of a "community law" type, would lack validity, not to mention efficacy, if such conflicts were to be resolved pursuant to the criterion of the supremacy of municipal law. This criterion, which has even been rejected repeatedly by The Hague International Court of Justice in relations of international law, is even more unsustainable in relations of community law. 112/

The last opinion is the one that ended up prevailing in the situation that arose in regard to Chilean Decree Law Number 600 which created the Estatuto de la Inversión Extranjera (Foreign Investment Code) published in the Diario Oficial of July 13, 1974. 113/ The statement of facts that follows clearly explains this observation.

The question on the compatibility of Decree Law No. 500 and the Common Regime for treatment of foreign capital, etc. (Decision 24) was formally raised in the framework of the Commission of the Cartagena Agreement in the course of its fifteenth regular session held from September 10 to 14 and September 19 to 20, 1974. The Board had submitted for consideration by the Commission an elaborate report on item 1 of the agenda, "Application of Decision 24 in the Member States". 114/ On this first occasion, the representatives of the Governments of

---

112. On this vast topic, particularly as concerns the European Community law, see Instituto Interamericano, op. cit. in footnote 108, pp. 193-290 and 937-957.

113. The complete text of the Decree Law also appears in doc. JUN/di 127 Rev. 1, July 22, 1974.

114. Cf. Informe de la Junta sobre las Disposiciones Legales de los Países Miembros en Relación con la Decisión 24 doc. COM/XV/di 1, September 8, 1974.

Bolivia, Colombia, Ecuador, Peru and Venezuela drew up
a declaration which indicated, among other things, "That
absolute respect of its community legal order is essential
to the nature and purposes of the Cartagena Agreement",
and that the Chilean Decree Law "is incompatible with the
Common Regime..." In relation to this declaration, the
Representative of Chile declared, among other things,
that his country "had been subjected to a condemnatory
declaration without foundation which put into doubt its
traditional policy with regard to international commitments",
and that "this contrasts with the fact that no mention is
made in this declaration on how other countries regulate
or apply Decision 24 in a manner inconsistent with the
stipulations of this Decision and that the Chilean delegation
would like to attribute to differences in interpretation". 115/

In the regular session just referred to the Commission resolved to hold a special meeting, at the request of
the Board, after it had carried out the investigations in
relation to the problems deriving from Item 1 of the
Agenda. 116/ On this second occasion the Commission
unanimously approved the following Declaration: 117/

> A. The Commission, in becoming aware of the
> measures adopted and to be adopted by the Govern-
> ment of Chile referred to in the Report of the Co-
> ordinator of the Board and the Statement of the re-
> presentative of that country, recognizes that Decree
> Law 746 issued by the Government of Chile on No-
> vember 6, 1974 reveals that Decision 24 is in full
> effect in that country and is part of the Chilean legal
> system. The Commission is pleased with this. 118/

---

115. Cf. Final Act, pp. 4 and 6, respectively.
116. Ibid., p. 6.
117. Cf. Decimosexto Período de Sesiones Ordinarias, Acta Final (November 12 to 14, 1974), p. 3.
118. In the new Decree Law No. 746 mentioned in
this passage of the declaration there is "a specific mention
that recognizes that Decision 24 constitutes an instrument
that is part of the Chilean legal order in the field of foreign
investments". Cf. ibid., Annex III, p. 3.

B. The Commission also understands that Decision 24, owing to its nature of international commitment, has greater force in all of the member states than domestic provisions on foreign investments and on trademarks, patents, licenses and royalties and consequently prevails over them.

The foregoing Declaration, as well as the passages cited from the first one, clearly indicate the position that has been adopted by both the Commission as such and, in the first declaration, the five member states individually, on the hierarchy of the Andean legal order. In this way of thinking, perhaps the only thing that should be stressed is the affirmation "That absolute respect of its community legal order is essential to the nature and purposes of the Cartagena Agreement", which is a postulate or principle upon which the position adopted by the Subregion appears to be based. 119/

---

119. Regarding the topic "Application of Decision 24 in the member states," the following information should be offered. In the Ninth Regular Session (July 10 to 14 and August 17 to 20 of 1972), the Commission analyzed the situation of the "force and application" of Decision 24 in the member states, and decided to request the Board to convene a meeting of experts for the purpose of considering certain points. Cf. Final Act, p. 6. In November 1972 a group of government experts was convened, but the information was inadequate, as shown in the report that the Board provided to the Commission in its Tenth Regular Session (doc. COM/X/dt. 4). After several postponements, the second meeting of the group of experts took place from July 22 to 24 of 1974. Greater progress could also not be obtained in that meeting, since in those days Chilean Decree Law No. 600 had been promulgated. Cf. Report from the Board cited in footnote 114, p. 1-2. In its Sixteenth Regular Session (Nov. 12-14, 1974) the Commission decided to entrust the Board with completing the analysis of the application of Decision 24 in the member states and requested from it: (i) a proposal for common regulation of Decision 24 on those matters that are the competence of the Commission, and (ii) a proposal aimed at achieving

The supremacy of the Andean legal order was also recognized by the Supreme Court of Justice of Colombia in one of the decisions mentioned in Subsection 4, b) of this chapter. Here are the two passages in which the Court specifically refers to the question. 120/

> International conventions are entered into to be complied with strictly and in good faith. It cannot be sustained that the Constitution, after making them mandatory, permits a subsequent act of State to disavow them.

> If international agreements have the force of law which the state cannot disavow, even by means of another law, it is evident that they prevail over the legislative act approving them. This is how the

---

119 (Cont.) the harmonious application of that decision on those topics that could cause problems of interpretation. Cf. Final Act, pp. 3-4. In compliance with the notice to attend the meeting issued by the Commission in its Eighteenth Regular Session, the First Meeting of the Consultative Committee of the Cartagena Agreement was held (November 12 to 14, 1975), to analyze Working Paper CC. De. 24/I/1, Bases para un Reglamento de la Decisión 24, prepared by the Board. The Committee limited itself to reviewing this document and entrusting the Board to prepare a more complete report in the near future. Cf. Final Act, pp. 1-2. In summary, all of these initiatives and efforts appear to be directed towards overcoming, by means of a "subregional" regulation of the Common Regime (Decision 24), the national legislative diversity that can be noted from the reading of the report from the Board cited in footnote 114. On this matter, see also Comparative Study of the Latin American Legislation on the Regulation and Control of Private Foreign Investment, doc. OEA/Ser. G, CP/INF. 680/75 rev. 1.

120. Cf. loc. cit. in footnote 90, p. 251.

Constitution considers it in very exceptional cases
(Article 3, in fine, 76-18, 120-20, 210).

It is true that the Court, in the passages transcribed,
refers only to the hierarchical relations between the Cartagena Agreement and the national laws, that is to say,
between the conventional Andean legal order and the domestic legislation. No reference is made in them, evidently, to the hierarchical relations between the legal order
emanating from the subregional acts and domestic legislation. But the decisions, as a whole, do contemplate
those relations. Furthermore, it suffices to read the
passages transcribed in subsection 4 b) to note that the
new position or doctrine of the Colombian Supreme Court
rests, precisely, in the supranational competences attributed to the subregional organs. If this were not so,
how would it have been possible to declare the unconstitutionality of the provisions of Law 8 that subordinated
the validity of certain subregional acts to the national
Legislative Branch?

RECAPITULATION

The intention to conclude this study with a recapitulation was merely to point out the most outstanding features and characteristics of the Andean legal order. Consequently, this is not an effort to fill the many gaps which the reader has surely found in the preceding chapters, but an attempt to present these salient features and characteristics in a summary and systematic form.

Concerning the Cartagena Agreement itself, a detailed summary of its sui generis characteristics was made in the last section of Chapter II, so that reference to the highlights will suffice. To begin, it is appropriate to repeat that these characteristics are due, for the most part, to the very close linkage and relationship of the Agreement to the Montevideo Treaty, and in general to the legal and institutional framework of LAFTA. Among the expressions of this linkage and relationship are the stipulation that the Agreement, as well as the amendments and rules for adherence to it, should be compatible with the Treaty; the transitory nature of the Agreement, i.e., the subjection of its validity to the condition that the commitments acquired within the general framework of the Treaty do not exceed those established in that Treaty; the normative interdependence of the two instruments, in the sense that in regard to certain matters the Agreement adheres to the provisions of the Treaty on the subject, to the point where one might think that upon expiration of the Treaty the subregional Agreement would also expire automatically; the subordination--from a hierarchical point of view and in regard to certain matters--of certain provisions of the Agreement, besides the general principle stated in Article 114, which explicitly states its provisions shall not affect the rights and obligations resulting from the Montevideo Treaty and the Resolutions of LAFTA.

Despite this linkage and relationship to the legal order of LAFTA, the Cartagena Agreement, on the one hand, contains substantive commitments much greater in scope than those stipulated in the Montevideo Treaty and, on the other hand, subjects the countries of the Subregion to an institutional framework considerably more dynamic than that of the Association. The former constitutes the very purpose of subregional agreements as they were conceived in the Bogotá Declaration and, above all, in the Declaration of Presidents of the Americas. The latter is consistent with the traité cadre character of the Andean Pact. By the same reasoning, it can be inferred that the Pact establishes competences ratione materiae and confers attributes or powers on the subregional organs capable of generating the new rights and obligations of member states which are necessary for the full achievement of the objectives of the Pact. This institutional framework, moreover, is essentially "communitarian," considering the operation of the two principal subregional organs--the Commission and the Board--and their relationship, which represent, respectively, the national interest and the subregional interest.

Concerning the competencies of the subregional organs, a general observation was made in Chapter IV on the system of the Cartagena Agreement of attributing competencies is worth repeating here. In contrast to other systems, such as those of the European Communities and LAFTA, which are distinguished by a true distribution or division of competencies and powers between the organs of integration and the member states, in the system of the Agreement this situation does not obtain, at least in regard to competencies ratione materiae. In effect, the so-called "material" competencies, with a few exceptions, are reserved to the subregional organs. This is precisely one of the most outstanding characteristics of the system of the Agreement, which reveals the amazingly vast sphere of action which has been entrusted to these organs, as well as the preponderant role which they play in the subregional integration process.

As for the rest, the competencies may be grouped into two broad categories, the normative and the executive. The former, on their part, generally conform to specific mandates which include the period within which they must be executed, although practice has repeatedly shown that, in principle, this type of competence does not run out or expire upon execution of the mandate. The presence of "implicit" competences or powers should also be referred to. Seemingly evident in some provisions of the Agreement and much more clearly evident in the practice of the subregional organs, they lend greater dynamism to the authority of said organs.

Perhaps the most interesting features and characteristics of the Andean legal order are those revealed by a study of the nature and validity of subregional acts, in particular the decisions of the Commission and the resolutions of the Board. Considered in light of the letter and, if you will, the spirit of the Cartagena Agreement and other pertinent instruments, the norms deriving from these acts must be observed by and/or in the member states. As was indicated at the time these acts were first examined in Chapter V, in reality we are dealing with a corollary of the principle pacta sunt servanda, in the sense that since the norms of the basic instrument are legally binding, and above all since it has this traité-cadre character, the norms generated by the exercise of competences attributed by that instrument to subregional organs are equally obligatory.

In this connection, the conditions stipulated for this purpose in the Agreement itself must be borne in mind, and they make it necessary to distinguish between two broad categories of acts: on the one hand, those which involve, besides the competence and the specific action of the subregional organ or organs, a complementary act on the part of the member states, on which the full validity and operation of the act depends, and on the other hand, those for which the Agreement does not require, at least explicitly, additional action on the part of member states besides the competence and specific action of those countries. In contrast to the first group, it is reasonable to presume in regard to the second that it deals with acts which, ab initio, are fully valid for and/or in the member states, i. e., acts which have validity or effect erga omnes.

When this topic is examined in light of the acceptance of subregional acts into the domestic law of the member states, unfortunately a certain lack of uniformity is observed, which is due in part to the absence of provisions in the Agreement which explicitly permit, as does the Treaty of Rome which established the European Economic Community, the direct applicability of those acts which fall into the second of the categories described above, and, to a greater extent, to the fact that deeply-rooted Latin American legal traditions and procedures remain an obstacle to the dynamic aspects of the law of integration. On this subject it is gratifying to recognize that in the long run the first experiments in this acceptance--with the Common Regime (Decision 24) and with the Agreement itself--have been highly successful, inasmuch as today, because of the new (1975) decisions of the Supreme Court of Justice of Colombia, all doubts about the supranationality of subregional competences and the consequent validity erga omnes of acts not specifically requiring a complementary national act have been completely clarified, for the moment at least in that country.

Elaborating on the topic, the Board of the Agreement took a fortunate initiative in incorporating into the proposed treaty for the creation of the jurisdictional organ or subregional tribunal provisions which affirm that the decisions of the Commission are binding on the member states from the date on which it approves them, and that they will be directly applicable in those countries. Although, in a strictly legal sense, the automatic validity and obligatory nature of subregional acts pertaining to the second of the abovementioned categories, as well as their direct applicability, are implicit in the context of the Andean Pact, the practical importance and utility of being able to count on this type of provision is undeniable. In any case, and above all while the initiative of the Board does not become reality, it would be well to insist again on the need for the pertinent national authorities to recognize, when the occasion arises, that the acts of subregional organs are valid by the mere fact of their approval, that the source of their validity lies in their having been approved by organs which have been granted competence to do so, and that the internal acts or measures required for their execution are merely a mechanical element in the process of creating and applying the Andean legal order as a whole.

This recapitulation should not be ended without a reference to the present standing which has already been recognized of Andean law in relation to the domestic law of the member states. In this respect, it is sufficient to remember the way in which the situation arising from Chilean Decree-law 600, which created the Statute of Foreign Investment, was surmounted. On that occasion five of the six members of the Commission declared jointly "That absolute respect for its communitarian legal order is essential to the nature and goals of the Cartagena Agreement", and that the Decree in question "is incompatible with the Common Regime..." Later the Commission itself, this time unanimously, declared "that Decision 24, because of its nature as an international commitment, has in all member states a higher status than domestic provisions on foreign investment..." It is evident that these are unequivocal pronouncements from an authoritative source favoring the supremacy of law derived from the acts of subregional organs over national law different and incompatible with it.

In conclusion, it need only be observed that the Andean institutional framework, the competences of the subregional organs and the validity of their acts, as well as the hierarchical relationship of the Andeal legal order toward the domestic law of the member states, permit one to consider the subregional legal order as new and genuine community law. Thus it is conceived in the organic instrument, the Cartagena Agreement, and thus it is also essentially being applied in practice.

APPENDICES

AGREEMENT ON SUBREGIONAL INTEGRATION
"CARTAGENA AGREEMENT"*

(Signed at Bogotá, Colombia, May 26, 1969)

THE GOVERNMENTS OF Bolivia, Colombia, Chile, Ecuador and Peru,

MOTIVATED by the Declaration of Bogotá and the Declaration of the Presidents of the Americas; and

BASED on the Montevideo Treaty, and on Resolutions 202 and 203 (CN-II/VI-E) of the Council of Foreign Ministers of the Latin American Free Trade Association (LAFTA),

HAVE DECIDED, through their duly accredited plenipotentiaries, to conclude the following

AGREEMENT ON SUBREGIONAL INTEGRATION

CHAPTER I

Objectives and Mechanisms

Article 1. The present Agreement has as its goals: to promote a balanced and harmonious development of the Member States, to accelerate this development through economic integration, to expedite their participation in the integration processes as stipulated in the Montevideo Treaty, and to create a climate favorable to the conversion of LAFTA into a common market, all of these designed to secure the progressive improvement of the living standards of the peoples of the Subregion.

Article 2. A balanced and harmonious development must be conducive to an equitable distribution of the benefits

---

* English version from International Legal Materials, Vol. III, No. 5, September 1969.

resulting from integration of the Member States by effecting a reduction of the existing discriminations that aggravate them. The achievements of the process should be periodically assessed, taking into account, among other factors, its effect on the expansion of global exports of each State, the conduct of its trade balance with respect to the Subregion, the development of its gross territorial product, the generation of new employment, and its capital formation.

Article 3. To achieve the goals set by the present Agreement, the enumerated operations and measures shall be employed, inter alia:

a) Coordination of economic and social policies, and unification of domestic law in pertinent fields;

b) Joint programming, intensified subregional industrialization processes, and execution of Sectorial Programs of Industrial Development;

c) Greater acceleration in the trade liberalization program than that adopted generally within the LAFTA framework;

d) A common external tariff, attained by progressive stages through a minimum common external tariff;

e) Programs directed toward stimulation of development in the agricultural and livestock sector;

f) Channelling of resources from inside and outside the Subregion to provide investment financing necessary to the Integration Process;

g) Physical integration; and

h) Preferential treatment to be accorded to Bolivia and Ecuador.

Article 4. For the better achievement of the present Agreement, the Member States shall undertake the necessary efforts to seek adequate solutions for the problems arising from the land encirclement of Bolivia.

CHAPTER II

Organs of the Agreement

Article 5. The principal organs of the Agreement are the Commission and the Board (Junta). The auxiliary organs shall be the Committees as defined under Section "C" of this Chapter.

Section A - The Commission

Article 6. The Commission is the supreme organ of the Agreement, constituted by one plenipotentiary representative from each of the Member State Governments. Each Government shall accredit one principal and one alternate representative.

The Commission shall express its will in the form of "Decisions."

Article 7. The following are attributes of the Commission:

a) To formulate the general policies of the Agreement and to adopt any measures necessary to achieve its objectives;

b) To approve the rules indispensable for coordination of development plans, and harmonization of the economic policies of the Member States;

c) To appoint and remove Board members;

d) To issue instructions to the Board;

e) To delegate its powers to the Board, when deemed desirable;

f) To approve, veto or amend proposals of the Board;

g) To supervise the coordinated compliance with obligations assumed under this Agreement and under the Montevideo Treaty;

h) To approve the annual budget of the Board and to fix the contributions of each Member State;

i) To enact its own internal rules of procedure, and those to govern the Committees; and to approve the Board's rules and any amendments thereto;

j) To propose to the Member States any reform to the present Agreement; and

k) To hear and deal with any other business of common interest.

In compliance with its functions, the Commission, in furthering the goals of the Agreement, shall give special consideration to the situation of Bolivia and Ecuador and the preferential treatment to be accorded to them.

Article 8. The Commission shall encourage concerted action by the Subregional nations relative to problems arising from international trade which affects any one of them; and it shall participate in international meetings and organizations of economic character.

Article 9. The Commission shall have a President, with a one-year term of office. This shall be a rotative office, to be exercised in turn by each of the Representatives in the alphabetical order of their States.

The first President shall be selected by lot.

Article 10. The Commission shall meet in regular session three times a year, and in special session whenever convened by its President, upon request of any Member State, or of the Board.

Its meetings shall be held at Board headquarters, but may also take place elsewhere. The Commission sessions must have a quorum of at least two-thirds of the Members.

Attendance at Commission meetings shall be compulsory, and non-attendance shall be taken to signify abstention.

Article 11.   The Commission's Decisions must be adopted by affirmative vote cast by two-thirds of the Member States.   Exceptions to this general rule are as follows:

a)   Matters covered in Annex I of the present Agreement, in which Commission Decisions must be adopted by a two-thirds affirmative vote, with no negative vote.

The Commission may incorporate new matters in said Annex by an affirmative vote of two-thirds of the Member States.

b)   Cases enumerated in Annex II, where the Board proposals must be approved by an affirmative vote cast by at least two-thirds of the Member States, with no negative vote.   The proposals receiving an affirmative vote of two-thirds of the Member States, but which are subject of a negative vote, must be returned to the Board for consideration of the reasons originating the said negative vote. Within a period of not less than two nor more than six months, the Board may renew its proposal for Commission consideration with the amendments deemed desirable and in such event, the amended proposal shall be considered as approved if it receives an affirmative vote of two-thirds of the Member States, and no negative vote; or if a negative vote is cast by the same State voting previously against it, it shall not be counted;

c)   Matters related to the special treatment to be accorded to Bolivia and Ecuador, listed in Annex III. In these cases, the Commission Decisions shall be adopted by an affirmative vote of two-thirds, provided one of these is cast either by Bolivia or Ecuador; and

d)   Appointment of Board members, to be approved by unanimous vote.

Article 12.   The Commission must consider Board proposals in all cases, and its Decisions issuing thereon shall conform to the rules established in Article 11.

Section B - The Board

Article 13. * The Board is the technical organ of this Agreement, consisting of three members, and it may act only in the concerted interest of the Subregion as a unit.

The members shall have three-year terms, and are eligible for reelection. In cases of vacancy, the Commission shall immediately proceed to designate a replacement, who shall also have a three-year term.

Article 14. Board members may be nationals of any Latin American state, they shall be answerable to the Commission for their actions; shall act in the common interest; shall refrain from any activity incompatible with the nature of their duties; may not exercise any other professional office , whether remunerative or not, for the duration of their terms; and shall not seek or receive instructions from any Government or from any national or international entity.

Article 15. The Board shall have the following functions:

a) To supervise the implementation of the present Agreement and of the Commission Decisions;

b) To comply with Commission assignments;

c) To prepare proposals for the Commission, conducive to expediting or accelerating compliance with the Agreement, in order to achieve its goals within the shortest possible time;

d) To undertake studies and submit recommendations necessary for applying preferential treatment to Bolivia and Ecuador, and generally any matter concerning participation in the Agreement by these two countries;

e) To participate in the Commission meetings, unless the latter deems it advisable to hold closed session

Notwithstanding, the Board shall have the right to participate in any discussion of its own proposals made to the Commission, and particularly those under Sections c) and d);

f) To assess annually the accomplishments of the implementation of this Agreement, and the progress in the achievement of its goals, giving special attention to compliance with the principle of equitable distribution of integration benefits; and to propose to the Commission any corrective measures of positive character that may be pertinent;

g) To undertake the technical studies entrusted to it by the Commission, and any other deemed desirable;

h) To perform the duties assigned to it by the Commission;

i) To perform the functions of Permanent Secretariat of the Agreement, and to maintain direct contacts with Governments of Member States through the organs designated by each for this purpose;

j) To draft its internal rules and submit same to the Commission for approval or modifications;

k) To submit the draft of annual budget estimates to the Commission;

l) To prepare its annual work schedule, giving priority to tasks entrusted to it by the Commission;

m) To present an annual report of its operations to the Commission;

n) To propose to the Commission an organic structure for its technical divisions and any reorganizations it may deem desirable;

o) To hire and dismiss technical and administrative staff;

p) To entrust the performance of specific tasks to experts in certain fields;

q) To call for periodic meetings of national entities charged with the formulation or execution of economic policy and, particularly, those in charge of planning; and

r) To exercise any other powers expressly conferred on it by the clauses of this Agreement.

Article 16. In the contracting of technical and administrative staff, who may be of any nationality, the Board shall consider solely the qualification, competency and reputation of the candidates, and shall, insofar as not incompatible with the above criteria, fill the positions to effect as broad a geographical subregional distribution as possible.

Article 17. The Board shall always act with the unanimous expression of all members, but it may present for consideration of the Commission any alternative proposals, also unanimously approved.

Article 18. The Board shall function as a permanent organ, and its headquarters shall be designated by the Governments of the Member States at any time they deem appropriate following the date of signature of the present Agreement.

Section C - The Committees

Article 19. The Advisory Committee is the organ through which the Member States shall maintain close ties with the Board. This Committee shall be composed of representatives from all Member States, who may be accompanied by advisers in attendance at meetings.

Article 20. The Advisory Committee shall meet at the Board Headquarters whenever convened by the Board or by the President of the Commission, at the request of any Member State.

Article 21. The Advisory Committee shall have the following duties:

a) To advise the Board and to collaborate in the performance of its work whenever so requested; and

b) To analyze the Board's proposals upon request, prior to their submission for consideration by the Commission.

The opinions of the Committee members shall be incorporated in the form of reports for transmission to the Commission and the Board for their consideration.

Article 22. There shall be an Economic-Social Advisory Committee composed of representatives of the sectors of management and labor in the Member States. The Commission, within the first year that the Agreement is in force, shall determine the composition, the procedure for filling the posts, and the functions of this Committee.

Section D - Settlement of Disputes

Article 23. The Commission shall be empowered to execute any procedures of negotiations, good offices, mediation and conciliation that may be necessary in cases of disputes arising from the interpretation or implementation of the present Agreement, or of the Commission Decisions.

If settlement is not obtained, the Member States shall observe the procedure established in the "Protocol for the Settlement of Disputes," signed in Asunción on 2 September 1967 by the Foreign Ministers of the Contracting Parties of the Montevideo Treaty.

For the purposes contemplated in Section 3 of Article 16 in said Protocol, the Member States declare that all members covered under the present Agreement and the Commission Decisions shall be included thereunder.

For purposes of Article 36 of said Protocol, the Member States pledge themselves to seek its ratification as soon as possible.

Section E - Coordination with the Andean Development Corporation

Article 24. In addition to the functions enumerated in
Articles 7 and 15, it shall be incumbent upon the Commission and the Board to maintain close contact with the Directors and the Executive President of the Andean Development
Corporation, to the end that adequate coordination with their
activities may result and thus facilitate the successful
achievement of the goals of the present Agreement.

CHAPTER III

Coordination of Economic Policy
and Development Planning

Article 25. The Member States shall adopt a strategy
for Subregional development based on the following fundamental goals:

a)   Acceleration of the economic development of the
     Member States on an equitable basis;

b)   Increased generation of employment opportunities;

c)   Improvement in the position of Member States and
     of the Subregion as a unit in matters of foreign
     trade and balance of payments;

d)   Overcoming of infrastructure problems which are
     presently hindering economic development;

e)   Reduction in the existing discrimination of develop
     ment levels among the Member States; and

f)   Achieving a maximum utilization of scientific and
     technological progress, and activation of research
     in these fields.

Article 26. The Member States shall initiate immediately a coordinated procedure in their development planning

in specific sectors, and harmonization of their economic and social policies, directed toward future adoption of a concerted planning system for the integrated development of the area.

These processes shall be employed simultaneously and in coordination with the formation of a subregional market, utilizing the following machinery, inter alia:

a) A system of industrial programming;

b) A special system for the agricultural-livestock sector;

c) Plans for physical and social infrastructure;

d) Coordination of exchange, monetary, financial and fiscal policies, whether use of Subregional capital is to be made within or outside of the area;

e) A common trade policy with respect to third countries; and

f) Harmonization of planning methods and techniques.

Article 27. Prior to 31 December 1970, the Commission, at the proposal of the Board, shall approve and present for consideration of the Member States, a common system for treatment of foreign capital and, likewise, systems for trademarks, patents, licenses and royalties, inter alia.

The Member States pledge themselves to adopt the measures necessary to implement such systems within the six months following approval by the Commission.

Article 28. Prior to 31 December 1971, the Commission, at the proposal of the Board, shall approve and recommend to the Member States a uniform system to govern multinational enterprises.

Within the same period of time, the Commission, at the proposal of the Board, shall issue directives to serve as a guide for the unification of legislation on industrial incentives in the Member States.

249

The States shall pledge themselves to adopt all measures necessary to implement this unification within the six months following Commission approval.

Article 29. The Commission, at the proposal of the Board, and at the latest by 31 December 1970, shall establish the permanent procedures and machinery necessary to achieve the coordination and unification defined in Article 26.

Article 30. The Commission, at the proposal of the Board, shall adopt a program of common instrumentation and machinery to govern foreign trade in the Member States, to be put into effect by the latter prior to 31 December 1972. An exception to the preceeding shall be the Common External Customs Tariff which shall be governed by the provision of Chapter VI.

Article 31. In their national development plans and in the formulation of their economic policy, the Member States shall incorporate those measures required to insure compliance with the preceding articles.

CHAPTER IV

Industrial Programming

Article 32. The Member States pledge themselves to undertake a process of industrial development of the Sub-region through joint programming to achieve the following goals, among others:

a) Greater expansion, specialization and diversification of industrial production;

b) Maximum utilization of available resources of the area;

c) Stimulation of greater productivity and more efficient utilization of production factors;

d) Utilization of large industry; and

e) Equitable distribution of benefits.

Article 33. For the above enumerated goals, the Commission, at the proposal of the Board, shall approve Sectorial Programs of Industrial Development, to be jointly implemented by the Member States.

Article 34. The Sectorial Programs of Industrial Development must include stipulations on the following aspects:

a) Identification of products to be subjected to the Program;

b) Joint programming of new investment on a subregional scale, and of measures to insure their financing;

c) Location of industries in the Subregional countries;

d) Unification of policies on aspects directly influencing the Program;

e) Programs for Exemptions which shall provide a different pace, by country and by product and, which in any case, shall permit free access to the subregional;

f) A common External Customs Tariff; and

g) The periods of time during which the rights and duties related to the Program must be continued in the case of denunciation of the Agreement.

Article 35. The Board shall propose to the Commission, in each case, those implementary measures indispensable to secure compliance with the respective Program and, particularly, those necessary to insure the installation of plants that may be assigned pursuant to the provisions of Section (c) of the preceding Article, and the effective utilization of the subregional market by said installations.

Article 36. With regard to existing industries of the Subregion whose production has not been incorporated in a

Sectorial Program of Industrial Development, the Commission, at the proposal of the Board, shall introduce program based on the criteria set forth in Article 32, tending to rationalize the production of merchandise in those cases in which, in its discretion, it is possible and desirable to do so pursuant to the aims of this Agreement.

The Board shall present at least annually to the Commission proposals for the Programs referred to in this Article.

Article 37. For the purposes of the preceding article, the Board shall take into account the following factors, among others:

a) Installation capacities of existing industries;

b) Financial and technical assistance needs for the installation, expansion, modernization or preservation of industrial plants;

c) Manpower capacity requirements;

d) Possibilities of agreement as to horizontal combination in specialization among companies within the same industry;

e) Perspectives for establishment of joint systems of trade, research, technology, and other forms of cooperation among similar enterprises.

The Member Countries shall hold systematic consultations within the framework of the Commission, with Board participation, on investment programs for the industries referred to above in this Article.

Article 38. The Commission, at the proposal of the Board, may recommend the creation of multinational enterprises for installation, expansion or complementarity of specific industries. Such enterprises must, among other goals, endeavor to achieve a more efficient utilization of investment opportunities offered by an expanded market and an improved organization and exploitation of the productive

resources of the Subregion, as well as a strengthening of
its negotiating capacity to secure collaboration from foreign
capital and the transmission of technological advice.

Article 39.   When the Board deems it desirable, but
in any event in its annual assessment of accomplishments,
it shall propose to the Commission those measures it considers indispensable to insure equitable participation by the
Member States in common Sectorial Programs of Industrial
Development, in the implementation of same, and in their
promotion of the goals.

Article 40.   The Commission is empowered to coordinate its work adequately with that of the Andean Development Corporation and to negotiate the collaboration of any
other national and international institutions whose technical
and financial contributions may be deemed desirable for the
following purposes:

a)   To expedite the coordination of policies and joint
investment programming;

b)   To channel an increasing volume of financial resources to overcome problems which may arise in
the Member States during the integration process;

c)   To promote the financing of specific projects that
are adopted in compliance with the Sectorial Program of Industrial Development; and

d)   To expand, modernize or convert existing industrial enterprises which are affected by the reciprocal exemptions.

CHAPTER V

Liberalization Program

Article 41.   The Liberalization Program has as its
goal the elimination of charges and restraints of all kinds
encumbering the importation of goods originating in the territory of the Member States.

Article 42.   The term "charges" shall be understood
to include customs duties and any other charges of equivalent effect, whether fiscal, monetary or exchange, that are
imposed on imports. Not included in this concept are those
fees and similar charges with respect to the estimated cost
of services rendered.

The term "restraints of all kinds" shall be understood
to signify any measure of administrative, fiscal or exchange
character, imposed by unilateral decision of a Member
State, which impedes or hinders importation. This concept
shall not include those situations covered by Article 53 of
the Montevideo Treaty.

Article 43.   For purposes of the preceding Articles
the Board may, at its own initiative or upon request of a
party, determine in the necessary instances whether a measure that is unilaterally imposed by a Member State constitutes a "charge" or a "restraint."

Article 44.   The provisions of Article 21 of the Montevideo Treaty shall be applicable in cases involving matters
of tax, assessment or other internal liens.

Article 45.   The Liberalization Program shall be automatic and irrevocable, and shall include all products, in
order to attain total liberalization not later than 31 December 1980. The various aspects of this Program shall be
applied:

a)   To goods which are subject to Sectorial Programs
of Industrial Development;

b)   To goods included, or to be included, in the Common Schedule defined in Article 4 of the Montevideo
Treaty;

c)   To commodities not being produced in any country
of the Subregion, which are included on the corresponding schedule; and

d)   To goods not comprised in any of the above sections.

254

Article 46. Restraints of all kinds shall be eliminated not later than 31 December 1970.

Exceptions to the above rule shall be made for restraints applied to goods reserved to the Sectorial Programs of Industrial Development, which restraints shall be eliminated whenever liberalization is effected pursuant to the respective program, or to the provisions of Article 53.

Bolivia and Ecuador shall eliminate restraints of all kinds at the time that they initiate compliance with the Liberalization Program for each product, pursuant to the rules established in Article 100, but they may substitute charges not to exceed the lowest level fixed by Section a) of Article 52, in which case application shall affect both the imports proceeding from the Subregion as well as those from outside the area.

Article 47. Within the term stipulated in the preceding article the Commission, at the proposal of the Board, shall prescribe what products are to be reserved for the Sectorial Programs of Industrial Development.

Prior to 31 December 1973 the Commission, at the proposal of the Board, shall approve the Sectorial Programs of Industrial Development with respect to those products which have been reserved pursuant to the preceding paragraph.

If at the expiration of said term the Board finds it possible to propose Programs with respect to products which have been reserved but not yet incorporated in Programs already adopted, the said period of time shall be understood to be extended to 31 December 1975.

Article 48. The Commission, at the proposal of the Board, shall at any time adopt new Sectorial Programs of Industrial Development and prescribe the pertinent measures, bearing in mind the experience gained from application of the provisions of Chapter IV, and considering the importance of industrial programming as the fundamental machinery of this Agreement.

Article 49. Goods that are included in the first stage of the Common Schedule described in Article 4 of the Montevideo Treaty shall be totally liberated from all charges and restraints within one hundred and eighty (180) days following the date that this Agreement becomes effective.

Prior to 31 December 1971 the Commission, at the proposal of the Board, shall establish the Liberalization Program to be applicable to goods included in the remaining stages of the Common Schedule.

Article 50. Prior to 31 December 1970 the Commission, at the proposal of the Board, shall prepare a schedule of goods not being produced within any of the Subregional countries, nor reserved for any Sectorial Program of Industrial Development, and shall select those to be reserved for production in Bolivia or Ecuador, establishing with respect to the latter the conditions and terms of such reservation.

The charges on the goods included on such a schedule shall be totally eliminated by 28 February 1971. The liberalization of goods reserved for production in Bolivia or Ecuador shall be for the exclusive benefit of these countries.

Notwithstanding the preceding, and within the terms stipulated in the first paragraph of the present Article, the Board may propose to the Commission that it assign some of the products on the prepared Schedule to benefit Colombia Chile and Peru. The beneficiary country of such assignment shall disencumber the respective products in the manner established by Article 52.

Upon expiration of four years from the date on which such assignment was made, should the Board prove that the beneficiary country has not yet initiated the corresponding production, or that the project is not in process of execution, the effects shall cease as of this time and the beneficiary shall proceed immediately to disencumber the respective product.

Article 51. At any time subsequent to the expiration of the indicated term in the second paragraph of the preceding Article the Commission, at the proposal of the Board, may incorporate new products on the Schedule described in the first paragraph of the preceding Article. Charges on said products shall be eliminated sixty days from the date of approval for their inclusion on said schedule.

When the Board deems it technically and economically feasible, it shall propose to the Commission that reservation of some of the new commodities be made for production in Bolivia and Ecuador, and with respect to these, that the corresponding terms and conditions for such reservation be established.

Article 52. Goods not included under Articles 47, 49 and 50 shall be liberated from charges in the following manner:

a) The point of departure shall be calculated on the minimum charge on each product listed on the national customs tariffs of Colombia, Chile and Peru, or in their respective National Schedules in effect on the date of signature of the present Agreement. Said point of departure may not exceed the ad valorem percentage of the CIF value of the merchandise;

b) On 31 December 1970, all charges in excess of the level stipulated in the preceding section shall be reduced to said level; and

c) The remaining charges shall be gradually eliminated through annual reductions of ten percent each until total liberalization is achieved by 31 December 1980.

Article 53. Products which had been selected for Sectorial Programs of Industrial Development, but were not included therein within the stipulated time periods of Article 47, shall comply with the Liberalization Program in the following manner:

a) Goods not being produced in any of the Subregional countries shall be exempt from charges on 31 December 1973, or 31 December 1975, as the case

257

may be. Without prejudice to the above the Commission at the proposal of the Board may select some of these commodities to be produced in Bolivi and Ecuador, and establish the conditions and terms of the reservation; and

b) For goods covered under the system of Article 52, which should commence elimination of charges on 31 December 1973, the percentage of reduction shall be adjusted to cover any time that may be lacking to complete the term stipulated in Article 45; those which must initiate the elimination on 31 December 1975 shall accomplish this through five annual reductions of five, ten, fifteen, thirty and forty percent, respectively.

In any of these cases, the Member States may agree on a selective elimination of products, provided is a more accelerated rate.

If the Board should exclude some commodities from the above reservation prior to 31 December 1975, the Liberalization Program shall be adjusted at this time to that which would correspond to them pursuant to the measures of Sections a) and b) of the present Article.

Article 54. The Member States shall abstain from altering any levels of charges and from introducing any new restraints of any kind on importation of goods originating in the Subregion, should this signify a less favorable situation than the one in existence at the time of the effective date of this Agreement.

Exceptions from this rule shall be made as to any alter ations in their tariffs introduced by Bolivia and Ecuador to justify their instruments of commercial policy, in order to insure the initiation or expansion of certain production activities within their territories. These exceptions must be certified by the Board and authorized by the Commission.

Similarly, exception from this rule may be made for an alteration in charges resulting from the substitution of charges for other restraints, referred to in Article 46.

Article 55.   Up to 31 December 1970, each Member State may present to the Board a Schedule of goods presently being produced in the Subregion as exceptions to the Liberalization Program, and the procedures for establishing an External Tariff.   These Exception Schedules may not include products listed in the Common Schedule; those schedules of Colombia and Chile may not list products which are already included among the more than two hundred and fifty items on NABALALC /LAFTA's Tariff Nomenclature/; that of Peru may not exceed four hundred and fifty items. If any State has not delivered its list of exceptions to the Board by the expiration of the term, it shall be understood to have renounced the rights conceded by this Article.

The Commission, at the proposal of the Board, may modify the number of Items referred to in the preceding paragraph up to November 30, 1970.

The products included on the Schedules of Exceptions shall be totally liberated of charges and other restraints, and protected by the Common External Tariff by 31 December 1985 at the latest.

Without prejudice to the above, Peru must reduce the number of Items on its Schedule of Exceptions to three hundred and fifty by 31 December 1974, and to two hundred and fifty by 31 December 1979. The products eliminated by Peru from its Schedule of Exceptions pursuant to this article shall enter the Liberalization Program and be adopted on the External Tariff at the levels corresponding to them as of the aforementioned dates.

In any case, the Board may authorize the maintenance of some exceptions beyond the stipulated sixteen year term in well-justified cases, fixing the duration of the extension and the conditions for future disencumbrance. This extension may not exceed four years and the number of exceptions may not exceed twenty items.

Article 56.   The incorporation of a product on the Schedule of Exceptions of a Member State shall prevent it from enjoying the advantages granted to said product by this Agreement.

259

A Member State may withdraw products from its Schedule of Exceptions at any time. In this event, it shall immediately adjust these to the Liberalization Program and the External Tariff in force for such products, under the corresponding terms and levels, and shall simultaneously commence to enjoy the respective advantages.

In duly qualified cases, the Board may authorize a Member State to incorporate on its Schedule of Exceptions those products which, although having been reserved for Sectorial Programs of Industrial Development, had not been so programmed.

Such incorporation may in no case signify an increase in the number of Items corresponding to the State.

Article 57. The Board should contemplate the feasibility of incorporating in the Sectorial Programs of Industrial Development those products included by Member States on their Schedules of Exceptions.

Similarly, in the programs adopted pursuant to Articles 36 and 37, concerning existing industries, priority should be given to those whose products are on the Exception Schedules, in order to enable them to confront Subregional competition within the briefest possible time.

For the purposes contemplated in the preceding paragraphs, interested countries shall communicate to the Board their intention to participate, and shall withdraw the product from their Exception Schedule pursuant to measures established in the respective program.

Within the second half of 1974, the Member States may effect negotiations for the purpose of finding formulas permitting them to obtain a gradual withdrawal of products from their Exception Schedules within the term expiring on 31 December 1985.

Article 58. The inclusion of products on Exception Schedules shall not affect the exportation of products originating in Bolivia or Ecuador which have been, during the preceding three years, the object of substantial trade between the respective country and Bolivia or Ecuador, or which may show certain signs to become significant trade within the immediate future.

The same shall apply in the future to those products originating in Bolivia or Ecuador, which are incorporated on the Schedule of Exceptions of any Member State, and concerning which there appears to be a definite and immediate expectancy of exportation from Bolivia or Ecuador to the country which had made them an exception from the reciprocal liberalization program.

The Board shall determine when substantial trade has existed, or whether there is a definite expectancy that it will exist.

Article 59. The Member States, as a unit, shall endeavor to conclude Complementarity Agreements with the other Contracting Parties of LAFTA in suitable production sectors, in conformity with the provisions of the Montevideo Treaty, and the respective Resolutions.

Article 60. The commitments adopted under the Montevideo Treaty in compliance with the LAFTA Liberalization Program shall prevail over the provisions of the present chapter to the extent that the former may be more advanced than the latter.

CHAPTER VI

Common External Tariff

Article 61. The Member States shall pledge themselves to make the Common External Tariff fully operative by 31 December 1980 at the latest.

Article 62. Prior to 31 December 1973 the Board shall prepare a Draft Common External Tariff, to be submitted for consideration of the Commission for approval within the following two years.

On 31 December 1976, the Member States shall commence a process directed toward adoption of a Common External Tariff by reconciling the charges levied by their domestic tariffs on imports from outside the Subregion, to be effected on an annual, automatic and parallel basis, and in a manner to make it fully operative by 31 December 1980.

Article 63. Prior to 31 December 1970, the Commission, at the proposal of the Board, shall approve a Minimum Common External Tariff, whose basic aims shall be:

a) To establish adequate protection for subregional production;

b) To create progressively a subregional preference margin;

c) To expedite the adoption of a Common External Tariff; and

d) To stimulate effective exploitation of subregional production.

Article 64. On 31 December 1971, the Member States shall initiate a reconciliation of the charges levied on imports from outside the Subregion with those established in the Minimum Common External Tariff, in those cases where the former are lower than the latter, and this procedure shall be effected by an annual horizontal and automatic progression, enabling it to become fully operative by 31 December 1975.

Article 65. Notwithstanding the provisions of Articles 62 and 64, the following rules shall be applicable;

a) The rules on the Common External Tariff established by Sectorial Programs of Industrial Development, shall govern with respect to those products subjected to the Programs; and

b) At any time that a product becomes liberated from charges and other restraints, in compliance with the Liberalization Program, it shall fully and simultaneously become subject to the charges established in the Minimum Common External Tariff, or in the Common External Tariff, as the case may be.

In the case of commodities not produced within the Subregion, each country may defer the application of common charges until such time as the Board can verify the fact that production has commenced within the Subregion. At any rate, if the Board, in its discretion, finds that the new production is insufficient to satisfy the normal supply demands of the Subregion, it shall propose to the Commission those measures necessary to balance the need for protection of the subregional product with the need to insure a normal supply.

Article 66. The Commission, at the proposal of the Board, may modify the levels of common tariffs in the measure and at the times considered desirable for the following reasons:

a) To satisfy the needs of the Subregion;

b) To consider the special status of Bolivia and Ecuador; and

c) To adjust these levels to those fixed in LAFTA's Common External Tariff.

Article 67. The Board may propose to the Commission any measures it deems indispensable to achieve normal conditions for subregional supply.

In order to cover temporary deficiencies in supply which may affect it, any Member State may raise this question with the Board, which shall verify the situation within a term compatible with the urgency of the matter. Once the Board has verified that the problem does exist and so informs the affected country, the latter may adopt such measures as a provisional reduction or a suspension of charges of the External Tariff, within the limits indispensable to correct its problematic situation.

Article 68. The Member States pledge themselves not to alter unilaterally any charges established during the various stages of the External Tariff. Likewise, they promise to enter into necessary consultations with the Commission before concluding agreements of a tariff nature with countries outside the Subregion.

The Member States shall harmonize the agreements under this chapter with their commitments under the Montevideo Treaty.

CHAPTER VII

Measures on Agriculture and Livestock

Article 69. With the aim of achieving the adoption of a common policy and the formulation of a plan covering the agro-livestock sector, the Member States shall coordinate their national policies and their plans for agro-livestock development, taking into consideration the following objectives, inter alia:

a) Raising the standard of living for the rural population;

b) Increased production and productivity;

c) Specialization, as a means for the better utilization of production factors;

d) Subregional substitution of imports, and diversification and increase in exports; and

e) Eventual and adequate supplying of subregional markets.

Article 70. In order to achieve the objectives enumerated in the preceding article, the Commission shall, at the proposal of the Board, take the following periodic measures, inter alia:

a) Joint programs by product or group of products, conducive to development of agriculture and stock raising;

b) Concerted trade systems and conclusion of agreements by the respective State organs on the supply of agro-livestock products;

c) Encouragement of agreements between the national organizations linked to planning and execution of the agro-livestock policies;

d) Proposals for export promotion;

e) Joint programs for applied research, and for technical and financial assistance to the agro-livestock sector; and

f) Common measures and programs on vegetable and animal health.

Article 71. The Commission and the Board shall negotiate all measures necessary to accelerate the agro-livestock development in Bolivia and Ecuador, and their participation in an expanded market.

Article 72. Trade in agro-livestock products, based on the Liberalization Program of this Agreement, even after expiration of the periods stipulated in Article 2 of the Montevideo Treaty, shall be fully subject to its Article 28, to the Resolutions which complement same, and to any future measures that may be adopted to amend or substitute these.

·Article 73. Any State imposing the measures described in the preceding article, must send notice to the Board immediately, together with a report as to motivation for their application.

Any Member State that considers itself injured by virtue of these measures may appeal to the Board.

The Board shall analyze the case and propose to the Commission what measures of a positive nature would be appropriate, in view of the objectives stipulated in Article 69.

The Commission shall render a decision on the applied restrictions and on the measures proposed by the Board.

Article 74. Prior to 31 December 1970, the Commission, at the proposal of the Board, shall prepare the list of agro-livestock products for purpose of the application of Articles 72 and 73. Said list may be amended by the Commission, at the proposal of the Board.

CHAPTER VIII

Competitive Commercial Practices

Article 75. Prior to 31 December 1971, the Commission, at the proposal of the Board, shall adopt the rules indispensable to forestall or to remedy any practices which might constitute unfair competition within the Subregion, such as "dumping," undue price manipulation, maneuvers intended to impede the normal supply of raw materials, and others of similar effect. In these matters, the Commission shall take under consideration those problems that might arise from the application of charges and other restraints on exports.

The Board is entrusted with surveillance over the application of said rules in any particular cases of complaint, for which purpose it must bear in mind the need to coordinate these measures with the provisions of Resolution 65 (II) of the Conference of Contracting Parties of LAFTA and those which complement or amend them.

Article 76. Until such time as the Commission may adopt the rules mentioned in the preceding article, the affected State may appeal to the Board to apply provisions of Resolution 65(II).

Article 77. The Member States may not adopt corrective measures unless authorized in advance by the Board. The Commission shall issue procedural rules for the application of the rules of the present Chapter.

CHAPTER IX

Saving Clauses

Article 78. If a Member State finds itself in one of the situations covered in Chapter VI of the Montevideo Treaty, caused by factors alien to the Liberalization Program of this Agreement, it may invoke the safeguards consonant with the provisions of the said chapters and of the pertinent Resolutions.

Article 79. If, as a result of the impostion of the Liberalization Program of this Agreement, serious disadvantages are caused or threaten the economy of a Member State, or a significant sector of its economic activity, said State may, with advance authorization of the Board, apply corrective measures of emergency nature and in a non-discriminatory manner. When necessary, the Board should propose to the Commission measures of collective coordination directed to overcoming the prejudices which have been caused.

Article 80. If monetary devaluation effected by one Member State should alter the normal competitive conditions, another State which considers itself prejudiced may bring the case to the Board, which shall render a brief and summary opinion. If the disadvantage is verified by the Board, the injured State may adopt corrective measures of provisional nature for the duration of the prejudicial situation, as limited by the Board recommendations. In any case, said measures may not signify a reduction in the customary import levels existing prior to the devaluation.

Without prejudice to the application of the said provisional measures, any Member State may request the Commission to render a final decision in the matter.

The Member State which has ordered the devaluation may request the Board at any time to review the situation in order to attenuate or suppress the above-mentioned corrective measures. The decision of the Board may be overruled by the Commission.

Article 81. No saving clauses of any kind may be invoked with respect to importation of products originating in the Subregion, which are incorporated in Sectorial Programs of Industrial Development.

Neither shall Articles 79 and 80 be applicable to the importation of products originating in the other member countries of LAFTA, when incorporated in the Liberalization Program of the Treaty of Montevideo.

CHAPTER X

Origin

Article 82. The Commission, at the proposal of the Board, shall adopt any special measures necessary to classify the origin of merchandise. Said measures should be incorporated in a dynamic instrument for subregional development and be adequate to achieve the objectives of this Agreement.

Article 83. The Board shall be empowered to fix the specific requirements of origin for products so requiring it. When necessary to fix specific requirements in a Sectorial Program of Industrial Development, the Board should establish these simultaneously with the approval of the corresponding program itself.

Within the year following the fixing of specific requirements, the Member States may request a review by the Board, which shall give its summary opinion.

Upon request of a Member State, the Commission should examine these requirements and render a final decision, within a term of more than six (6) and less than twelve (12) months, as computed from the date of the establishment of these by the Board.

The Board may at any time upon its own initiative or at the request of a party amend any requirements established pursuant to this article, in order to adapt them to the economic and technological progress of the Subregion.

Article 84. Upon adopting and establishing the special norms or the specific requirements of origin, as the case may be, the Commission and the Board shall avoid the creation of any obstacles to enjoyment by Bolivia and Ecuador of the advantages deriving from application of the Agreement.

Article 85. The Board shall implement compliance measures for the norms and requirements of origin within the subregional trade. Likewise, it shall propose any measures considered necessary to settle conflicts of origin which might hinder the achievement of the goals of this Agreement.

CHAPTER XI

Physical Integration

Article 86. The Member States shall undertake concerted action to solve infrastructural problems that affect unfavorably the process of economic integration of the Subregion. Such action may be exercised principally in the fields of energy, transportation and communications and shall particularly include measures necessary to expedite border trade among the Member States.

Towards this end, the Member States shall endeavor to establish entities or enterprises of multinational character, where feasible and desirable, to expedite the execution and administration of said projects.

Article 87. Prior to December 31, 1972, the Board shall draft initial programs in the fields mentioned in the preceding article, and present these for the consideration of the Commission. Such programs shall include, as far as possible:

a) Identification of specific projects to be incorporated in national development plans and an order or priority in which they should be implemented;

b) Urgent measures to finance the necessary pre-investment studies;

c) Technical and financial assistance needs to insure the execution of the projects; and

d) Methods for instituting joint action before international credit institutions and particularly, the Andean Development Corporation, to insure the provision of financing not available within the Subregion.

The undertaking of these initial programs shall mark the commencement of a continuing process, directed toward the expansion and modernization of the physical infrastructure of the Subregion.

Article 88.   The programs enumerated in the preceding article, as well as the Sectorial Programs of Industrial Development, must include measures of collective coöperation, enabling satisfaction of the infrastructure requirements indispensable for their execution in an adequate manner, and must give special consideration to the status of Ecuador and the territorial characteristics and landlocked position of Bolivia.

CHAPTER XII

Financial Matters

Article 89.   The Member States shall coordinate their national policies in matters of finance and payments in the measure necessary to expedite achievement of the goals of this Agreement.

To such end, the Board shall present to the Commission proposals on the following matters, inter alia:

a) Channelling of subregional funds of public and private savings for financing of investments aimed at development of industry, agriculture and the infrastructure, within the context of an expanded market;

b) Financing of trade among the Member States and with those outside the Subregion;

c) Measures to expedite the Subregional circulation of capital and especially funds for the development of industry, services and trade, within the context of an expanded market;

d) Strengthening of the multilateral clearing system of reciprocal balances in effect among the Central Banks of LAFTA, to fulfill subregional trade needs, and the eventual creation of a Subregional Compensation Payments Fund and a system of reciprocal credits;

e) Measures to solve conflicts that may arise from double taxation; and

f) Creation of a common reserve fund.

Article 90. If, as a consequence of compliance with the Liberalization Program of the Agreement, a Member State should encounter difficulties with respect to its fiscal income, the Board may propose to the Commission, at the request of the affected State, measures to remedy these disadvantages. In its proposals, the Board shall consider the degree of economic development of the Member State.

CHAPTER XIII

Special Regime for Bolivia and Ecuador

Article 91. In the progressive elimination of the differences presently existing in the development of the Subregion, Bolivia and Ecuador shall enjoy special treatment to permit them to achieve a more accelerated rate of economic development, through effective and immediate

271

participation in the advantages of area industrialization and liberalization of trade.

To achieve this aim, the organs of the Agreement shall propose and adopt the necessary measures, in conformity with its rules.

Section A - Harmonization of Economic Policies and Coordination of Development Planning

Article 92.   In the harmonization of economic and social policies, and in coordination of planning, as covered under Chapter III, adequate preferential and incentive treatment should be accorded to Bolivia and Ecuador to compensate their structural deficiencies and insure for their benefit the mobilization and assignment of the resources indispensable in the implementation of the goals contemplated by this Agreement.

Section B - Industrial Policy

Article 93.   Industrial policy of the Subregion shall grant special consideration to the status of Bolivia and Ecuador in the way of priority assignments in production benefits and the consequent placement of enterprises in their territories, particularly through participation in the Sectorial Programs of Industrial Development.

Article 94.   The Sectorial Programs of Industrial Development shall offer exclusive advantages and effective preferential treatment in favor of Bolivia and Ecuador, so as to expedite the effective utilization of the subregional market.

Article 95.   The Board, upon requesting the Commission to act on the complementary measures contemplated in Article 35, should envision exclusive advantages and preferential treatment to favor Bolivia and Ecuador, in those cases deemed necessary.

Section C - Commercial Policy

Article 96. To permit immediate participation by
Bolivia and Ecuador in the benefits of an expanded market,
the Member States shall concede, in an irrevocable and
nonextendible form, the elimination of charges and barriers
on all types of imported products originating within those
jurisdictions, under terms of the following Articles 97 and
98.

Article 97. As indicated in the preceding article,
products originating in Bolivia and Ecuador shall be governed by the following criteria:

a) By 31 December 1973, at the latest, those products
described under Section d) of Article 45 shall be
granted free and definite access to the Subregional
market. To this end, the charges shall be automatically eliminated in three annual and successive reductions of forty, thirty and thiry percent, respectively, the first reduction to be instituted on 31
December 1971, using as a point of departure those
levels defined in Section a) of Article 52;

b) The Commission, at the proposal of the Board and
prior to 31 December 1970, shall approve schedules
of goods to be liberated for the benefit of Bolivia
and Ecuador on 1 January 1971;

c) Charges on the products referred to in Article 53
shall be totally eliminated to the benefit of Bolivia
and Ecuador on 1 January 1974, or 1 January 1976,
depending upon whether or not these were subject
to extension under terms of Article 47;

d) Prior to 31 March 1971, the Commission, at the
proposal of the Board, shall fix preferential margins favoring a number of items of production of
special interest to Bolivia and Ecuador, and shall
fix the periods of time during which said margins,
effective on 1 April 1971, shall be maintained at
that level.

The schedule referred to in this section shall incorporate those products covered by Section d) of Article 45; and

e) The same procedure indicated in Section c) shall be applied to the schedule of goods selected from among those which had been reserved to Sectorial Programs of Industrial Development, but not incorporated therein within the time limits set by Article 47.

Article 98. The non-extendible concessions to Bolivia and Ecuador, granted by Member States in the liberalization of products on the Common Schedule, shall govern exclusively to their benefit. This exclusiveness shall be limited to the State which is granting the concession.

Article 99. The corrective measures referred to in Articles 72 and 79 shall extend to all imports proceeding from Bolivia and Ecuador only in duly justified cases and following Board verification of the fact that serious and substantial disadvantages would result from said importation. The Board shall follow the procedures of the said Article 70, and of Article 4 of LAFTA Resolution 173 (CM-I/III-E) for these operations.

Article 100. Bolivia and Ecuador shall comply with the Liberalization Program in the following form:

a) Liberation of products incorporated in Sectorial Programs of Industrial Development in the manner established for each;

b) Liberation of products which, although reserved to said programs, were not in fact included therein in the manner or within time limits set by the Commission, at the proposal of the Board. The Commission and the Board, upon making such decision, shall weigh basically those benefits to be derived from the programming and the placement of industry referred to in Article 93;

c) The period set by the Commission may not exceed by more than five (5) years, that stipulated in Article 52, Section c);

d) Products incorporated or to be incorporated in the Common Schedule shall be liberated in the manner and time limits provided in the Montevideo Treaty and in the pertinent Conference Resolutions;

e) Commodities not as yet being produced within the Subregion, and not forming part of the reserve set aside for their benefit under Article 50, shall be liberated within sixty days after such reserve has received Commission approval.

Nevertheless, exceptions may be made from this treatment with respect for those goods which the Board, upon its own initiative or as petitioned by Bolivia or Ecuador, may qualify for this purpose as being luxuries or non-essential.

These commodities shall be governed by procedures established in Section f) of the present Article, for their subsequent liberalization; and

f) The commodities not included in the preceding sections shall be eliminated from the national tariffs through annual and successive reductions of ten (10) percent each, the first to be made on 31 December 1976. Nevertheless, Bolivia and Ecuador may initiate the liberalization of these products during the course of the first six (6) years that this Agreement is in force.

Article 101. The Board shall periodically evaluate the results achieved by Bolivia and Ecuador in their interchange with the other Member States, and the extent to which they may be effectively benefitting from the expanded market. Based on such evaluations, the Commission may revise the periods of time stipulated in Sections c) and f) of the preceding article.

Article 102.   The Bolivian schedule of exceptions may include commodities comprised in no more than three hundred fifty (350) Items and in fifty (50) subclasses of NABALAL /the LAFTA Brussels Tariff Nomenclature/. The Ecuadorean list may not include more than six hundred (600) Items. This number may be modified by the Commission under the same terms of the second paragraph of Article 55.

Total elimination of charges and other barriers on commodities included by Bolivia and Ecuador on their schedules of exceptions shall be completed by 31 December 1990, at the latest. This term may be extended by the Board in duly qualified instances.

Otherwise, the provisions of Articles 55, 56 and 57 shall apply in all aspects to the Bolivian and Ecuadorean schedules of exceptions.

The rule incorporated in the first paragraph of Article 54 shall not be applicable to goods that Bolivia and Ecuador have included on their schedules of exceptions.

Article 103.   In preparing the programs referred to in Articles 36 and 37, the Commission and the Board shall give special and priority attention to those industries in Bolivia and Ecuador whose products have been listed by them as exceptions to the Liberalization Program, in order to enable these industries to become eligible at the earliest possible opportunity for participation in the Subregional market.

Section D - The Common External Tariff

Article 104. On 31 December 1976, Bolivia and Ecuador shall initiate the process directed toward adoption of the Common External Tariff through annual, automatic and lineal reductions, and they must complete liberalization by 31 December 1985.

Bolivia and Ecuador shall be compelled to adopt the Minimum Common External Tariff only in application to commodities not being produced within the Subregion, defined in Article 50. With respect to such products, minimum charges shall be adopted through a lineal and automatic process to be completed within three years computed from the date on which the production of these goods has been initiated within the Subregion.

Without prejudice to the provisions of the first paragraph of this Article, the Commission, at the proposal of the Board, may determine when Bolivia and Ecuador shall adopt minimum tariff levels relative to products of interest to the other Member States, provided that the application of such levels does not constitute a disadvantage to Bolivia or Ecuador.

The Commission, at the proposal of the Board, may also render decisions as to adoption of minimum tariff levels by Bolivia and Ecuador with respect to commodities, the importation of which from outside the Subregion may cause substantial prejudice to them.

Article 105. As authorized by the Commission, at the proposal of the Board, Bolivia and Ecuador may establish some exceptions to the application of the progressive reconciliation of their National Tariffs with the Common External Tariff, which will permit them to enforce their present industrial incentive legislation, principally as it relates to importation of capital goods, semi-manufactured products and raw materials necessary for their development.

Such exceptions shall not be applicable to any case after 31 December 1985.

Section E - Financial Cooperation and Technical Assistance

Article 106. The Member States pledge themselves to take joint action in confronting the Andean Development Corporation and other national or international Subregional organizations for the purpose of obtaining technical assistance and financing for high priority installation in Bolivia and Ecuador of industrial enterprises and complexes.

The assignment of funds for such projects shall be based on the fundamental goals of reducing present differences in the development levels among the States, and accentuating beneficial efforts on behalf of Bolivia and Ecuador.

Moreover, the Member States, with respect to the Andean Development Corporation, shall join efforts to secure the distribution of regular and special resources in

such manner as to enable Bolivia and Ecuador to receive
substantially greater shares than those which might have
resulted were the distribution of such resources to be proportionate to their capital contributions to the Corporation.

Section F - General Provisions

Article 107. In its periodic evaluations and annual reports, the Board shall give special and individual consideration to the status of Bolivia and Ecuador within the Subregional Integration processes, and propose to the Commission any measures deemed adequate to improve their development potentials substantially and to activate their participation progressively within the area industrialization.

Article 108. Wherever no provision is made in this
Agreement as to special treatment for Bolivia and Ecuador,
the principles and provisions of the Montevideo Treaty, as
well as the LAFTA Resolutions favoring the Relatively Less
Economically Developed Countries, shall be considered as
incorporated therein.

CHAPTER XIV

Adherence, Effective Date and Denunciation

Article 109. The present Agreement may not be signed
with reservations, and shall remain open to adherence by
the other Contracting Parties of the Montevideo Treaty.
Those Relatively Less Economically Advanced Countries
which adhere hereto shall have the right to treatment similar to that accorded in Chapter XIII to Bolivia and Ecuador.

The conditions for adherence shall be defined by the
Commission, bearing in mind that acceptance of new members must be adjusted to the goals of the Agreement.

Article 110. The present Agreement shall be submitted for consideration by the Permanent Executive Committee of LAFTA, and once the Committee has declared it compatible with the principles and objectives of the Montevideo
Treaty and of Resolution 203 (CM-II/VI-E), each Member

State shall approve it in conformity with its respective legislative procedures and forward the corresponding ratification instrument to the Executive Secretariat of LAFTA.

The Agreement shall become effective upon communication of approval by three States to the Executive Secretariat of LAFTA.

The effective date for the remaining States shall be that on which their respective instruments of approval of the Agreement are communicated, pursuant to the procedure stipulated in the first paragraph of this Article.

The present Agreement shall remain effective as long as the goals achieved within the general framwork of the Montevideo Treaty do not surpass those established herein.

Article 111. Any Member State desiring to withdraw from this Agreement shall communicate with the Commission. As of that date, the rights and obligations deriving from its status as a Member shall cease, with the exception of those benefits received and granted pursuant to the Subregional Liberalization Program, which shall remain in force for five years following the date of withdrawal.

The period of time indicated in the preceding paragraph may be reduced in duly justified cases, by decision of the Commission and at the request of the interested Member State.

The provisions of Section g) of Article 34 shall be applicable with respect to the Sectorial Programs of Industrial Development.

CHAPTER XV

Final Provisions

Article 112. The Commission, at the proposal of the Board, and based on the latter's reports and periodic evaluations, shall prepare by 31 December 1980 at the latest, the necessary machinery to insure the achievement of the goals, once the process of reciprocal liberalization has been concluded and the Common External Tariff adopted. This machinery should contemplate the special treatment to be accorded to Bolivia and Ecuador, as long as the present differences subsist in their rate of development.

Article 113. The advantages pledged under this Agreement shall not be extended to non-member Countries, nor create for them any obligations based thereon.

Article 114. The clauses of this Agreement shall not affect the rights and obligations derived from the Montevideo Treaty and the LAFTA Resolution which shall be applied in supplementary manner.

Transitional Provision: Exceptions from the provisions of Article 54 shall be based on changes in levels caused by the conversion made by Ecuador in its National Customs Tariff, as a consequence of its adoption of the Brussels Tariff Nomenclature.

APPENDIX I

1. Delegate to the Board whatever duties are considered appropriate.

2. Approve the modifications to the present Agreement.

3. Amend the proposals of the Board.

4. Approve the norms necessary to make possible the coordination of development plans and the harmonization of economic policies of the member states.

5. Approve the harmonization program for instruments regulating the foreign trade of the member states.

6. Approve the physical integration programs.

7. Accelerate the Liberalization Program, by products or product groupings.

8. Approve the joint agricultural development programs.

9. Approve and modify the list of agricultural products dealt with in Article 74.

10. Approve the measures for joint cooperation established in Article 79.

11. Modify the number of items referred to in Articles 55 and 102.

12. Reduce the number of matters included in the present Appendix.

13. Establish the conditions for adherence to the present Agreement.

APPENDIX II

1. Approve the list of products reserved for Industrial Development Sectorial Programs.

2. Approve the Industrial Development Sectorial Programs.

3. Approve the rationalization and specialization programs referred to in Article 36.

4. Approve the Common Minimum External Tariff and the Common External Tariff in accordance with the terms stated in Chapter VI, establish the conditions for their application, and modify the common tariff levels.

5. Approve the list of products not produced in any country of the Subregion.

6. Approve the special norms regarding source.

APPENDIX III

1. Approve the list of products for immediate liberalization according to Article 97 (b).

2. Fix margins of preference and indicate terms of enforcement for the lists of products of special interest for Bolivia and Ecuador $\overline{/}$Article 79 (d) and (e)$\overline{/}$.

3. Determine the form and the terms in which Bolivia and Ecuador will liberalize products reserved for Industrial Development Sectorial Programs and which may not have been included in them $\overline{/}$Article 100 (b)$\overline{/}$.

4. Revise the liberalization terms for the products referred to in items (c) and (f) of Article 100.

5. Determine the minimum tariff levels that Bolivia and Ecuador may adopt for products of interest of the other Member Countries (Article 104).

6. Approve the list of products not produced, reserved for production in Bolivia and Ecuador, and fix the conditions and reservation terms (Article 50).

In testimony whereof the undersigned Plenipotentiaries, having deposited their full powers, which were found to be in good order, affix their signatures to this Agreement in behalf of their respective governments.

Done in the city of Bogotá on the twenty-sixth day of the month of May in the year nineteen hundred sixty nine, in five originals, all of them equally valid.

For the Government of the Republic of Colombia:
JORGE VALENCIA JARAMILLO

For the Government of the Republic of Bolivia:
TOMAS GUILLERMO ELÍO

For the Government of the Republic of Chile:
SALVADOR LLUCH

For the Government of the Republic of Ecuador:
JOSÉ PONS VIZCAÍNO

For the Government of the Republic of Peru
VICENTE CERRO CEBRIÁN

FINAL ACT OF THE NEGOTIATIONS BETWEEN THE COMMISSION OF THE CARTAGENA AGREEMENT AND THE GOVERNMENT OF VENEZUELA FOR THE ADHERENCE OF THAT COUNTRY TO THE AGREEMENT*

(Done at Lima, Peru, February 13, 1973)

I

Antecedents

1. By Decision No. 35 the Commission of the Cartagena Agreement created a working group to study the proposals of the Government of Venezuela for the purpose of determining the form of its incorporation into the Cartagena Agreement.

2. The efforts of this working group having been concluded, the Commission approved Decision No. 42 in which it expressed its desire to initiate negotiations for the purpose of establishing the conditions for the incorporation of Venezuela into the Cartagena Agreement, in conformity with an agreed upon procedure.

3. On January 14, 1972 the Government of Venezuela notified the **Standing** Executive Committee of the Latin American Free Trade Association of its desire to initiate negotiations for the purpose of determining the conditions for its incorporation into the Cartagena Agreement subject to the provisions of Resolution 165 of the Committee.

4. Having fulfilled the procedures established in the second Article of the cited Resolution 165, the Government of Venezuela accredited Ambassador Julio Sosa Rodríguez as its Special and Plenipotentiary Representative to undertake with the Commission the negotiations referred to in the same Resolution and these were initiated on March 17, 1972, during the Eighth Period of Ordinary Sessions of the Commission.

---

* English version from International Legal Materials, Vol. XII, N° 2, March 1973.

5.   The Commission and the Special Representative of
Venezuela approved by common agreement the procedure
and the agenda for the negotiations and they agreed that their
conclusion would be embodied in a Final Act.

6.   The negotiations were continued during the following
periods of sessions of the Commission: Seventh Extraordinary
Eighth Extraordinary, Ninth Extraordinary and Tenth Extrao
dinary. During the latter, the Commission and the Special
Representative of Venezuela reached a complete understandin
on all of the matters discussed, in consequence of which and
as a result, they approved on this date the Consensus of Lime
in which is embodied all of the agreements which were achiev

II

The following Plenipotentiary and Alternate Representatives, under the Presidency of Lieutenant General Luis
Barandiaran Pagador, of the Air Force of Peru, the Plenipotentiary Representative of Peru, were present at the
meeting:

Bolivia: Juan Pereira Fiorilo, Adolfo Gutiérrez Rivero
Chile: Juan Somovia Altamirano, Gaston Illanes Fernand
Colombia: Raul Arbelaez Uribe, David Barbosa Mutis
Ecuador: Francisco Rosales Ramos, Alfredo Luna Tobar
Peru: Luis Barandiaran Pagador, Juan de la Piedra Villalong
Venezuela: Julio Sosa Rodríguez

Accredited as advisors were ..... ⌐names¬..... for
Bolivia; ..... ⌐names¬..... for Chile; .....⌐names¬
..... for Colombia; ..... ⌐names¬..... for Ecuador;
.....⌐names¬..... for Peru; .....⌐names¬..... for
Venezuela.

Also present were the members of the Junta, Messrs.
Felipe Salazar Santos, Coordinator, Germánico Salgado
Penaherrera and Salvador Lluch Soler; and the Secretary of
the Commission, Mr. Javier Silva Ruete, who was assisted
by Mr. Alberto Fabini Gómez.

The Andean Development Corporation was represented by its Executive President, Mr. Adolfo Linares Arraya, and the Coordinator at the Junta, Mr. Edgard Camacho Omiste; and the Executive Secretary of LAFTA was represented by Mr. Juan Pascual Martinez.

III

CONSENSUS OF LIMA

1. The Government of Venezuela, through its Special and Plenipotentiary Representative, in the presence of the Plenipotentiary Representatives of the member countries of the Cartagena Agreement, signed on this date the original text of said Agreement which is deposited in the Ministry of Foreign Affairs of Peru.

2. The Governments of Bolivia, Chile, Colombia, Ecuador, Peru and Venezuela signed on this same date, through their duly accredited Plenipotentiary Representatives, the Additional Instrument to the Cartagena Agreement for the Adherence of Venezuela, the original text of which shall be deposited in the Executive Secretariat of LAFTA and one copy of which shall be incorporated into this document as Annex A and it shall form an integral part of the Consensus of Lima.

3. On this same date the Commission has approved the Final Act of its Eleventh Period of Extraordinary Sessions during which Decision No. 70, establishing the conditions for the adherence of Venezuela to the Cartagena Agreement, was approved. This Decision shall also be incorporated into this document as Annex B and it shall form an integral part of the Consensus of Lima.

4. The documents referred to in the preceding paragraphs shall be approved by the signatory countries of this Final Act in conformity with their respective legal procedures.

IV

The adherence of Venezuela in accordance with the provisions of this Act shall be deemed to have occurred, in every respect, when the respective instrument of adherence has been deposited in the Executive Secretariat of LAFTA and the Additional Instrument to the Cartagena Agreement for the Adherence of Venezuela has entered into effect.

V

One copy of this Act with the Annexes thereto, duly certified by the Secretary of the Commission, shall be sent to the Executive Permanent Committee of the Latin American Free Trade Association so that these documents shall be in conformity with the relevant Resolutions of the Conference of the Contracting Parties and of the Committee.

In witness whereof, the Plenipotentiaries whose signatures accompany this document, having deposited their credentials in the Secretariat of the Commission and these having been found to be in correct and proper form, sign this Final Act with all of its Annexes in the name of their respective governments.

Done in the City of Lima this thirteenth day of the month of February of nineteen hundred and seventy-three, in seven equally authentic copies, one of which shall be deposited in the Secretariat of the Commission of the Cartagena Agreement

For the Government of Bolivia	Juan Pereira Fiorilo
For the Government of Chile	Juan Somovia Altamirano
For the Government of Colombia	Raul Arbeláez Uribe
For the Government of Ecuador	Francisco Rosales Ramos
For the Government of Peru	Luis Barandiaran Pagador
For the Government of Venezuela	Julio Sosa Rodríguez

ADDITIONAL INSTRUMENT TO THE CARTAGENA AGREEMENT FOR THE ADHERENCE OF VENEZUELA

The Governments of BOLIVIA, CHILE, COLOMBIA, ECUADOR, PERU AND VENEZUELA;

IN VIEW OF Article 109 of the Cartagena Agreement, Resolution 165 of the Standing Executive Committee of LAFTA, Decision No. 42 of the Commission of the Cartagena Agreement and the communication of January 14, 1972, sent by the Government of Venezuela to the Permanent Executive Committee of LAFTA;

UNITED in the common goal of strengthening and advancing the integration process in Latin America and, in particular, in establishing favorable conditions for the conversion of LAFTA into a common market;

IN THE REALIZATION that Venezuela has participated since the Declaration of Bogotá in the negotiations leading to subregional integration and is a contracting party to the Constitutional Convention of the Andean Development Corporation, the Andrés Bello Convention and the Hipolito Unanue Convention;

INSPIRED by the spirit of the Cartagena Agreement and determined to attain its objectives on an equitable and just scale;

Have agreed to the following:

Article 1. The Commission shall approve the common external tariff, establish the conditions of its application, modify the common tariff levels and approve the rationalization and specialization programs referred to in Article 36 of the Agreement by a two-thirds affirmative vote and without there being a negative vote.

In the preparation of its proposals on the common external tariff, the Junta (Board) shall take into account the provisions of Article 4 of the Cartagena Agreement in favor of Bolivia.

Article 2. Within 120 days following the date on which it deposits its instrument of adherence to the Agreement, Venezuela may present to the Junta a list of products which are presently produced in the subregion in order to except them from the liberalization program and from the process of establishing the common tariff. This list may not encompass products which are included in more than 250 items of the NABALALC and it will be subject to the provisions of Articles 55, 56, 57 and 58 of the Agreement and to the others which are applicable.

Article 3. Also, within the same period of time established in the preceding Article, Venezuela may present to the Junta an additional list of exceptions which may not encompass products which are included in more than 200 items of the NABALALC, which shall be subject to the following provisions:

a) Venezuela may distribute, at its discretion, the number of items of this additional list to except products originating in Chile, Colombia and Peru, provided that the additional list applicable to any of these three countries is not greater than 110 items of the NABALALC;

b) In all cases the additional list of exceptions shall only be applicable with respect to those products of the country to which it is directed; and

c) In the event that the same NABALALC item is included on more than one additional list of Venezuela, each item shall be computed separately for the purpose of calculating the total sum established in this Article.

Article 4. Chile, Colombia and Peru, in turn, may each compose their own additional lists of exceptions to their present lists of exceptions, which may not include more than 30 items of the NABALALC. Also, these countries may include new items in their additional lists of exceptions, so long as the total number in each of these lists does not exceed the number of items of the NABALALC which Venezuela has incorporated in its additional list of exceptions, in regard to each respective country. The additional lists of exceptions of Chile, Colombia and Peru, prepared in accordance with the provisions of this Article, shall only be applicable with respect to Venezuela.

Article 5. Bolivia and Ecuador may each compose additional lists of exceptions to their present lists of exceptions, which lists may not include more than 30 items of the NABALALC and which shall only be applicable with respect to Venezuela.

Article 6. Bolivia, Chile, Colombia, Ecuador and Peru shall present their additional lists of exceptions to the Junta within 30 days following the date on which Venezuela has presented its additional list.

Article 7. The Junta shall verify if the products included in the additional lists of exceptions of Bolivia, Chile, Colombia, Ecuador, Peru and Venezuela are currently produced in the country which included the product on its additional list or if there are possibilities for its production. If the Junta finds that the indicated conditions do not exist, the product must be excluded from the corresponding additional list of exceptions.

Article 8. The additional lists of exceptions shall be in force, except that the countries may withdraw some of the products from them in conformity with the provisions of Article 56 of the Agreement, until December 31, 1979, on which date Bolivia, Chile, Colombia, Ecuador, Peru and Venezuela may substitute some of the products included in their original lists of exceptions by others which were included in their respective additional lists, but in all cases the single lists of exceptions of Chile, Colombia, Peru and Venezuela, from that date, may not encompass products which are included in more than 250 items of the NABALALC, and the lists of Bolivia and Ecuador may not exceed the limits established in Article 102 of the Agreement.

Without prejudice to the provisions of the preceding paragraph, the Junta may authorize Peru to maintain some additional exceptions beyond the 250 mentioned above after December 31, 1979, though it must establish the time period for such extension and the conditions for their future tariff liberalization. Such extension may not extend beyond December 31, 1985, nor may the number of exceptions be more than 20 items of the NABALALC. In this case, Venezuela may also be authorized to maintain a similar number of exceptions against Peru.

Article 9. The Decisions approved by the Commission, upon the proposal of the Junta, in accordance with Article 73 of the Agreement shall be approved by an affirmative vote of two-thirds of the member countries in defining if the application of the restrictions exceeds the provisions of paragraphs (a) and (b) of Article 28 of the Treaty of Montevideo or contravenes the provisions of paragraph (d) of Article 69 of the Agreement.

When such Decisions concern measures of a positive character proposed by the Junta in light of the objectives cited in Article 69, the voting system provided for in paragraph (a) of Article 11 of the Agreement shall be applied.

Article 10. When the economic harm referred to in Article 79 of the Agreement is so grave that immediate corrective measures are called for, the member country which is being affected may apply temporary corrective measures of an emergency nature, subject to the subsequent action of the Junta.

These measures must cause the least possible disruption to the liberalization program and, for as long as they are being applied unilaterally, they may not cause a decrease in the importation of the product or products against which they are applied below the level of the average of the preceding twelve months.

The member country which adopts such measures must communicate this fact in all of its particulars to the Junta immediately and the Junta, within 30 days, shall take action to authorize, modify or suspend their use.

Article 11. In the situations referred to in Article 80 of the Agreement, the country which considers itself to be harmed may, in the presentation of its case to the Junta, propose the protective measures it feels are adequate for the magnitude of the proposed modification, which must be accompanied by the technical bases on which its proposals are founded. The Junta may request any complementary information which it deems appropriate.

The brief and summary conclusion of the Junta must be presented within one month from the date on which the request was received. If the Junta has not acted within this time period and the requesting country considers that the delay may cause it harm, it may adopt the initial measures contained in its proposal, which fact shall be immediately communicated to the Junta; the Junta, in its later decision, must decide about the maintenance, modification or suspension of the applied measures.

In its decision the Junta shall take into account, among other judgmental factors, the relevant economic indicators of the conditions of commercial competition in the subregion which the Commission is to approve as a general standard, upon the proposal of the Junta, the particular characteristics of the exchange systems of the member countries and the relevant studies of the Monetary and Foreign Exchange Council.

Until the system of economic indicators has been approved by the Commission, the Junta shall proceed on the basis of its own judgment.

Notwithstanding the provisions of the above paragraphs, if, during the lapse of time between the presentation of the request referred to and the decision of the Junta, in the judgment of the requesting member country there exist antecedents which cause a well-founded concern that, as a result of the devaluation, immediate grave harm will again be done to its economy requiring the adoption of emergency protective measures, it may present its case to the Junta which, if it feels that the case is well founded, may authorize the application of adequate measures which may be applied for a period of 60 continuous days. The definitive decision of the Junta regarding the modification of the normal conditions of competition shall determine, in every case, the maintenance, modification or suspension of the emergency measures which were authorized.

The measures which are adopted in accordance with the provisions of this Article may not cause a decrease in the level of existing commerce below the levels prior to the devaluation.

The second and third paragraphs of Article 80 shall be fully applicable to all of these measures.

<u>Article 12.</u> This instrument shall be submitted for consideration by the Permanent Executive Committee of LAFTA and once it has been declared compatible with the principles and objectives of the Treaty of Montevideo and with Resolution 203 (CM-II/VI-E), each of the member countries shall approve it in conformity with their respective legal procedures and shall send the corresponding acts of approval to the Executive Secretariat of LAFTA.

This instrument shall enter into force when all of the member countries and Venezuela have communicated their approval to the Executive Secretariat of LAFTA.

In witness whereof, and having found their credentials to be sufficient and in correct and proper form, the respective Representatives sign this instrument.

Done in the City of Lima on the thirteenth day of the month of February in the year nineteen hundred and seventy-three.

This instrument shall be deposited in the Executive Secretariat of LAFTA, which shall send duly authenticated copies of the same to the governments of the member countries.

For the Government of Bolivia   Juan Pereira Fiorilo
For the Government of Chile   Juan Somavia Altamiranc
For the Government of Colombia   Raul Arbeláez Uribe

For the Government of Ecuador   Francisco Rosales Ramos
For the Government of Peru   Luis Barandiaran Pagador
For the Government of Venezuela Julio Sosa Rodriguez

Annex B

Decision No. 70

CONDITIONS FOR THE ADHERENCE OF VENEZUELA
TO THE CARTAGENA AGREEMENT

The COMMISSION of the CARTAGENA AGREEMENT;

IN VIEW OF Article 109 of the Agreement and Decision
No. 42 of the Commission, and as a result of the negotiations between the Commission and the Plenipotentiary Representative of Venezuela;

DECIDES:

To approve the following conditions for the adherence
of Venezuela to the Cartagena Agreement:

CHAPTER I

LIBERALIZATION PROGRAM

Article 1. Within 120 days following the date on which
Venezuela deposits in the Secretariat of the Commission the
instrument of its adherence to the Cartagena Agreement,
that country shall begin to totally eliminate all tariffs and
trade restrictions of every nature applied against the importation of the following products originating in the member
countries:

a) Those included in the first round of the Common
    List as defined in Article 4 of the Treaty of
    Montevideo, in conformity with the provisions of
    Articles 49 and 98 of the Agreement;

b)   Those included in the list defined by Article 50 of the Cartagena Agreement, approved by Decision No. 26 of the Commission;

c)   Those included in Annex I of Decision No. 28 of the Commission, in favor of Bolivia;

d)   Those included in Annex II of Decision No. 28 of the Commission, in favor of Ecuador;

e)   Those included in Annex I of Decision No. 29 of the Commission, in favor of Bolivia; and

f)   Those included in Annex II of Decision No. 29 of the Commission, in favor of Ecuador.

In the cases of paragraphs (c) and (d) of this Article, the conditions established in Decision No. 28 of the Commission shall be fulfilled.

Article 2. Within the same period of time established in the preceding Article, Venezuela shall adopt the measures established in Decision No. 34 with respect to the products included in the Annex thereto, in order to establish and maintain the margins of preference for Bolivia and Ecuador established in that Decision.

Article 3. The tariffs which Venezuela applies on the importation of products originating in the member countries shall be converted for the subregion into ad valorem terms on the CIF price of the goods. For this purpose a group of experts, coordinated by the Junta, shall be formed which shall employ the same method used to determine the initial points of the tariff reduction program, as established in Decisions Nos. 15 and 23 of the Commission and later expressed in terms of the NABANDINA by Decision No. 64.

Article 4. With respect to the products referred to in Article 52 of the Cartagena Agreement, which list was approved by Decision No. 27 of the Commission, Venezuela shall proceed in the following manner:

a) Within 120 days from the date on which the Government of Venezuela deposits in the Secretariat of the Commission its instrument of adherence to the Cartagena Agreement, that country shall take as a starting point for the fulfillment of the liberalization program the level reached as of that date by Chile, Colombia and Peru by virtue of the tariff reductions effectuated to that date;

b) When the tariff on a product is less than the starting point defined in the preceding paragraph, Venezuela may maintain that tariff until Chile, Colombia and Peru reach that level by virtue of the annual reductions referred to in paragraph (c) of Article 52. From that moment Venezuela shall eliminate the remaining tariff by means of annual reductions of 10% of the initial starting point as approved in Decisions Nos. 15 and 23 of the Commission until total liberalization is reached on December 31, 1980; and

c) With respect to the same list of products referred to in this Article and which originate in Bolivia or Ecuador, Venezuela shall reduce, within the time period established in paragraph (a) of this Article, the tariffs which are included in the initial starting point to the level reached by Chile, Colombia and Peru as of the same date. In all cases, such products shall have free and absolute access to the Venezuelan market by December 31, 1973.

Article 5. As of the same date on which Venezuela fulfills the provisions of the preceding Article, the tariff reductions effectuated by Chile, Colombia and Peru in fulfillment of Articles 49, 50 and 52 of the Agreement shall be extended to Venezuela.

Article 6. Venezuela shall eliminate all restrictions of every nature applicable to the importation of all products originating in the other member countries within the period of time indicated in paragraph (a) of Article 4, with the exception of those which are applied to the products reserved for sectorial industrial development programs by Decision

No. 25 of the Commission, to which shall be applied the provisions of the second paragraph of Article 46 of the Agreement.

Notwithstanding the provisions of the preceding paragraph, Venezuela may substitute, in this instance, restrictions by tariffs so long as the level applicable to imports from the subregion does not exceed that established as the starting point for the fulfillment of the liberalization program for that country, in conformity with the provisions of paragraph (a) of Article 4 of this Decision. In no case may Venezuela apply a lower tariff than that resulting from the above-mentioned formula to imports from outside the subregion, but it may, if it so desires, maintain for such imports restrictions of every nature.

The group of experts referred to in Article 3 shall consider the tariffs and restrictions established by Venezuela in its national tariff schedule promulgated on January 1, 1973, including its transitory provisions.

Based on the conclusions of the group of experts and the substitution referred to in this Article, the Junta shall send a proposal to the Commission for its determination, within the time period referred to in paragraph (a) of Article 4 of this Decision, of the tariff levels of Venezuela which are related to the liberalization program.

Article 7. For the purpose of fulfilling, by Venezuela, the provisions of Article 54 of the Agreement, reference will be made to the tariffs and restrictions prevailing in that country on May 1, 1973.

CHAPTER II

THE MINIMUM COMMON EXTERNAL TARIFF

Article 8. As the starting point for the fulfillment, by Venezuela, of the minimum common external tariff, the tariffs established in the Decision of the Commission in accordance with Article 6 of this Decision shall be taken.

Starting from these levels, Venezuela shall initiate the process of approximating those of the minimum common external tariff beginning on December 31, 1973 and it shall complete this process in an annual, lineal and automatic manner so that the minimum common external tariff will be in full effect for that country by December 31, 1975.

Article 9. Venezuela shall present to the Junta any observations which it considers necessary regarding the tariff levels of the minimum common external tariff, approved by Decision No. 30 of the Commission. Immediately after receiving the observations of Venezuela the Junta shall convene a group of experts from the member countries to examine such observations and, within the following 60 days, shall present a proposal to the Commission.

Article 10. For the purposes of the application of the final paragraph of Article 65 of the Agreement, which refers to the minimum common external tariff, the Commission, upon the proposal of the Junta, shall approve, before December 31, 1973, a list of products expressed in items of the NABANDINA for which there is no existing subregional production.

Article 11. For the purpose of fulfilling the objective of the preceding Article, the member countries shall supply to the Junta, before June 30, 1973, information regarding items of the NABANDINA in regard to which they consider there to be no existing subregional production.

Article 12. The Junta may include new products on the list referred to in Article 10 of this Decision when it finds, on its own or upon the request of a member country, that there is no existing production in the subregion.

When a member country requests the inclusion of new products on the above-mentioned list, it must present to the Junta the bases on which it founds its request.

Article 13. The member countries may defer the application of the tariffs of the minimum common external tariff for the products included in the list referred to in Article 10 of this Decision, until the Junta verifies that production in the subregion has been initiated. The member countries must notify the Junta of any such decisions effectuated in conformity with this Article.

Article 14. Whenever the Junta learns, either directly or through information supplied by any of the member countries, that the production of any product included in the list referred to in Article 10 of this Decision has been initiated it shall take steps to verify if in fact such production has been initiated and if it has such product shall be withdrawn from the list and the Junta shall so notify the member countries.

Article 15. The member countries exercising the option granted in the final paragraph of Article 65 of the Agreement deferring the application of the tariffs of the minimum common external tariff for the products included in the list referred to in Article 10 of this Decision shall begin to apply such tariff from the date on which the Junta withdraws the product from the list and so notifies the member countries.

Article 16. When a member country is about to initiate production of any product included in the list referred to in Article 10 of this Decision and has a well-founded reason to fear that stockpiles of that product, in quantities which could harm the new production, are being accumulated in the subregion, it shall communicate this fact to the Junta along with the bases for its concern. The Junta shall examine such bases and such other information which it can collec and, if it finds that the fears of the interested country are well founded, it shall recommend to the other member countries the adoption of the necessary measures to avoid such harm. Among such measures, the Junta may include the full and immediate application of the tariffs of the minimum common external tariff.

Article 17. Whenever, in the judgment of the Junta, such new production is insufficient to normally satisfy the acquirements of the subregion, it shall propose to the Commission, acting on its own or upon the request of any member country, the measures which it considers necessary to facilitate the importation of the relevant products in quantities which are sufficient to overcome the deficit.

Article 18. The measures referred to in the preceding Article shall be based on the objectives of reconciling the need to protect subregional production with that of assuring a normal supply and avoiding disturbances in the conditions of competition. These measures may include, among others, a reduction of the common tariffs or deferring their application.

The Junta must periodically analyze the evolution of the situation in order to prevent the adopted measures from being prologed longer than is strictly necessary and it may propose to the Commission the adoption of the measures which it deems appropriate.

Article 19. Without prejudice to that which was established in Decision No. 49-a, the Commission shall approve, upon the proposal of the Junta, before December 31, 1975, regulations for the final paragraph of Article 65 of the Agreement in regard to the application of the common tariffs. Until the referred to regulations are approved, the application of the final paragraph of Article 65 shall be governed by the rules of this Decision.

Article 20. Any member country which is affected by temporary insufficiencies of subregional supply, in terms of Article 67 of the Agreement, may present its case to the Junta, along with the necessary background materials, specifying, at the least, the quantities and nature of the demand. The Junta shall notify the other member countries of such a situation within two working days following such presentation and it shall request such information as it deems appropriate.

Article 21. The member countries shall supply to the Junta the information referred to in the preceding Article within ten working days following the date on which the request was received. In cases of urgency, duly authenticated by the Junta in its request for information, this must be provided in a maximum period of five working days.

Article 22. If any of the member countries do not provide the information requested by the Junta within the periods established in the preceding Article it shall be considered that those countries cannot supply any or all of the requirements of the member country which considers itself to be affected.

Article 23. Within three working days following the termination of the time periods established in Article 21 of this Decision, the Junta, based on the request of the interested country, the information supplied by the other member countries and the conclusions of its own investigations, shall issue an appropriate Resolution and communicate it immediately to the member countries.

Article 24. In the event that the Resolution of the Junta verifies that there is a temporary insufficiency of supply, the member country which made the request may adopt measures such as the temporary reduction or suspension of the common tariffs, within the terms established by the Junta in conformity with the provisions of the preceding Article.

CHAPTER III

THE COMMON TARIFF NOMENCLATURE
OF THE MEMBER COUNTRIES OF
THE CARTAGENA AGREEMENT (NABANDINA)

Article 25. Venezuela shall put its national tariff nomenclature in the terms of the NABANDINA no later than December 31, 1973.

Article 26. Venezuela shall present to the Junta the observations which it considers necessary to adapt the NABANDINA to the conditions of its production and external commerce. The Junta shall immediately convene a group of experts from the member countries to examine such observations, and, based on the conclusions of the group, shall present a proposal to the Commission within the following 60 days.

CHAPTER IV

SECTORAL INDUSTRIAL DEVELOPMENT PROGRAM FOR THE METALWORKING INDUSTRIES

Article 27. Within six months following the date on which the Government of Venezuela deposits in the Secretariat of the Commission its instrument of adherence to the Cartagena Agreement, the Junta shall present to the Commission a complementary proposal to Decisions Nos. 57 and 57-a for the participation of Venezuela in the Metalworking Program. This proposal must be approved by an affirmative vote of two-thirds of the member countries, provided that there is no negative vote.

Article 28. The participation of Venezuela in the Metalworking Program shall not affect the effectiveness of the assignments made to Bolivia, Chile, Colombia, Ecuador and Peru in Decisions Nos. 57 and 57-a. The Junta in its proposal may include measures which entail the sharing or withdrawing of assignments, but only after previously consulting with and gaining the acceptance of the country or countries favored by such assignments.

Article 29. Until the Commission approves the proposal referred to in Article 27 of this Decision, Venezuela shall endeavor not to encourage the production, in its territory, of the products assigned to Bolivia, Chile, Colombia, Ecuador and Peru in Decisions Nos. 57 and 57-a.

Article 30. Until the Commission approves the proposal referred to in Article 27 of this Decision, the products assigned to Bolivia, Chile, Colombia, Ecuador and Peru in Decisions 57 and 57-a shall not benefit from the opening of the Venezuela market, nor shall the same products, when they originate in Venezuela, benefit from the opening of the markets of the other member countries.

CHAPTER V

EVALUATION

Article 31. When a member country, as a result of the internal evaluations which it undertakes regarding the consequences of its participation in the integration process, considers that, as a result of such process, a significant deterioration of its global economic relations with the sub-region has been caused, it may present its situation to the Commission, within the annual periods established for evaluation, so that it can analyze the actual situation and adopt, if necessary, the necessary positive corrective measures to resolve the problem which was presented.

Article 32. Without prejudice to the provisions of Article 15, paragraph (f), of the Agreement, a member country may, on the occasion of the annual evaluations, request that the Junta specially analyze any situation within the terms of the preceding Article so that, if the Junta deems it appropriate, it may make recommendations to the Commission for the correction of the difficulties presented by the affected country.

CHAPTER VI

COMMON CODE FOR THE TREATMENT OF FOREIGN CAPITAL, TRADEMARKS, PATENTS, LICENSES AND ROYALTIES

Article 33. Add to Article 1 of Decision No. 24 the following definition:

Portfolio Development Bonds: These are titles or obligations issued for development purposes and publicly offered by the state, state entities, quasi state entities, national and mixed enterprises or by the Andean Development Corporation the acquisition of which does not confer, in any case, the right to participate in the technical, financial, administrative or commercial direction of the issuing entity and which must always be qualified, for this purpose, by the competent national authority.

Article 34. Add the following paragraphs to Article 13 of Decision No. 24:

The governments of the member countries may allow foreign enterprises, without the necessity of special authorization, to apply their undistributed earnings to the acquisition of Portfolio Development Bonds when the total of these purchases plus reinvested earnings, in conformity with the preceding paragraph, does not exceed, when considered together, 5% of the capital of the particular enterprise. In these cases, the purchase of such bonds shall be considered to be a reinvestment and the obligation to register them shall continue to prevail.

The foreign enterprise may apply its other undistributed earnings to the acquisition of Portfolio Development Bonds, but in such cases they will not benefit from the treatment referred to in the preceding paragraph.

CHAPTER VII

UNIFORM CODE FOR MULTINATIONAL
ENTERPRISES AND REGULATIONS FOR THE
TREATMENT APPLICABLE TO SUBREGIONAL CAPITAL

Article 35. Substitute Article 3 of Decision No. 46 with the following text:

Each member country shall establish in its internal laws the requirements which its nationals must meet in order to invest in multinational enterprises or to transfer capital to any other member country.

The competent national authorities shall only authorize the reexportation of capital or the transfer of earnings to the territory of the member country where the capital originated.

CHAPTER VIII

ADDITIONAL LIST OF PRODUCTS TO THE LIST
CONTAINED IN ANNEX A OF DECISION No. 16

Article 36. Add the following products to the list contained in the Annex to Decision No. 16 of the Commission:

NABALALC

01.01.1.91	Racehorses
01.02.1.99	Live cattle
01.03.1.99	Live pigs
01.05.1.01	Baby chicks
02.01.1.31	Fresh pork, refrigerated
02.01.1.32	Fresh pork, frozen
02.01.1.33	Bacon
02.06.2.01	Salted or brined pork, dry or wet
02.06.2.02	Salted or brined beef, dry or wet
02.06.2.99	Other meats salted or brined, dry or wet
04.01	Fresh milk and cream, unconcentrated and unsweetened
04.02.1	Milk with or without sugar, canned, concentrated or sweetened
07.01.0.05	Fresh or refrigerated onions
07.06.0.01	Cassava roots
08.01.0.03	Pineapple
10.05.0.02	Unhusked ears of corn
12.04.0.02	Sugarcane
17.01.1	Unrefined sugar
17.01.2	Semirefined or refined sugar
41.01.1	Untreated cattle hides (fresh, salted, dried, pickled or limed)
41.02.1	Cattle hides and skins (including buffalos) prepared differently than as specified in Positions 41.06 to 41.08, inclusive
44.05.2	Wood sawed lengthwise, sliced or peeled, of more than five millimeters in width, nonconiferous

CHAPTER IX

GENERAL PROVISIONS

Article 37. The adherence of Venezuela to the Cartagena Agreement signifies its acceptance of the Decisions approved by the Commission until this date, without prejudice to the time periods and conditions established in this Decision.

Likewise, the Resolutions of the Junta, issued until this date, shall be fully applicable to it.

Article 38. In all matters not expressly referred to in this Decision and in the Final Act of the negotiations between the Commission and Venezuela, it shall be understood that Venezuela is in the same category as Chile, Colombia and Peru and, consequently, it shall enjoy all of the same rights and assume all of the same obligations which the Agreement establishes for the mentioned countries.

In witness whereof, the Plenipotentiaries whose signatures accompany this document, having deposited their credentials in the Secretariat of the Commission and these having been found to be in correct and proper form, sign this document in the name of their respective governments.

Done in the City of Lima the thirteenth day of the month of February of the year nineteen hundred and seventy-three, in seven equally authentic copies, one of which shall be deposited in the Secretariat of the Commission of the Cartagena Agreement.

For the Government of Bolivia   Juan Pereira Fiorilo

(all of the other names are identical to
the Consensus of Lima)

LIMA PROTOCOL
ADDITIONAL TO THE CARTAGENA AGREEMENT*

(Signed by the Governments of Bolivia, Colombia,
Ecuador, Peru and Venezuela the 30th of October
of 1976)

THE GOVERNMENTS OF Bolivia, Colombia, Ecuador,
Peru and Venezuela

AGREE, through their duly authorized Plenipotentiary
Representatives, on the following:

Article 1. To extend for three years the term
stipulated in Article 47 of the Agreement for the close of
the reservation period and in Article 45, the third, fourth
and fifth paragraphs of Article 55, the final paragraph of
Article 57, Article 61, Section c) of Article 97, the second
paragraph of Article 102, Article 104, the second paragraph of Article 105 and Article 112 of the Agreement for
completion of the liberalization program and the Common
External Tariff. Also, to extend for three years the
terms stipulated in Article 8 of the Additional Instrument
for the Adherence of Venezuela.

Article 2. To replace Article 62 of the Agreement
with the following:

The Commission, at the proposal of the Board, and
by December 1978, shall approve the Common External
Tariff that must provide levels of maximum and minimum
protection to subregional production, taking into account
the objective of the Agreement to harmonize the economic
policies of the member states and the present existence

---

* Translation by the Department of Legal Affairs,
General Secretariat of the Organization of American
States.

306

of different economic policies which include _inter alia,_ monetary, exchange and paratariff policies.

On December 31, 1979, the member states shall commence a process directed toward adoption of a Common External Tariff by harmonizing the charges levied by their domestic tariffs on imports from outside the Subregion, to be effected on an annual, automatic and parallel basis, and in a manner to make it fully operative by December 1988 in Bolivia and Ecuador.

Article 3. Prior to October 31, 1977, the Commission, at the proposal of the Board, shall approve a list of products which shall be excluded from the reserve list for programming and shall reserve from among those not produced, a separate list of the products to be produced in Bolivia and Ecuador, indicating the conditions and terms of the reservation.

On December 31, 1977, the member states shall adopt for the products of this list the point of departure referred to in Section a) of Article 52 of the Agreement and shall eliminate all charges levied on imports of those products.

The remaining charges shall be eliminated through six annual reductions of five, ten, fifteen, twenty, twenty-five percent, the first of which shall be made on December 31, 1978.

Colombia, Peru and Venezuela shall eliminate by December 31, 1977 the charges levied on imports originating from Bolivia and Ecuador.

Bolivia and Ecuador shall liberate the importation of these products in the form indicated in Section b) of Article 100 of the Agreement.

Article 4. To replace Article 53 of the Agreement with the following:

With respect to products which had been selected for Sectoral Programs of Industrial Development but were not included therein within the time periods stipulated in

Article 47, the member states shall comply with the Liberalization Program in the following manner:

a) The Commission, at the proposal of the Board, shall select lists of commodities not produced, to be produced in Bolivia and Ecuador, and shall establish the conditions and terms of the reservation;

b) On December 31, 1978, the member states shall adopt for the remaining countries the point of departure referred to in Section a) of Article 52 of the Agreement and shall eliminate all charges levied on imports of those products;

c) The remaining charges shall be eliminated through five annual successive reductions of five, ten, fifteen, thirty and forty percent, the first of which shall be made on December 31, 1979;

d) Colombia, Peru and Venezuela shall eliminate by December 31, 1978 all charges levied on imports originating from Bolivia and Ecuador.

Article 5. To delete item 2 of Annex II of the Agreement and add the following paragraphs to Article 11:

The Sectoral Programs of Industrial Development must be adopted by affirmative vote cast by two-thirds of the member states, with no negative vote.

The proposals receiving an affirmative vote of two-thirds of the member states, but which are subject of a negative vote, must be returned to the Board for consideration of the reasons originating the said negative vote.

Within a period of not less than one nor more than three months, the Board may renew its proposal for Commission consideration with amendments deemed desirable and in such event, the amended proposal shall be considered as approved if it receives an affirmative vote of two-thirds of the member states.

Article 6. The country or countries that have cast a negative vote may abstain from participating in the program, in which case it shall enter into force under the following conditions:

a) At least four member states must participate;

b) The country which does not participate shall include the products which are subject of the program in its schedule of exceptions, if they are not already there. The Commission, at the proposal of the Board, shall determine the period and conditions for liberalization and adoption of the Common External Tariff for these products. In its proposals the Board shall consider the results of the negotiations held for this purpose between the countries participating in the program and the country not participating;

c) The member states participating in this type of program shall commit themselves not to encourage for two years the manufacture of products that have been assigned exclusively for inclusion for the benefit of the nonparticipating member state. When this period has expired, the countries participating in the program shall decide on the distribution of those products, at the proposal of the Board.

Article 7. A member state that does not participate initially in a sectoral program of this type may request its inclusion at any time. The Commission, at the proposal of the Board, shall approve the conditions for the inclusion through the voting method stipulated in Section b) of Article 11 of the Agreement. In its proposals the Board shall consider the results of the negotiations held for this purpose between the countries participating in the program and the country not participating.

Article 8. To replace Section c) of Article 52 of the Agreement with the following:

309

After the reduction made on December 31,1975, the remaining charges shall be eliminated through seven annual successive reductions of six percent each, the first to be made on December 31,1976, and a final reduction of eight percent, to be made on December 31, 1983.

Article 9.   To replace Section f) of Article 100 with the following:

The commodities not included in the preceding sec- tions shall be eliminated from the national tariffs through annual successive reductions, three of five percent each, beginning December 31, 1979; five of ten percent each, beginning December 31,1982; one of fifteen percent on December 31,1987, and a final reduction of twenty percent on December 31, 1988.

Article 10.   Prior to December 31,1977, Bolivia may present an additional schedule of exceptions compris- ing up to two hundred thirty six (236) item of NABALALC in order to complete, in the same terms as Ecuador, the schedule authorized by Article 102 of the Agreement.

Article 11.   To add to Article 45 of the Agreement the following paragraph:

Notwithstanding the provisions of the first paragraph of this Article, the Commission, at the proposal of the Board, may include in the Sectoral Programs of Industrial Development liberalization programs ex- tending beyond December 31, 1983, thus establishing for the benefit of Bolivia and Ecuador terms ad- ditional to those of the other member states.

Article 12.   The Commission, at the proposal of the Board, shall adopt the necessary measures to ensure the effectiveness and benefit of the assignments granted to Bolivia and Ecuador, especially those intended to strengthen agreements relative to the assignments granted to those countries, to the extension of periods for the maintenance of the assignments,   and the execution of the projects assigned in the sectoral programs.

CHAPTER II

Attributes of the Commission

<u>Article 5</u>.   The following are attributes of the Commission:

a)   To formulate the general policies of the Agreement
and to adopt any measures necessary to achieve
its objectives;

b)   To approve the rules indispensable for coordination
of development plans and harmonization of the economic policies of the member countries;

c)   To appoint and remove Board members;

d)   To issue instructions to the Board;

e)   To delegate its powers to the Board, when deemed
desirable;

f)   To approve, reject or amend proposals of the
Board;

g)   To supervise the coordinated compliance with
obligations assumed under this Agreement and
under the Montevideo Treaty;

h)   To approve the annual budget of the Board and to
fix the contributions of each member country;

i)   To enact its own internal rules of procedure and
those to govern the Committees, and to approve
the Board's rules and any amendments thereto;

j)   To propose to the member countries any reforms
to the present Agreement; and

k)   To hear and resolve any other matters of common
interest.

<u>Article 6</u>.   Board members shall be appointed by the
Commission by unanimous vote.

Except in the case of resignation, death or removal of a Board member, appointments shall be made no later than sixty days prior to the initiation of the term for which the member is appointed.

In case of resignation, death or removal, a replacement shall be appointed within thirty days thereafter.

Article 7. No Board member may be removed by the Commission except in case of serious wrongdoing or when he systematically impedes the Board's work.

Article 8. Either on its own initiative or at the request of a member country, the Commission shall proceed to examine the facts of which it is aware in relation to the preceding article and, following a hearing of the Board member concerned, shall decide whether he should be removed.

The Commission's decision shall be adopted by the affirmative vote of two-thirds of the member countries.

The functions of a Board member who is to be removed shall cease on the date of notification of his removal.

CHAPTER III

Meetings

Article 9. The Commission shall meet in regular session three times a year beginning the second Monday of March, July and November.

Regular sessions may be postponed only by written request of at least two member countries sent to the President of the Commission 20 days prior to opening date of the session, except in case of force majeure.

Article 10. The Commission shall meet in special session whenever called by its president, at the request of any of the member countries or the Board.

The request for a special session must state the purpose of the meeting and propose a date.   The president shall call the meeting within 15 days of receipt of the request.

Article 11. Regular and special sessions shall be held at Board headquarters but they may take place elsewhere if the Commission so decides or at least three member countries so request.

Article 12.   The Board shall be responsible for preparing the provisional agenda of meetings and remitting it to the president of the Commission and to the representatives of the member countries not later than 30 days prior to the opening of the respective meeting.   Furthermore, the Board shall transmit the documents 15 days in advance.

If any of the member countries wish to include new items in the provisional agenda they should communicate this in writing to the president of the Commission, to the other member countries and to the Board so that they will be informed at least 15 days prior to the opening of the corresponding session, accompanied by the documentation, when pertinent, that will serve as a basis for the discussion and eventual decision on the topics suggested for inclusion. Unless this procedure has been followed, no new topics may be introduced unless agreed to unanimously by the Commission.

The agenda must be approved in the first session of the Commission.

In the case of special sessions, the agenda may include topics other than those for which the meeting was called only with the consent of all the representatives.

Article 13.   An officer of the Board shall be appointed to act as secretary of the meetings.

Article 14.   The Commission may set up working groups to study specific points of the agenda.

CHAPTER IV

The President

Article 15.   The Commission shall have a president whose term shall be one year.   His function shall be exercised successively by each of the representatives in turn according to the alphabetical order of the countries.

The president shall assume his functions on the last day of the regular session in November of each year.

The first president shall be selected by lot.

In case of the absence or impediment of the incumbent the duties of the president shall be performed temporarily by the next principal representative according to the alphabetical order of countries indicated above.

<u>Article 16</u>. The functions of the president are:

a) To represent the Commission;

b) To call the Commission to regular and special sessions;

c) To receive the credentials of the principal and alternate representatives;

d) To receive the communications by which the member countries accredit advisors to attend each meeting of the Commission;

e) To issue invitations to observers and advisors approved by the Commission;

f) To preside over the sessions;

g) To submit the agenda to the Commission for approval;

h) To fix the order of the day, submit matters relating thereto for consideration by the Commission, direct the deliberations, call matters to a vote and announce the results thereof;

i) To resolve questions of order. Should such a resolution be appealed, the case shall be submitted at once to the Commission, which may revoke it by a two-thirds vote of the member countries;

j)   To see that the regulations are complied
     with;

k)   To install the working groups;

l)   To limit the length and the number of interventions
     by each representative in discussions on a single
     matter;

m)   To convoke the Advisory Committee whenever re-
     quested by any member country to do so;

n)   To appoint a recording secretary for closed ses-
     sions; and

o)   To perform any other duties entrusted to him by
     the Commission.

Article 17.   The simultaneous exercise of the functions
of president with those of representative is incompatible in
sessions of the Commission.

CHAPTER V

Quorum and Voting

Article 18.   The Commission may meet with the presence of at least two thirds of the member countries.

Attendance at meetings is compulsory and nonattendance
shall be considered as an abstention.

Article 19.   The Commission shall express its will in
its "Decisions", which shall be enumerated consecutively.

Article 20.   The Decisions of the Commission shall
contain:

a)   The term "The Commission of the Cartagena
     Agreement";

b) When applicable, an indication of the provisions that serve as a basis for the Decision, preceded by the words "Having Seen", and the reasons that motivate the Decision, preceded by the word "Whereas"; and

c) The text of the Decision, following the word "Decides".

Article 21. The text of a Decision in its resolutive part shall be divided into articles. In cases where its provisions involve obligations for the member countries or for the organs of the Agreement, the date of their entry into force shall be indicated in the final article. Otherwise it shall be understood that the effective date is the date of approval of the final act of that particular meeting.

Article 22. The Decisions shall be adopted by the affirmative vote of two thirds of the member countries. Each representative shall have the right to one vote and, in counting the two thirds, any fraction left over shall be converted to the whole number nearest to it.

Article 23. The general voting principle indicated in the preceding article shall exclude the appointment of Board members, which requires a unanimous vote, and the matters indicated below, which must be approved by a two-thirds affirmative vote, with no negative vote:

1) Delegation to the Board of whatever functions are considered appropriate;

2) Approval of modifications to the Agreement;

3) Amendment of proposals of the Board;

4) Approval of rules that may be necessary for the coordination of development plans and the harmonization of the economic policies of the member countries;

5) Approval of the program for harmonization of the instruments for regulation of the foreign trade of the member countries;

6) Approval of physical integration programs;

7) Acceleration of the liberalization program, by products or groups of products;

8) Approval of joint programs of agricultural development;

9) Approval and modification of the list of agricultural products dealt with in Article 74 of the Agreement;

10) Approval of the joint measures for cooperation established in Article 79 of the Agreement;

11) Modification of the number of items referred to in Articles 55 and 102 of the Agreement;

12) Reduction of the number of matters included in this article; and

13) Establishment of the conditions for adherence to the Agreement.

Article 24. In the matters indicated below Board proposals receiving an affirmative vote of two thirds of the member countries, but which receive a negative vote, must be returned to the Board for consideration of the reasons for the said negative vote:

1) Approval of the list of products reserved for sectorial programs of industrial development;

2) Approval of the sectorial programs of industrial development;

3) Approval of the rationalization and specialization programs referred to in Article 36 of the Agreement;

4) Approval of the common minimum external tariff and the common external tariff in accordance with the formalities provided for in Chapter VI of the Agreement, establishment of conditions for their application, and modification of common tariff levels;

5) Approval of the list of products not producted in any country of the subregion; and

6) Approval of the special rules of origin.

Within a period of not less than two months nor more than six, the Board shall raise the proposal again for consideration by the Commission with the modifications it considers advisable and, in that case, the proposal thus modified shall be deemed approved if it receives the favorable vote of two thirds of the member countries, with no negative vote; however, the vote of the country that had voted negatively on the previous occasion shall not be counted as a negative one.

Article 25. When dealing with the following matters, related to the special treatment for Bolivia and Ecuador, the Commission shall adopt its decisions by a two-thirds affirmative vote, provided one of these is cast either by Bolivia or Ecuador:

1) Approval of the list of products for immediate liberalization according to Article 97 (b) of the Agreement;

2) Establishment of margins of preference and indication of enforcement dates for the lists of products of special interest to Bolivia and Ecuador (Article 9 (d) of the Agreement);

3) Determination of the manner and the time periods in which Bolivia and Ecuador shall liberalize the products reserved for sectorial programs of industrial development and not included in them (Article 100 (b) of the Agreement);

4) Review of the liberalization periods for the products referred to in Article 100 (c) and (f) of the Agreemer

5) Determination of the minimum tariff levels to be adopted by Bolivia and Ecuador for products of interest to the other member countries (Article 104) of the Agreement; and

6) Approval of the list of products not produced but reserved for production in Bolivia and Ecuador, and fixing the conditions and time periods for reservation (Article 50 of the Agreement).

CHAPTER VI

Obligations of the Representatives

Article 26. The representatives in the Commission have the following attributes:

1) To present to the Commission in due course the instruments by which the various obligations arising from the Agreement are put into force in their respective countries; and

2) To see that the obligations imposed on their respective countries by the Agreement are complied with.

CHAPTER VII

Settlement of Disputes

Article 27. If differences arise regarding interpretation or application of the Agreement or Decisions of the Commission, the affected countries must seek a solution by direct negotiation. In any case, they shall inform the Commission of the results of such negotiations.

Article 28. If a solution by direct negotiation is not forthcoming, or if disputes are only partially solved, the Commission must interpose its good offices with the countries in dispute.

If the Commission feels that its good offices are insufficient or that the matter in dispute requires more direct intervention on its part, it shall offer to mediate and shall seek an agreement by proposing formulas that it considers appropriate within a time period that it shall establish for this purpose.

Article 29. If the efforts indicated in the two preceding articles should fail, the Commission shall undertake the procedure of conciliation. For this purpose it shall appoint a conciliation committee composed of one national from each of the countries in disagreement and one national from each of the other member countries.

This committee must investigate the facts and hear the parties in dispute. Following this procedure the committee, with the majority vote of its members shall issue a report containing proposals that it believes will lead to a final solution. This report must be placed in the hands of the Commission within a period of three months from the date of constitution of the conciliation committee.

Article 30. If the procedures of negotiation, good offices, mediation and conciliation, mentioned in the above articles, should fail, the countries in dispute shall observe the procedure of arbitration established in the protocol for the settlement of disputes, signed in Asunción on September 2, 1967.

CHAPTER VIII

Minutes and Other Documents

Article 31. The order of the day and the documents that must be considered in the meetings shall be distributed to the representatives at least twenty-four hours in advance of the pertinent meeting, unless the Commission should agree to a shorter period in certain cases.

Article 32. Minutes shall be drawn up of all the meetings of the Commission, and shall contain an accurate version of the deliberations; they shall be attached as appendices to the proposals of the Board and the reports issued on the matters relating to them.

Article 33. There shall be a final act of the meeting, which shall be signed by the representatives and contain as appendices the decisions of the Commission and the proceedings of all the sessions held.

Article 34. The Board shall be the depository of all documents relating to the execution of the Agreement.

REGULATIONS OF THE BOARD OF THE
CARTAGENA AGREEMENT

(Decision N° 9 of the Commission, March 13, 1970)

CHAPTER I

Members of the Board

Article 1. The Board is the technical organ of this Agreement, consisting of three members, and it may act only in the concerted interest of the Subregion as a unit. Its seat is the city of Lima.

Article 2. Board members may be nationals of any Latin American country. They shall have three-year terms and be eligible for reelection.

The term shall be counted from the date that the Board member assumes his functions, which shall be certified by the director-secretary.

Article 3. Board members shall assume their functions within 60 calendar days of the date of their election or within the period fixed in the election proceedings.

Article 4. Board members shall be answerable to the Commission for their actions; shall act in the common interest; shall refrain from any activity incompatible with the nature of their duties; may not exercise any other professional office, whether remunerative or not, for the duration of their terms; shall not seek or receive instructions from any government or from any national or international entity; and shall not accept any honors or decorations without the consent of the Commission.

Article 5. For the purposes of the provision of the second paragraph of Article 13 of the Agreement, it shall be understood that vacancies shall occur in the following cases:

a) Accepted resignation;

b) Death;

c) Removal;

d) Permanent physical or mental disability, understanding to be such any disability which, in the
opinion of physicians chosen by the Board, is permanent or may last more than six months.

A vacancy shall also occur if a Board member does not
assume his functions within the prescribed time, except in
case of force majeure.

Article 6. Vacations, leave, in-service travel and
temporary physical impairment shall be understood as temporary absence.

No temporary absence on account of leave, vacation or
in-service travel may extend beyond 60 days.

CHAPTER II

Functions of the Board

Article 7. The Board shall have the follwing functions:

1. To supervise the implementation of the Agreement
   and of the Commission Decisions (Art. 15 (a) of
   the Agreement);

2. To comply with Commission assignments (Art. 15
   (b));

3. To prepare proposals for the Commission, conducive to expediting or accelerating compliance
   with the Agreement, in order to achieve its goals
   within the shortest possible time (Art. 15 (c));

4. To undertake studies and submit recommendations
   necessary for applying preferential treatment to
   Bolivia and Ecuador, and generally any matter concerning participation in the Agreement by these two
   countries (Art. 15 (d));

5. To participate in the Commission meetings, unless the latter deems it advisable to hold closed sessions (Art. 15 (e));
Notwithstanding, the Board shall have the right to participate in any discussion of its own proposals made to the Commission, and particularly those under Sections 3 and 4 (Art. 15 (e));

6. To assess annually the accomplishments of the implementation of this Agreement, and the progress in the achievement of its goals, giving special attention to compliance with the principle of equitable distribution of integration benefits; and to propose to the Commission any positive corrective measures that may be pertinent (Art. 15 (f));

7. To undertake the technical studies entrusted to it by the Commission, and any others deemed desirable (Art. 15 (g));

8. To perform the duties assigned to it by the Commission (Art. 15 (h));

9. To perform the functions of Permanent Secretariat of the Agreement, and to maintain direct contacts with governments of member countries through the organs designated by each of them for this purpose (Art. 15 (i));

10. To draft its internal rules and submit them to the Commission for approval or modification (Art. 15 (j));

11. To submit the draft of annual budget estimates to the Commission (Art. 15 (k));

12. To prepare its annual work schedule, giving priority to tasks entrusted to it by the Commission (Art. 15 (l));

13. To present an annual report of its operations to the Commission (Art. 15 (m));

14. To propose to the Commission an organic structure for its technical divisions and any reorganizations it may deem desirable (Art. 15 (n));

15. To hire and dismiss technical and administrative staff (Art. 15 (o));

16. To appoint the secretary of the Commission (Art. 13, Regulations of the Commission);

17. To entrust the performance of specific tasks to experts in certain fields (Art. 15 (p) of the Agreement);

18. To call for periodic meetings of national entities charged with the formulation or execution of economic policy and, particularly, those in charge of planning (Art. 15 (q));

19. To request the president of the Commission to call special meetings (Art. 10);

20. To convoke the Advisory Committee (Art. 20);

21. To maintain close contact with the directors and the executive chairman of the Andean Development Corporation for the purpose of establishing an adequate coordination of activities (Art. 24);

22. To determine, at its own initiative or upon request of a party, whether a measure that is unilaterally imposed by a member country constitutes a "charge" or a "restraint" (Art. 43);

23. To decide whether it is possible to propose programs with respect to products which have been reserved but not yet incorporated in programs already adopted, for the purposes of the extension of the period of time indicated in Article 47 to December 31, 1975;

24. To exclude some products from the list of those reserved for sectorial programs of industrial development (Art. 53, last par.);

327

25. To verify whether Colombia, Chile or Peru have not initiated the production of goods reserved for their benefit, or whether their projects are not in process of execution, for the purposes of application of the last section of Article 50 of the Agreement. In this case, the Board shall communicate the results of its verification to the member countries. The benefits derived from the reserve established in Article 50 of the Agreement shall cease from the date of the Junta's communication (Art. 50);

26. To certify as exceptions from the rules determined by Article 54 of the Agreement any alterations introduced by Bolivia and Ecuador in their tariffs (Art. 54);

27. To authorize the maintenance of some products in the schedules of exceptions of the member countries beyond the terms indicated in Articles 55 and 102 of the Agreement by fixing the duration of the extension and the conditions for future disencumbrance (Arts. 55 and 102);

28. To authorize a member country to incorporate in its schedule of exceptions those products which, although having been reserved for sectorial programs of industrial development, had not been so programmed (Art. 56);

29. To determine when substantial trade has existed or whether there is a definite expectancy that it will exist between Bolivia or Ecuador and the remaining member countries, for the purposes of application of Article 58 of the Agreement;

30. To verify the fact that production in certain commodities has commenced in the Subregion for the purposes of application of the final paragraph of Article 65 of the Agreement;

31. To verify the existence of temporary deficiencies in supply which may affect any member country, for the purposes of application of Article 67 of the Agreement;

32. To supervise the application of rules on commercial competition (Art. 75);

33. To authorize a member country to adopt corrective measures in compliance with the rules on commercial competition (Art. 77);

34. To negotiate all measures necessary to accelerate agro-livestock development in Bolivia and Ecuador and their participation in an expanded market (Art. 71);

35. To authorize member countries to apply corrective measures of a temporary nature and in nondiscrimatory manner and to analyze periodically the progress of the situation in conformance with the prosions of Article 79 of the Agreement;

36. To verify the existence of disorders caused by a monetary devaluation effected by one member country, making the recommendations and reviewing the situation referred to in Article 80 of the Agreement;

37. To fix or amend, upon its own initiative or at the request of a party, the specific requirements of origin for products so requiring it (Art. 83);

38. To supervise compliance with the norms and requirements of origin (Art. 85);

39. To certify whether imports proceeding from Bolivia and Ecuador result in serious disadvantages to the other member countries, for the purposes of application of Articles 72 and 79 of the Agreement (Art. 99);

40.	To qualify as luxuries or nonessential certain commodities not as yet being produced within the Subregion, for the purposes of their liberalization by Bolivia and Ecuador (Art. 100 (e));

41.	To evaluate periodically the results achieved by Bolivia and Ecuador in their interchange with the other member countries (Art. 101);

42.	To maintain relations with international organizations and other entities for purposes of information and examination of matters of interest to the subregional integration process;

43.	To negotiate for technical assistance with governments, international advisory agencies and other entities and arrange the terms under which such assistance can be furnished;

44.	To maintain and administer the patrimony of the Cartagena Agreement;

45.	To organize the secretariat services required by the Commission, the committees, government expert groups, international advisory working groups and other meetings called by the Commission or the Board;

46.	To exercise any other powers expressly conferred on it by the Cartagena Agreement (Art. 15 (r)).

CHAPTER III

Coordinator of the Board

Article 8. The Board shall have a coordinator who shall perform his functions for a period of one year.

The members of the Board shall exercise this function in an order to be determined by lot. In case of absence or impediment of the incumbent, his functions shall be performed temporarily by the Board member next in line according to the order determined by lot.

Article 9. The coordinator shall legally represent the Board and perform other internal functions that the Board may entrust to him.

CHAPTER IV

Proposals of the Board

Article 10. The Board shall adopt its proposals by the unanimous vote of its members, but it may present for consideration of the Commission alternative proposals also approved unanimously.

In the same way, the Board may modify its proposals while they are being discussed by the Commission.

CHAPTER V

Resolutions of the Board

Article 11. In those matters in which the Board has its own decision-making powers, as contained in the text of the Agreement or delegated by the Commission, it shall express its will in the form of Resolutions, which shall be numbered consecutively.

The director-secretary shall authenticate the Resolutions and other acts of the Board.

Article 12. The will of the Board shall be expressed in its Resolutions by the unanimous vote of its members.

Article 13. The Resolutions of the Board shall enter into force on the date in which they are approved. They shall be communicated to the member countries through the national organs referred to in Article 15 (i) of the Agreement by letter sent by the director-secretary.

Furthermore, within 24 hours following the approval of a Resolution, the director-secretary shall cable an extract of its text to the national organ referred to without disregarding other additional forms of publicity that may be considered opportune.

The director-secretary shall leave a record of his compliance with the above formalities and the date of the communications.

Article 14. The Resolutions of the Board shall contain:

1. The form "The Board of the Cartagena Agreement";

2. An indication of the provisions that serve as a basis for the Resolution, preceded by the words "Having Seen", and the reasons that motivate it, preceded by the word "Whereas"; and

3. The text of the Resolution, following the word "Resolves".

Article 15. The resolutive part shall be divided into articles. In cases where its provisions involve obligations for the member countries, the date of their entry into force shall be indicated.

CHAPTER VI

Internal Organization of the Board

Article 16. The internal organization of the Board shall be the following:

1. Office of the Board

2. Departments and technical offices.

Article 17. The Board shall organize its Office and its technical departments as well as any other dependencies in the form which it considers most convenient to carry out in the best manner the functions that have been assigned to it in the Agreement. On its organization and its reforms it shall report to the Commission in due course.

COMMON REGIME OF TREATMENT OF FOREIGN CAPITAL AND OF TRADEMARKS, PATENTS, LICENSES, AND ROYALTIES *

(Decision 24 of the Commission, December 31, 1970, as amended) **

THE COMMISSION OF THE CARTAGENA AGREEMENT

IN VIEW of Articles 26 and 27 of the Cartagena Agreement and Proposal No. 4 of the Board;

WHEREAS In the Declaration of Bogotá it was recognized that foreign capital "can make a considerable contribution to the economic development of Latin America, provided it stimulates capital formation in the country where it is established, facilitates extensive participation of national capital in that process, and does not create obstacles to regional integration."

In the same document the governments proposed the adoption of "standards that will facilitate the use of modern technology, without limiting the market for products manufactured with foreign technical assistance and the coordination of foreign investments with general development plans."

In the Declaration of Punta del Este the Presidents of America stated: "Integration must be fully at the service of Latin America. This requires the strengthening of Latin American enterprise through vigorous financial and

---

* English version from International Legal Materials, Vol. XVI, No. 1, 1977.
** This text of Decision 24 incorporates the amendments introduced by Decision 37 (June 1971), 37-a (July 1971) and 70 (February 1973), of the Commission, as well as the more recent and substantive ones that were introduced by Decisions 103 and 109 (1976).

technical support that will permit it to develop and supply the regional market efficiently. " And they recognized that: "Foreign private enterprise will be able to fill an important function in assuring achievement of the objectives of integration within the pertinent policies of each of the countries of Latin America";

The Ministers of Foreign Affairs of the Member Countries of the Cartagena Agreement, at their first meeting in Lima, confirmed the conviction expressed in the Consensus of Viña del Mar that "economic growth and social progress are the responsibilites of their peoples and that attainment of national and regional objectives depend fundamentally on the effort of each country"; reaffirmed their determined support of "the sovereign right of every country to dispose freely of its national resources"; adopted as a common policy "to give preference in the economic development of the subregion to authentically national capital and enterprises of the Member Countries" and recognized that the investment of foreign capital and the transfer of foreign technology constitute a necessary contribution to the development of Member Countries and that they "must receive guaranties of stability in the measure in which they really constitute a positive contribution".

DECLARES:

1. The programming of subregional development and the expansion of the market will generate new investment requirements in the various sectors of production. Consequently, it is necessary to establish common rules for foreign investment which will be consistent with the new conditions created by the Cartagena Agreement, in order that the advantages deriving from it may benefit national or mixed enterprises as defined therein.

2. The contribution of foreign capital and technology can play an important part in subregional development and help with the national effort to the extent that it constitutes an effective contribution toward attaining the objectives of integration and reaching the goals indicated in national development plans.

3. The standards of the common regime must clearly set forth the rights and obligations of foreign investors and the guaranties that will protect foreign investments in the subregion. In addition, they must be stable enough to work for the mutual benefit of the investors and the Member Countries.

4. The treatment given to foreign capital may not discriminate against national investors.

5. One of the fundamental objectives of the common regime must be the strengthening of national enterprises, in order to enable them to participate actively in the subregional market.

6. In line with this order of ideas, national enterprises must have the best possible access to the modern technology and new administrative practices of the contemporary world. At the same time, it is necessary to establish efficient mechanisms and procedures for the production and protection of technology in the territory of the subregion and to improve the terms under which foreign technology is acquired.

7. With the purpose of attaining the objectives set forth herein, common standards must contemplate mechanisms and procedures which are sufficiently efficient to make possible a growing participation of national capital in existing or future foreign enterprises in Member Countries, in such a way as to lead to the organization of mixed enterprises in which national capital has the majority interest and in which national interests will have the capacity to participate in determining fashion in the basic decisions of such companies. When the participation of national capital is represented by contributions of the State or of State enterprises, it may be less than the majority interest, provided its determining capacity in decision-making is guaranteed.

8. In compliance with the general spirit of the Cartagena Agreement and with the provisions of Article 92 thereof, the common regime must set standards "that will compensate for the structural deficiencies of Bolivia

and Ecuador and ensure the mobilization and assignment of the resources needed for fulfillment of the objectives contemplated in the Agreement in their favor. "

9. The common regime should also tend to strengthen the negotiating capacity of the Member Countries vis-à-vis other countries, enterprises which supply capital and technology, and international organizations which are concerned with these matters.

DECIDES

To approve the following:

COMMON REGIME OF TREATMENT OF FOREIGN
CAPITAL AND OF TRADEMARKS, PATENTS,
LICENSES, AND ROYALTIES

CHAPTER I

Article 1. For the purposes of this regime, the following definitions are understood:

Direct Foreign Investment: Contributions, coming from abroad and belonging to foreign natural or juridical persons, made to the capital of an enterprise, in freely convertible currency, or the physical or tangible goods indicated in II (b) of Annex No. 1, and having the right to repatriation of their value and the transfer of profits abroad.

Likewise, investments in national currency from funds which are entitled to be transferred abroad and the reinvestments which are made in accordance with this regime shall be considered to be foreign investments.

National investor: The State, national individuals, national non-profit entities, and the national enterprises defined in this Article.

Foreign nationals with consecutive residence in the recipient country of no less than one year, who renounce before the competent national authority the right to repatriate the capital and to transfer profits abroad, shall also be considered to be national investors. In cases when it may be justified, the national competent entity of the host country may exempt said persons from the requirement of uninterrupted residency for not less than one year.

Each Member Country may exempt foreign natural persons whose investments have been generated internally from the obligation to renounce established in the preceding paragraph.

Likewise, the investments of property of subregional investors shall be considered (equivalent to the investments of) national investors under the following conditions: *

a) The investment must be previously authorized by the country of origin of the investor, when the corresponding national legislation so provides;

b) The investment must be submitted for the prior approval of the host country and be registered by the national competent entity which shall request certification from the national competent entity of the country of origin notifying it of the investment made;

c) The repatriation of capital and the transfer of earnings syall be subject to the provisions of this Decision and the national competent entities shall not authorize such remissions except to the territory of the Member Country of origin of the capital;

d) The national competent entities shall not authorize subregional investments in enterprises which produce or exploit products assigned in an Industrial Sectoral

---

* /Translator's note: These provisions are almost identical to those of Article 3 (as modified by Article 35 of Decision 70) and Article 5 of Decision 46 on Andean multinational enterprises./

Development Program to a Member Country different from the host country, except in cases of programs of co-production or complementation previously agreed upon.

Subregional Investor: The national investor of any Member Country different from the host country.

Foreign Investor: The owner of a direct foreign investment.

National Enterprise: An enterprise organized in the recipient country, more than 80% of whose capital belongs to national investors, provided that in the opinion of the competent national authority, that proportion is reflected in the technical, financial, administrative, and commercial management of the enterprise.

Mixed Enterprise: An enterprise organized in the recipient country and whose capital belongs to national investors in a proportion which may fluctuate between 51% and 80%, provided that in the opinion of the appropriate national authority, that proportion is reflected in the technical, financial, administrative, and commercial management of the enterprise. *

_____

   * /Decision 110 of November 30, 1976, addresses the need to define the treatment to be accorded the investment of a mixed enterprise. It states:
   "Art. 1.   The Commission, upon the proposal of the Junta, shall decide at its XXII Regular Sessions the treatment to be accorded to the investments of a mixed enterprise.
   "Art. 2.   The Junta shall present its proposal no later than February 14, 1977.
   "Art. 3.   Until then, for the purpose of classifying the resulting enterprise, the investments of a mixed enterprise shall be calculated in the same national and foreign proportion as the national and foreign contributions made to the capital of the mixed enterprise; in the cases of Bolivia and Ecuador, the classification of such investments shall be governed by that which is established by the national competent entities."/

Foreign Enterprise: An enterprise organized or established in the recipient country whose capital in the hands of national investors amounts to less than 51% or, if that percentage is higher, it is not reflected in the opinion of the proper national authority, in the technical, financial, administrative, and commercial management of the enterprise.

New Investment: Investment made after July 1, 1971, in either existing or new enterprises.

Reinvestment: Investment of all or part of undistributed profits resulting from a direct foreign investment, in the same enterprise which produced them.

Portfolio Development Bonds: * These are titles or obligations issued for development purposes and publicly offered by the State, State entities, quasi-State entities, national and mixed enterprises or by the Andean Development Corporation the acquisition of which does not confer, in any case, the right to participate in the technical, financial, administrative or commercial direction of the issuing entity and which must always be qualified, for this purpose, by the competent national authority.

Recipient Country: The country in which the direct foreign investment is made.

Commission: The Commission of the Cartagena Agreement.

Board: The Board of the Cartagena Agreement.

Member Country: One of the Member Countries of the Cartagena Agreement.

Article 2. All foreign investors who wish to invest in one of the Member Countries must submit an application

---

* /Note: Added by Article 33 of Decision 70. Decision 70 appears at 12 I. L. M. 349./

to the competent national authority, which, after evaluating it, will authorize the investment when it corresponds to the development priorities of the recipient country. The application must follow the model indicated in Annex No. 1 of the regime.

Upon the proposal of the Board, the Commission may approve common criteria for the evaluation of direct foreign investments in the Member Countries.

Article 3. Member Countries shall not authorize any direct foreign investment in activities which they consider are adequately covered by existing enterprises.

Likewise, they shall not authorize any direct foreign investment of which the purpose is to acquire shares, participations, or rights owned by national or subregional investors.

Direct foreign investments made in a national enterprise to prevent its imminent bankruptcy are excepted from the provisions of the preceding paragraph, provided the following conditions are met:

a) That the agency in charge of supervising corporations in the respective country, or its equivalent, verifies that bankruptcy is imminent;

b) That the enterprise proves that it has granted an option to purchase preferably to national or subregional investors; and

c) That the foreign investor agrees to place on sale the shares, participations, or rights that he may acquire in the enterprise for purchase by national investors, in a percentage necessary to constitute a national enterprise, within a period not exceeding 15 years, which period will be established in each case according to the characteristics of the business sector. The authorization issued by the competent national authority shall specify the period of time and the conditions under which that obligation will be met, the way in which the value of the shares, participations, or rights will be determined at the time they are sold, and,

341

if pertinent, the systems by which the transfer of the latter to national investors will be ensured.

Article 4. Authorization for foreign investors to participate in national or mixed enterprises may be given, provided that it signifies increasing the capital of the respective enterprise and that the enterprise at least maintains its mixed classification.

Article 5. All direct foreign investments shall be registered with the competent national authority, together with the agreement specifying the terms of the authorization. The amount of the investment shall be registered in freely convertible currency.

Article 6. The authority which registers the investment, in coordination with the competent state divisions or bureaus in each case, shall be responsible for supervising the fulfillment of the obligations contracted by foreign investors.

In addition to the functions indicated in other provisions of this regime and those established in the regulations, the competent national authority shall:

a) Supervise fulfillment of the commitments for national participation in the enterprise's technical, administrative, financial, and commercial management, and in its capital;

b) Authorize in exceptional cases the purchase of shares, participations, or rights of national or mixed enterprises by foreign investors, in accordance with the provisions of Articles 3 and 4 of the present regime;

c) Establish an information and price control system of the intermediate products that may be furnished by suppliers of foreign technology or capital;

d) Authorize the transfer abroad, in freely convertible currency, of all amounts which enterprises or investors are entitled to transfer in accordance with this regime and with the national laws of the country concerned;

e) Centralize the statistical, accounting, information, and supervisory records connected with direct foreign investments; and

f) Authorize licensing contracts for the use of imported technology, trademarks and patents.

Article 7. Foreign investors shall be entitled to re-export the invested capital when they sell their shares, participations, or rights to national investors or when liquidation of the enterprise occurs.

The sale of shares, participations, or rights, of a foreign investor to another foreign investor must be previously authorized by the competent national authority and will not be considered as re-exportation of capital.

The subregional investor shall have the right to repatriate the capital invested when the shares, participations or other rights are sold to national or subregional investors, or when the enterprise is liquidated.

Article 8. Re-exportable capital is understood to be the capital formed by the total of the original direct foreign investment which is registered and actually made, plus the reinvestments made in the same enterprise in accordance with the provisions of this regime and minus the net losses, if any.

In cases of participation of national investors, the foregoing provisions shall be understood to be limited to the percentage of direct foreign investment in connection with the reinvestments made and with the net losses.

Article 9. In the case of liquidation of the enterprise, the difference between the real value of the net assets and the re-exportable capital as defined in the previous article shall be considered as capital gain and may be transferred abroad after payment of the pertinent taxes.

Article 10. Foreign investors shall have the right to transfer abroad the amounts obtained from the sale of their shares, participations, or rights, after payment of the pertinent taxes.

Article 11. Conversion of the amounts that a foreign investor may have the right to transfer abroad shall be made at the rate of exchange prevailing at the time of drawing the draft.

Article 12. Reinvestment of profits earned by foreign enterprises shall be considered to be new investments and may not be made without previous authorization and registration.

Article 13. Governments of the Member Countries may permit reinvestment of the profits received by a foreign enterprise without any special authorization, up to an amount not exceeding 7% per year of the company's capital. In these cases, the obligation to register is still in force.

The governments of the Member Countries may allow foreign enterprises, without the necessity of special authorization, to apply their undistributed earnings to the acquisition of Portfolio Development Bonds when the total of these purchases plus reinvested earnings, in conformity with the preceding paragraph, does not exceed, when considered together, 7% of the capital of the particular enterprise. In these cases, the purchase of such bonds shall be considered to be a reinvestment and the obligation to register them shall continue to prevail.

The foreign enterprise may apply its other undistributed earnings to the acquisition of Portfolio Development Bonds, but in such cases they will not benefit from the treatment referred to in the preceding paragraph. *

Article 14. Foreign credits contracted by an enterprise require previous authorization by, and must be registered with, the appropriate agency.

---

* /Note: Paragraphs 2 and 3 were added by Article 34 of Decision 70. By Decision 103 the percentage was raised from 5% to 7%./

Global limits on foreign indebtedness may be authorized for specified periods. Credit contracts concluded
within the authorized global limits must be registered with
the appropriate authority.

Article 15. Governments of the Member Countries
shall refrain from endorsing or guaranteeing in any form,
either directly or through official or semi-official institutions, external credit transactions carried out by foreign
enterprises in which the State does not participate.

Article 16. Transfers abroad made by enterprises
covering amortization or interest because of the use of
foreign credits shall be authorized in accordance with
terms of the registered contract.

For foreign credit contracts concluded between the
parent company and its affiliates or between affiliates of
the same foreign enterprise, the real rate of annual interest may not exceed by more than three points the rate of
interest of first-class securities prevailing in the financial
market of the country of origin of the currency in which the
transaction is registered. For external credit contracts
other than those indicated above, the real rate of annual
interest to be paid by the enterprises will be determined by
the competent national authority and it must be closely related to the prevailing conditions of the financial market of
the country in which the transaction has been registered.

For the purposes of this article, real interest is
understood to be the total cost that must be paid by the
debtor for the use of the credit, including commissions
and expenses of all kinds.

Article 17. In regard to domestic credit, foreign
enterprises shall not have access to long-term credit.
The terms and conditions of access to short- and medium-
term credit shall be those established in the respective
national legislation covering this matter, with medium-
term credit considered as that which does not exceed three
years.

Article 18. All contracts on the importation of technology and on patents and trademarks must be examined and submitted for the approval of the competent authority of the Member Country, which must appraise the effective contribution of the goods incorporating the technology, or other specific forms of measuring the effects of the imported technology.

Article 19. Contracts on importation of technology must contain, at least, clauses on the following subjects:

a) Identification of the terms of the transfer of technology;

b) Contractual value of each of the elements concerned in the transfer of technology, expressed in a form similar to that followed in the registration of direct foreign investments; and

c) Determination of the time period involved.

Article 20. Member Countries shall not authorize the conclusion of contracts for the transfer of foreign technology or patents which contain:

a) Clauses by virtue of which the furnishing of technology imposes the obligation for the recipient country or enterprise to acquire from a specific source capital goods, intermediate products, raw materials, and other technologies or of permanently employing personnel indicated by the enterprise which supplies the technology. In exceptional cases, the recipient country may accept clauses of this nature for the acquisition of capital goods, intermediate products or raw materials, provided that their price corresponds to current levels in the international market;

b) Clauses pursuant to which the enterprise selling the technology reserves the right to fix the sale or resale prices of the products manufactured on the basis of the technology;

c) Clauses that contain restrictions regarding the volume and structure of production;

d) Clauses that prohibit the use of competitive technologies;

e)   Clauses that establish a full or partial purchase option in favor of the supplier of the technology;

f)   Clauses that obligate the purchaser of technology to transfer to the supplier the inventions or improvements that may be obtained through the use of the technology;

g)   Clauses that require payment of royalties to the owners of patents for patents which are not used; and

h)   Other clauses with equivalent effects.

Save in exceptional cases, duly appraised by the competent authority of the recipient country, no clauses shall be accepted in which exportation of the products manufactured on the basis of the technology is prohibited or limited in any way.

In no case shall clauses of this nature be accepted in connection with subregional trade or the exportation of similar products to third countries.

Article 21.   Intangible technological contributions shall grant the right to payment of royalties, upon authorization by the competent national authority, but they may not be computed as capital contributions.

When these contributions are furnished to a foreign enterprise by its parent company or by another affiliate thereof, no payment of royalties shall be authorized and no deductions will be allowed in this connection for tax purposes.

Article 22.   National authorities will undertake a continuous and systematic task of identification of available technologies on the world market for the various industrial fields, in order to have available the most favorable and advisable alternative solutions for the economic conditions of the subregion, and will forward the results of their work to the Board. This action will be carried on in coordination with the action adopted under Chapter V of this regime in connection with the production of national or subregional technology.

Article 23. Before November 30, 1972, the Commission, upon the recommendation of the Board, will approve a program directed toward promoting and protecting the production of subregional technology, as well as the adaptation and assimilation of existing technologies.

This program shall contain, among other elements:

a) Special tax or other benefits to encourage the production of technology and especially that connected with the intensive use of input items of subregional origin or those designed to make efficient use of subregional productive factors;

b) Development of exports to third countries of products manufactured on the basis of subregional technology; and

c) Channeling of domestic savings toward the establishment of subregional or national research and development centers.

Article 24. The governments of the Member Countries shall give preference in their purchases to products that include technology of subregional origin in such form as the Commission may consider advisable. On the recommendation of the Board, the Commission may propose to the Member Countries the establishment of charges on products which use trademarks of foreign origin for which royalties have to be paid when generally known or easily accessible technology is used in their production.

Article 25. Licensing contracts for the utilization of trademarks of foreign origin in the territory of the Member Countries may not contain certain restrictive clauses such as:

a) Prohibition or limitation on the exportation or sale in certain countries of the products manufactured under the trademark concerned, or similar products;

b) Obligation to use raw materials, intermediate goods, and equipment supplied by the owner of the trademark or his affiliates. In exceptional cases, the recipient country may accept clauses of this nature provided the prices correspond to current levels on the international market;

    c)   Fixing of sale or resale prices of the products manufactured under the trademark;

    d)   Obligation to pay royalties to the owner of the trademark for unused trademarks;

    e)   Obligation permanently to employ personnel supplied or indicated by the owner of the trademark; and

    f)   Other obligations of equivalent effect.

Article 26. At the proposal of the Board, the Commission may indicate production processes products, or groups of products, with respect to which no patent privileges may be granted in any of the Member Countries. Likewise, it may decide on the treatment of privileges already granted.

CHAPTER II

Article 27. The advantages deriving from the duty-free program of the Cartagena Agreement shall be enjoyed only by products produced by national or mixed enterprises of the Member Countries, as well as by foreign enterprises which are in the process of being transformed into national or mixed enterprises, pursuant to the terms of this Chapter.

Article 28. Foreign enterprises that currently exist in the territory of any Member Country and that wish to enjoy the advantages deriving from the duty-free program of the Cartagena Agreement for their products must agree with the competent authority of the recipient country, within three years following the date the present regime enters into force, to their gradual and progressive transformation into national or mixed enterprises, in accordance with the provisions of Article 31.

At the end of the aforesaid three-year period, there must be in all cases a participacion of national investors in the capital of the enterprises of no less than 15%.

The time period in which this transformation must be carried out may not exceed 15 years in Colombia, Peru, and Venezuela, nor 20 years in Bolivia and Ecuador, starting from January 1, 1974.

Upon completion of two-thirds of the time period agreed for the transformation, there must be a participation of national investors in the capital of the said enterprise of no less than 45%.

Foreign enterprises that currently exist will be understood to be those that are legally organized or established in the territory of the respective country on January 1, 1974.

Article 29. The national authorities responsible for issuing certificates of origin of merchandise shall grant such certificates to products produced by currently existing foreign enterprises which, within the period of three years referred to in the first paragraph of Article 28, formally express to the government of the recipient country their intention to transform into national or mixed enterprises.

The products of currently existing foreign enterprises which do not enter into the agreement to transform themselves into national or mixed enterprises within the aforesaid three-year period may not enjoy the advantages deriving from the duty-free program of the Agreement, and consequently they shall not be issued a certificate of origin by the competent authority.

Article 30. Foreign enterprises that may be established in the territory of any Member Country after July 1, 1971, shall agree, in representation of their shareholders, to place on sale for purchase by national investors, gradually and progressively, in accordance with the provisions of Article 31, the percentage of their shares participations or rights necessary for the transformation

of such enterprises into mixed enterprises, within a period
which may not exceed 15 years in Colombia, Chile and
Peru, and 20 years in Bolivia and Ecuador.

In the case of Colombia, Chile, and Peru, the agreement must stipulate a participation of national investors
in the capital of the enterprise of no less than 15% at the
time production begins, no less than 30% upon completion
of one-third of the agreed period, and no less than 45%
upon completion of two-thirds of that period.

In the case of Bolivia and Ecuador, the progressive
participation of national investors in the capital of the
enterprise must be no less than 5% three years after production begins, no less than 10% upon completion of one-
third and no less than 35% upon completion of two-thirds of
the agreed period.

/In figuring the percentages referred to in this Article, any participation of subregional investors or of the
Andean Development Corporation shall be counted as national investors./ *

In all cases the period of 20 years with respect to
Bolivia and Ecuador shall start to be counted two years
after production begins.

Article 31. Agreements on the transformation of
foreign enterprises into mixed enterprises must stipulate
the following items, among others:

a)   The period of time for compliance with the obligation to transform the foreign enterprise into a mixed
enterprise;

b)   The gradual scale for the transfer of shares,
participations, or rights to national investors, including

---

* /This paragraph as well as Article 2(2) of Decision
46 were deleted by Article 4 of Decision 109. With the addition of subregional investors these paragraphs became
superfluous./

in that gradual scale, at least, the rules on minimum percentages referred to in Articles 28 and 30;

c) Regulations that will ensure the progressive participation of national investors or their representatives in the technical, financial, commercial, and administrative management of the enterprise, at least as of the date on which the enterprise begins production;

d) The method of determining the value of the shares, participations, or rights at the time of their sale; and

e) The systems that will ensure the transfer of shares, participations, or rights to national investors.

The transformation of a foreign enterprise to national or mixed, in the terms of this Decision, may also occur as a result of an increase of capital.

Article 32. The products of foreign enterprises shall enjoy the advantages deriving from the duty-free program of the Cartagena Agreement during the period of time agreed for their transformation into mixed enterprises under the conditions agreed to in the pertinent agreement. If the enterprise should fail to fulfill the obligations of the agreement or if at the end of the agreed period the transformation of the foreign enterprise into a mixed enterprise has not been carried out, its products will cease to enjoy the advantages of the duty-free program, and consequently they will not be covered by certificates of origin.

Article 33. With respect to the matters covered by this regime, the rights established herein for foreign and mixed enterprises are the maximum which may be granted to them by the Member Countries.

Article 34. Foreign enterprises of whose production 80% or more goes into exports to the markets of third countries shall not be obligated to abide by the provisions of this Chapter. In that case, the products of such enterprises may not enjoy in any way the advantages deriving from the duty-free program of the Cartagena Agreement.

In the same manner as foreign enterprises of whose production 80% or more is for exportation to third country markets, foreign or mixed enterprises in the tourism sector shall not be subject to the norms of Chapter II of Decision 24.

Article 35. The obligation upon foreign enterprises to place on sale certain percentages of the shares, participations, or rights of foreign enterprises in favor of national investors referred to in Articles 3, 28, and 30 shall be controlled by the competent national authority concerned. This obligation shall be fulfilled by sale to private individuals, to the State, or to State enterprises of the recipient country.

Article 36. Mixed enterprises shall be considered to be those in which the State or State enterprises participate, even if the participation is less than 51% of the capital, provided that the State representation has a determining capacity in the decisions of the enterprise. It shall be the duty of the Commission, on recommendation of the Board, to establish the minimum percentage of participation of the State or of the State enterprises referred to in this article, within three months following the date on which the present regime enters into force.

Article 37. Upon authorization by the competent national authority, the owners of a direct foreign investment shall have the right to transfer abroad, in freely convertible currency, the verified net profits resulting from the direct foreign investment, but not in excess of 20% of that investment annually.

However, each Member Country may authorize greater percentages and shall communicate to the Commission the provisions or decisions taken in this respect.

The national competent entity may also authorize the investment of excess distributed earnings, in which case (such investments) shall be considered (to be) direct foreign investment.

CHAPTER III

SPECIAL REGULATIONS BY SECTORS

Article 38. Each Member Country may reserve sectors of economic activity for national, public, or private enterprises and determine whether the participation of mixed enterprises in those sectors shall be admitted.

Without prejudice to the provisions of other articles of this Chapter, the Commission, on the recommendation of the Board, may determine the sectors which all the Member Countries shall reserve for national, public, or private enterprises, and determine whether participation of mixed enterprises shall be admitted in them.

Article 39. Foreign enterprises in the sectors referred to in this Chapter shall not be obligated to abide by the provisions of the previous Chapter regarding the transformation of foreign enterprises into national or mixed enterprises. However, they shall be subject to the other provisions of the common regime and to special provisions specified in Articles 40 to 43, inclusive.

Article 40. During the first ten years of the life of this regime, the activities of foreign enterprises in the sector of basic products under the concession system may be authorized, provided the duration of the contract does not exceed 20 years.

For purposes of this regime, the basic-products sector is understood to mean the one comprising the primary activities of exploration and exploitation of minerals of any kind, including liquid and gaseous hydrocarbons, gas pipelines, oil pipelines, and exploitation of forests. For Bolivia and Ecuador, this sector also includes primary agricultural and livestock activities.

Member countries shall not authorize deductions on account of depletion to be made for tax purposes by enterprises investing in this sector.

The participation of foreign enterprises in the exploration and exploitation of liquid and gaseous hydrocarbons shall be authorized preferably in the form of contracts of association with State enterprises of the recipient country.

Member Countries may grant foreign enterprises established in this sector treatment different from that provided in Article 37.

Article 41. The establishment of foreign enterprises or new direct foreign investment shall not be permitted in the sector of public services. Investments which had to be made by currently existing foreign enterprises in order to operate under technically and economically efficient conditions are excepted from this rule.

For these purposes, public services are considered to be those that provide drinking water, sewers, electric power and lighting, cleaning and sanitary, telephone, postal and telecommunications services.

Article 42. New direct foreign investment shall not be permitted in the sector of insurance, commercial banking, and other financing institutions.

Foreign banks which currently exist in the territory of the Member Countries shall cease receiving local deposits in current accounts, savings accounts, or time deposits within a period of three years from the date on which this regime enters into force.

Currently existing foreign banks which desire to continue accepting local deposits of any kind must convert into national enterprises, for which purpose they must place on sale shares representing at least 80% of their capital to be purchased by national investors within the period of time indicated in the previous paragraph.

355

Article 43. New direct foreign investment shall not
be permitted in domestic transportation enterprises, ad-
vertising enterprises, commercial radio stations, tele-
vision stations, newspapers, magazines, or enterprises
engaged in domestic marketing enterprises of products of
any kind.

Foreign enterprises which currently operate in these
sectors must convert into national enterprises, for which
purpose they must place on sale at least 80% of their shares
for purchase by national investors within a period not exceeding three years from the date on which this regime
enters into force.

Article 44. When, in the opinion of the recipient
country, special circumstances exist, that country may
apply other regulations than those provided in Articles 40
to 43 inclusive.

The products of foreign enterprises included in the
sectors of this Chapter which do not agree to convert into
national or mixed enterprises, or with respect to which
the Member Countries apply different regulations than
those referred to in the previous paragraph, shall not
enjoy the advantages of the duty-free program of the
Cartagena Agreement.

CHAPTER IV

Article 45. The capital of stock companies must be
represented in registered shares.

Bearer shares that currently exist must be converted
into registered shares within a period of one year from
the date on which this regime enters into force.

Article 46. When projects are concerned that per-
tain to products reserved for Bolivia or Ecuador by application of Article 50 of the Cartagena Agreement, the
four remaining countries agree not to authorize direct
foreign investment in their territories, except as stipulated in contracts signed before December 31, 1970.

Article 47. Upon the proposal of the Board, the Commission shall approve, no later than November 30, 1971, an agreement to avoid double taxation among the Member Countries.

Within the same period of time, the Commission, acting on the recommendation of the Board, shall approve a model agreement for the conclusion of arrangements on double taxation between the Member Countries and other states outside the subregion. In the meantime, the Member Countries shall refrain from concluding agreements of this nature with any country outside the subregion.

Article 48. The Member Countries agree to keep each other informed and to inform the Board regarding the implementation of this regime in their territories, particularly regarding the rules of Chapter II. Likewise, they agree to establish a continuing system for the exchange of information regarding authorizations for foreign investment or the importation of technology that they may grant in their territories, in order to facilitate a growing harmonization of their policies and to improve their negotiating capacity in order to obtain conditions no less favorable for the recipient country than those that have been negotiated in similar cases with any other Member Country.

Likewise, they agree closely to coordinate their action in the international organizations and forums which consider subjects relating to foreign investments or the transfer of technology.

Article 49. Without prejudice to the provisions of Articles 79, 81, and 99 of the Cartagena Agreement, any Member Country which considers that it is being harmed by imports of products from foreign enterprises made under the duty-free program of the Agreement, may apply to the Board for authorization to adopt the necessary corrective measures to prevent the damage.

Article 50. Member Countries shall not grant to foreign investors any treatment more favorable than that granted to national investors.

Article 51.   In no instrument relating to invest‐
ments or the transfer of technology shall there be clauses
that remove possible conflicts or controversies from the
national jurisdiction and competence on the recipient coun‐
try to allow the subrogation by States to the rights and
actions of their national investors.

Differences between Member Countries of this re‐
gime in regard to its interpretation or implementation
shall be resolved by following the procedure indicated in
Chapter II, Section D, "on the settlement of controversies"
of the Cartagena Agreement.

CHAPTER V

Article 52.   In accordance with the provisions of
this regime and of Chapter II of the Cartagena Agreement,
the Committee and the Board shall have the following
powers and duties:

The Commission

a)   Decides on recommendations submitted by the
Board for its consideration with respect to the treatment
of foreign capital, industrial property, and the system of
the production and marketing of technology, in compliance
with this regime;

b)   Approves, on the recommendation of the Board,
the regulations necessary for effective implementation of
the common regime; and

c)   Adopts other measures which tend to facilitate
the attainment of its objectives.

The Board

a)   Supervises the implementation and fulfillment
of the regime and of the regulations approved by the
Commission on this subject;

b)   Centralizes statistical, accounting, and other types of information relating to foreign investments or the transfer of technology, coming from Member Countries;

c)   Compiles economic and legal information regarding foreign investments and transfers of technology and furnishes it to Member Countries; and

d)   Recommends to the Commission necessary measures and regulations for the effective implementation of this regime.

Article 53.   In adopting decisions on the matters covered by this regime, the Commission shall follow the procedures established in Article 11 (a) of the Cartagena Agreement.

Article 54.   Member Countries shall establish a Subregional Industrial Property Office, which shall have the following functions:

a)   To serve as liaison between the national industrial property offices;

b)   To compile information on industrial property and distribute it to the national offices;

c)   To prepare model licensing contracts for the use of trademarks and patents in the Subregion;

d)   To advise national offices on all matters connected with the implementation of common regulations on industrial property adopted in the regulations referred to in Provisional Article G;

e)   To carry out studies and to submit recommendations to the Member Countries on invention patents.

Article 55.   Upon the recommendation of the Board, the Commission shall establish a subregional system for the development, promotion, production, and adaptation of technology, which shall also have the duty of centralizing the information referred to in Article 22 of this regime and distributing it among the Member Countries, together with the information it obtains directly on the same subjects and on the conditions for the marketing of technology.

TEMPORARY PROVISIONS

Article A. This regime shall enter into force when all the Member Countries have deposited in the Office of the Secretary of the Board the instruments by which they put it into practice in their respective territories, in accordance with the provisions of the second paragraph of Article 27 of the Cartagena Agreement.

Article B. Foreign investments existing in the territory of the Member Countries on the date this regime enters into force must be registered with the competent national authority within the following six months.

These investments shall continue to enjoy the benefits granted by the provisions currently in force in every respect that is not contrary to this regime.

Article C. Until the regulations called for in Temporary Article G hereof enter into force, the Member Countries shall refrain from signing unilateral agreements on industrial property with third countries.

Article D. Within the three months following the date on which this regime enters into force, each Member Country shall designate the authority or authorities that are competent to authorize, register, and supervise foreign investments and the transfer of technology, and shall inform the other Member Countries and the Board of such designation.

Article E. All contracts on the importation of technology and licenses for the use of trademarks and patents of foreign origin signed prior to the date on which this regime enters into force must be registered with the competent national authority within six months following that date.

Article F. Within six months following the date on which this regime enters into force, the Commission, at the recommendation of the Board, shall approve the regulations of the Subregional Industrial Property Office.

Article G. Within six months following the date on which this regime enters into force, the Commission, at the recommendation of the Board, shall adopt regulations for implementing the rules on industrial property, which shall cover, among others, the subjects listed in Annex 2.

Article H. The Member Countries agree not to establish incentives for foreign investment other than that contemplated in their industrial development legislation at the time this regime enters into force, as long as the obligation referred to in Article 28, second paragraph, of the Cartagena Agreement, on the harmonization of industrial development legislation, has not been fulfilled.

Likewise, before November 30, 1972, the Commission, on the recommendation of the Board, shall adopt the necessary measures to harmonize the system of incentives applicable to the other sectors.

Article I. Within three months following the date on which this regime enters into force, the Commission, on the recommendation of the Board, shall determine the treatment applicable to capital belonging to national investors of any Member Country other than the recipient country.

Within the same period of time, the Commission, on the recommendation of the Board, shall determine the rules to be applied to investments made by the Andean Development Corporation in any of the Member Countries.

Article   .*   The investments of public international financial entities or of foreign governmental entities of economic cooperation, whatever may be their juridical nature, shall be considered to be neutral capital and, consequently, they shall not be computed as either national or foreign in the enterprise in which they participate.

To determine the status of the enterprise as national, mixed or foreign in which these investments participate, the neutral capital shall be excluded from the calculation base and only the percentages of participation of the national and foreign investors in the remainder of the capital shall be taken into account.

Article   .   The Commission, upon the proposal of the Junta, shall determine the necessary conditions and requirements to consider as neutral capital the investments referred to in the preceding Article and shall approve a list of the entities which may receive this treatment.

The entities referred to in the preceding paragraph shall be exempt from the obligation to sell their shares, participations or rights, but if they so decide, they may sell their shares, participations or rights to national or subregional investors, or, upon the prior authorization of the national competent entity, to foreign investors, provided that the recipient enterprise maintains at least the same proportion of national capital.

In all other respects, the investments of these entities shall be subject to the general regime established by this Decision.

---

* This and the following articles were added to Decision 24 by Decision 103. The first two were in turn modified by Decision 109. In accordance with the new Transitory Article B, these are to be numbered and incorporated into the text of Decision 24 when it is codified by the Commission.

Article ____ . The Commission, upon the proposal of the Junta, may accord, with other countries of Latin America which are not members of the Cartagena Agreement, a special treatment for the capital of their nationals.

TRANSITORY PROVISIONS

Article A. The existing (foreign) enterprises which have entered into transformation agreements prior to the entry into effect of this Decision may accord with the national competent entity that the term established for transformation begin as of January 1, 1974.

Article B. The Commission, once the Junta so proposes, shall proceed to codify Decision 24, taking into account Decision 102. *

_____
* /Decision 102 addresses the question of Chile's rights and obligations deriving from the Cartagena Agreement. /

Guide Lines for the Authorization,
Registration, and Supervision of
Foreign Investments

Every application for foreign investment must contain:

I. Identification of the investor

    a) Name or firm name;

    b) Nationality;

    c) Membership of Board of Directors;

    d) Composition of personnel and management;

    e) Economic activity;

    f) Copy of articles of incorporation.

II. Details of the investment

    a) Financial resources in foreign exchange or credit;

        Currency in which the investment is made;
        Capital of national origin;
        Capital of foreign origin;
        Credit from parent company;
        Credit from other sources;
        Actual interest to be paid on credits.

    b) Physical or tangible resources, such as:

        Industrial plants;
        New and reconditioned machinery;
        New and reconditioned equipment;
        Spare parts;
        Loose parts and accessories;
        Raw materials;
        Intermediate products.

c)   Resources derived from technology or intangibles, such as:

   Trademarks;
   Industrial designs;
   Management capacity;
   Technical know-how, patented or not patented;
   Possible alternative know-how.

Technical know-how may be presented in the following forms:

   i.   Objects:

   Samples;
   Nonregistered models;
   Machinery, apparatus, parts, tools;
   Working devices.

   ii.   Technical documents :

   Formulas, estimates;
   Plans, drawings;
   Unpatented inventions.

   iii.   Instructions:

   Notes on preparation, manufacture, and functioning of the product or the process;

   Explanations or practical advice for use;
   Technical booklets;
   Supplementary explanations of patents;
   Manufacturing diagrams;
   Supervisory methods;
   Amounts to be paid for royalties;
   Identification of the recipient of royalties.

III.   Requirements which are satisfied

   a)   Shortage of domestic savings;

   b)   Shortage of foreign exchange;

c) Lack of directive or administrative capacity;

d) Need of access to scarce technological knowledge;

e) Lack of capacity or of commercial contacts for the sale of merchandise in international markets;

f) Lack of local entrepreneurial spirit.

IV. Plan for progressive national participation

a) Percentage of shares to be placed in the hands of national investors;

b) Operating capacity;

c) Exportable production;

d) Additional employment generated;

e) Importation of raw materials or intermediate products in annual production;

f) Use of national input items.

ANNEX No. 2

Provisions of the Regulations for the
Application of Standards on
Industrial Property

a) Determination of the signs, words, symbols, or names that may be registered as trademarks;

b) Provisions on ownership of the trademark, procedures for acquiring it, persons holding the right, etc. ;

c) Standard classification of products for trademark purposes;

d) Publication and terms of opposition to the registration;

e) Priority of right to opposition;

f) Use of the privilege;

g) Lapse for failure to use;

h) Term of the privilege;

i) Negotiation of the trademark;

j) Standard causes on nullity, failure to renew, cancellation by previous registrations, etc.;

k) Classification of patents;

l) Determination of the industrial products and processes that may be patented according to the objectives of the global strategy for development of the subregion;

m) Conditions of patentability and, particularly, standard criteria to establish the innovation and the industrial application of the patent;

n) Owners of the patent;

o) Procedure for registration, opposition, method of putting the invention into practice, etc.;

p) Term of the privilege; and

q) Standards on industrial models and designs.

REGULATIONS FOR THE APPLICATION OF
RULES ON INDUSTRIAL PROPERTY *

(Decision No. 85 of the Commission
June 5, 1974)

THE COMMISSION OF THE CARTAGENA AGREEMENT

HAVING CONSIDERED: Article 27 of the Cartagena
Agreement, Transitional Article g) of Decision 24, and
Proposal 19/mod. 1 of the Board;

DECIDES:

To approve the following:

REGULATIONS FOR THE APPLICATION OF RULES
ON INDUSTRIAL PROPERTY

CHAPTER I

INVENTION PATENTS

SECTION I

Requirements for Patentability

Article 1. An invention patent shall be granted for
new creations capable of industrial application and for
those which may complement such creations.

Article 2. An invention shall not be considered
novel if already incorporated in the technical state, that
is, if it has been made publicly accessible anywhere, by
oral or written description, or by use or exploitation, or
by any other means adequate to permit its execution prior
to the date of the filing of the application for the patent.
Notwithstanding the stipulation of this article, a revelation
made within a year prior to the application filing shall not
constitute loss of novelty of the invention should the revelation be the result of:

* English version from International Legal Materials, vol.
13, November 1974, p. 1489.

368

a) Obvious abuse to the detriment of the applicant or his assignees, such as theft of plans or documents, disloyalty or breach of faith by agents or collaborators, or by employees of the inventor, industrial espionage, or other similar acts;

b) The fact that the applicant or his assignees have exhibited the invention to an exposition officially sponsored and recognized in one of the Member Nations, or when experimentation has been undertaken to prove its applicability to industry.

Article 3. An invention is capable of industrial application if the object can be employed in manufacture, or is useful in any type of industry.

Article 4. The following shall not be considered to be inventions:

a) Principles and discoveries of scientific nature;

b) Mere discovery of matter existing in nature;

c) Commercial, financial, accounting, or similar plans, rules of the game; or other systems in the measure that these may be purely abstract in character;

d) Therapeutic or surgical methods for the treatment of humans or animals, and diagnostic measures;

e) Purely aesthetic creations.

Article 5. Patents shall not be granted for:

a) Inventions which contravene public order or good morals;

b) Vegetable varieties or animal races, and essentially biological processes for obtaining vegetables or animals;

369

c) Pharmaceutical products, medications, active therapeutic substances, beverages and food for human, animal or vegetable consumption;

d) Foreign inventions, the patent for which is requested one year after the date of the filing for patent registration in the first country in which it was sought. Upon expiration of this term, no rights may be asserted deriving from said application.

e) Inventions which affect the development of the respective Member Nations or the procedures, products or groups of products, the patentability of which has been excluded by the Governments.

SECTION II

Owners

Article 6. Owners of patents may be physical or corporate persons.

The right to a patent is presumed to belong to the first applicant.

If several persons make an invention jointly, the right shall correspond to them jointly.

Article 7. If a patent application covers an invention which has been misappropriated from the inventor or his assignees, or as the result of a default in a contractual or legal obligation, the injured party may claim title as true owner within the term of ninety work days following the date of publication of the patent application, or he may bring it to court should the patent already have been granted and the interested party had not alleged his right thereto through administrative procedure.

In the event of the objection covered under this article, the competent national office, upon its receipt, shall forward it to the competent judicial organ. At this time, the patent applicant, upon being summoned, shall answer the objection as provided under the procedure of the respective Member Nation.

The suit described above may only be brought within the two years subsequent to the granting of the patent.

Article 8. Unless otherwise stipulated, an invention by an employee or agent contracted to do research shall belong to the employer or principal. In any other case, the invention shall be the irrenounceable property of the employee or agent unless he has had access to secrets or confindential studies because of the nature of his duties.

Article 9. An inventor shall have a right to be described as such in his patent or similarly he may refuse to be so mentioned. These rights are non-waivable.

Article 10. The first application for an invention patent initially filed in any Member Nation shall give its owner a priority right for a term of one year, computed from the date of said application, to request a patent on the same invention in the other Member Nations.

SECTION III

Patent Applications

Article 11. Applications to secure invention patents must be presented to the respective competent national office and must include:

a) Name and surname, or firm name, and address of applicant, or those of the inventor, as the case may be;

b) Title or name of the invention; and

c) Object or purpose of the invention.

Article 12. The following must be appended to the application:

371

a) Powers (of attorney), if applicable;

b) Receipts showing payment of corresponding fiscal fees, if applicable;

c) Documents to accredit the existence and representation of a corporate applicant;

d) Plans and drawings, if applicable;

e) Precise and complete description of the invention in such terms as to permit a person conversant in the field to execute it;

f) One or more justifications to categorize the extent of the novelty and industrial application of the invention; and

g) Certified copy of the first patent application filed on the same invention.

Article 13. No patent may cover more than a single creation or invention, or group of inventions so directly related as to constitute a unit.

SECTION IV

Processing of Applications

Article 14. Upon presentation of the application, the competent national office shall examine it to verify whether it complies with the contents of paragraphs a) and d) of Article 5, and with the provisions of Articles 11 and 13, and whether the documents referred to in Article 12 have been appended.

Article 15. Should the examination reveal that the application failed to comply with the requirements of the preceding article, it (the office) shall formulate its objections, so that the applicant may present his comments or supplement the data within the term of sixty work days, extendable for a similar term under duly justified circumstances, without loss of his priority right.

Upon expiration of the designated time, if the applicant should fail to satisfy the formulated requirements, the application shall be considered to be abandoned without need of a declaration to this effect.

The description, justifications and the plans and drawings may not be altered except to the extent required to remedy the objected portions indicated by the respective office.

Article 16. If the application does not merit any objection, or it has been duly completed, publication shall be ordered, for a single time, in an adequate publicity medium, in extract form from the description of the invention and justifications requested.

Article 17. Within the terms of ninety work days following the date of publication any person may present supportee observations that may detract from the patentability of the invention.

Article 18. If such observations have been presented within the stipulated term of the preceding article, the competent national office shall notify the applicant so that, within sixty work days, he may endorse his own assertions and documents, or re-draft the justifications or description of the invention.

Article 19. Upon expiration of the terms stipulated in Articles 17 and 18, as the case may be, the competent national office shall proceed to examine whether the application is patentable in conformity with provisions of Articles 2, 3, 4 and of paragraphs b), c), and e) of Article 5, and in the case of an improvement patent, whether the object will signify such improvement.

Article 20. Should the final examination be favorable, the letters patent shall be granted.

If partially favorable, the patent may be granted by a founded resolution, to include only the acceptable justifications.

If unfavorable, it shall be rejected by a duly founded resolution.

Article 21. The Member Nations may decide that complete examinations are necessary on the status of the technique, which may affect the patentability of the invention in determined sectors of the industry.

Article 22. The competent national offices may request opinions from experts or from scientific and technological centers that they deem competent to issue opinions as to the novelty and industrial application of the invention.

Article 23. The competent national office shall assign a number to the owner and order of publication of the justification or justifications on the invention.

Any person may, at his own expense, obtain a copy of any patent granted.

Article 24. In the area of inventions of interest to national security or related to processes, products, or groups or products reserved to the Government, or when so determined by law, the granting of a patent may be subjected to conditions as to its exploitation. In such event, the administrative act granting it shall be dully supported or founded.

Article 25. For purposes of regulation and classification of patents, the Member Nations agree to adopt the International Classification of Invention Patents, signed on 19 December 1954, within one year computed from the enforcement of the present Decision.

Article 26. The Member Nations agree to keep each other informed and to inform the Board concerning patents granted or rejected by their respective competent national offices. To this end, the Board shall forward to the Member Nations the necessary instructions for the interchange of this data.

SECTION V

Rights Conferred by Patents

Article 27. The extent of protection conferred by a patent shall be determined by the tenor of the justifications, the description, and of the drawings or plans interpreting same.

Article 28. With the limitations stipulated in the present Regulation, the patent shall confer on its owner the right to exploit the invention itself in an exclusive manner, to grant one or more licenses for its exploitation, and to receive royalties or compensation deriving from its exploitation by third persons.

The patent shall not confer an exclusive right to import the patented product or one manufactured under his patented process.

Article 29. A patent shall be granted for a maximum term of ten years, computed from the date of the administrative resolution granting it. Initially it shall be granted for five years and in order to obtain an extension, the owner must prove to the competent national office that the patent is being adequately exploited.

A patent for an improvement shall expire with the original patent.

SECTION VI

Duties of the Patent Owner

Article 30. The patent owner is under duty:

a) To communicate to the competent national organs, within a term of three years computed from the date of the granting of the patent, that exploitation has been initiated. Omission of such communication shall give rise to the presumption that the exploitation has not been commenced for purposes of the concession of compulsory licenses, as stipulated in Article 34.

b) To register with the competent national organ all contracts covering assignment, license, or other type of utilization of the patent by third persons, or any other forms.

The duties outlined in paragraphs a) and b) shall be observed by the owner, or by his assignees, transferees, licensees, or any other person holding a right deriving from the patent.

Article 31. Exploitation shall be understood to mean the permanent and stable use of a patented process, or the manufacture of a product protected by the patent, to supply the market with its final results under reasonable trade conditions, provided these acts take place on the soil of the Member Nations which granted the patent, save for the stipulations on the Sectorial Programs of Industrial Development, covered under Articles 33 and 34 of the Cartagena Agreement.

SECTION VII

Licensing Rules

Article 32. The owner of a patent may grant to another person a license for its exploitation only through a written contract.

Licence contracts must be approved and registered with the competent national office.

Article 33. The competent national office may not authorize the celebration of a license contract for exploitation of patents if these fail to comply with the provisions of Article 20 of Decision 24 of the Commission of the Cartagena Agreement.

Article 34. Upon expiration of three years, computed from the date of concession of the patent, any person

may apply to the competent national office for a grant of
a compulsory licence to exploit that patent if, at the time
of the request and with the exception of a justifiable,
legitimate excuse by said office, one of the following acts
has occurred:

a) That the patented invention has not been exploited within the country;

b) That the exploitation of said invention has been
suspended for more than one year;

c) That the exploitation does not satisfy reasonable
conditions of quantity, quality, or price as
demanded by the national market;

d) That the patent owner has not granted any contractual licenses under reasonable conditions
in such manner that the holder thereof can
satisfy the demands of the national market, under
reasonable conditions of quantity, quality or
prices.

The term of five years having expired, as computed
from the date of concession of the patent, a compulsory
license may be granted by the competent national office
without need to prove the existence of any of the above
listed acts of paragraphs b), c) and d) of this Article.

The holder of a compulsory license must pay an
adequate compensation of the patent owner.

Article 35. The competent national office may grant
a license at any time if so requested by the owner of a
patent, the exploitation of which necessarily requires the
use of the other (license), a fact to be culy proved to the
respective office.

Article 36. The amount of compensation shall be
fixed by the competent national office, following a hearing
of the parties. Once the administrative procedure has
been exhausted, a suit may be filed with the competent
judicial organ within a term of thirty work days following
notification.

The filing of such claims shall not prevent exploitation (of the license) nor will it exercise any influence over the running of any periods of time. The filing of the suit shall not in the meantime prevent the patent owner from receiving the royalties fixed by the office on the uninvolved portions.

Article 37. At the request of the patent owner or of any licensee, the conditions of the licenses may be modified by the authority which had approved them with prior hearing of the parties, should there be justification by new facts and particularly when the patent owner has granted a license under more favorable conditions than those already established.

Article 38. The owner of a license may not transfer it nor grant sublicenses without authorization of the patent owner and of the competent national office, and in every case the respective patent must continue to be adequately exploited.

The obligation of the patent owner to prove initiation of exploitation shall be likewise applicable to the holder of the license.

Article 39. In the case of patents of interest to public health, or based on national development needs, the Government of the respective Member Nation may submit the patent to compulsory licensing at any time, and in such cases, the competent national office may grant the licenses requested to it.

Article 40. Licenses failing to comply with the provisions of this regulation shall be void.

SECTION VIII

Legal Protection

Article 41. Upon request of any person, or ex officio, with prior hearing of the parties, the competent national office may cancel a compulsory license when its holder makes inadequate use of the invention.

Article 42. Any person exploiting a patent without having entered into a license contract with owner of same, or without authorization of the competent national office, shall be penalized by the latter, ex officio, or at the request of a party, after hearing the presumed violator, by imposition of a fine in favor of the national treasury, while leaving open the appeals and actions provided by the laws of the respective Member Nations.

Article 43. The exploitation of a patent by virtue of a contract not authorized by the competent national office shall give rise to imposition of a fine on the contracting parties.

SECTION IX

Nullity of a Patent

Article 44. The national office which has granted a patent may decree its nullity ex officio, or at the request of any person, following a hearing with the patent owner and license holders, should the invention not be patentable pursuant to Articles 1, 2, 3, 4 and 5 of the present Regulation, or when there has been non-observance of the stipulations of paragraph e) of Article 12.

If the provisions referred to in the preceding paragraph are only partially applicable to a patent, the nullity shall be declared only with respect to that claim or claims subject to the objection.

CHAPTER II

INDUSTRIAL DRAWINGS AND MODELS

Article 45. Novel industrial drawings and models shall be registrable.

A drawing shall be understood to be any composite of lines or combination of colors incorporated in an industrial or mechanical product to give it a special appearance without altering the purpose of said product; and a model shall be understood to be any plastic form serving as a sample for the manufacture of industrial or mechanical products, giving them a special appearance and not implying any technical effects.

Drawings or models referring to wearing apparel are non-registrable.

Excluded from this protection shall be drawings or models which contravene good morals or public order.

Article 46. A drawing or model is not novel if, prior to the date of the application or to the date of a validly justified priority, it has been made publicly accessible in any place or at any time, by description, utilization, or by any other means.

A drawing or model is not novel by the mere fact that secondary differences are presented with respect to previous creations, or because reference is made to another class of products, differing from said creations.

Article 47. An application for registration must include: a) name and surname, or firm name, and address of applicant; b) indication of the type of products for which the drawing or model is to be used, as also the classification to which said products belong.

To this application there must be appended: a) any powers (of attorney) that may be necessary; b) documents to accredit the existence of the applicant of a corporation or legally constituted society; and c) a sample of the object bearing the drawing or model, or a graphic or photographic facsimile thereof.

Article 48. The application having been filed, the competent national office shall examine it to verify compliance with the stipulations of Articles 45 and 47.

Article 49. If an examination of the application shows that it has failed to comply with provisions of Article 45, it shall be rejected, and in all other cases objections shall be formulated so that the applicant may complete the data, effect the corrections, or attach the documents required by Article 47, within a term of sixty work days, without loss of his priority rights.

If at the expiration of the designated time, the applicant has not satisfied the formulated objections, the application shall be considered as abandoned without need of a declaration to this effect.

Article 50.   If the application does not merit any objections, or it has been duly completed, publication shall be ordered, for a single time, in an adequate publicity organ.

Article 51.   Within the following thirty work days after publication, any interested person may present objections to the registration.

Article 52.   If no objections are filed, or if these have been rejected, the competent national office shall proceed to test the industrial drawing or model for novelty.

Should this test prove acceptable, the corresponding registration shall be made.

Article 53.   An application validly filed with a Member Nation shall confer a right of priority for a term of six months within which registration in the other Member Nations may be requested.

Article 54.   The registration of industrial drawings or models shall confer on the owner the right to exclusive use for a term of five years computed from the date of the corresponding administrative act.

The owner of a drawing or model may freely grant licenses or conveyances thereof.

Any license or change of ownership must be recorded in the competent national office.

Article 55.   Member Nations agree to adopt the International Classification established by the Locarno Agreement of October 8, 1968, within a term of one year computed from the enforcement date of the present Regulation.

CHAPTER III

TRADEMARKS

SECTION I

Requirements for Registration of Trademarks

Article 56.   Registration of emblems that are novel, visible and sufficiently distinctive, may be recorded as trade or service marks.

Article 57.   Cooperatives, associations of public or private enterprises, communities, collective societies, and any other groups of legal entities, may register collective trademarks to distinguish their products or services.

Article 58.   The following may not be registered as trademarks:

a)   Those adverse to good morals or to public order, or those likely to deceive commercial resources or the consumer public, as to the nature, origin, means of manufacture, characteristics, or capabilities of the product or service for their intended use;

b)   Customary or necessary forms of products, their dimensions and colors;

c)   Descriptive or generic names, in any language, and signs that serve to designate species, quality, quantity, use, value or time, of the production of the products or the rendering of services;

d)   Terms that in current language or commercial customs of the Member Nations have been converted into a common description of the products or services in question, and their equivalents in other languages;

e) Those which unauthorizedly reproduce or imitate coats of arms, flags and other emblems, or denominations of any State, or of any intergovernment international organization, or of any created by international treaty;

f) Those that might be confused with others already registered, or previously applied for by a third person, or subsequently requested as a valid priority claim, covering products or services comprised within the same class;

g) Those that might be confused with other prominently known and registered marks within the country or abroad, covering identical or similar products or services;

h) Names, pseudonyms, signatures, and pictures of living persons, save with their written consent; names of deceased persons, save with consent of their heirs; and historical names;

Nevertheless, consent is not required in case of a physical person requesting registration of his own name, provided it is presented in a unique and sufficiently distinctive form to differentiate it from the same name used by other persons;

i) Names, signs or denominations that imply ties with living or deceased persons, institutions, creeds, national places or symbols, or that may expose them to discredit or ridicule;

j) Translation of trademarks already registered in another language, or of well-known foreign marks, save by the owners themselves; and

k) Translation into other languages of non-registrable terms.

Article 59. When the trademark consists of a word in a foreign language or of a geographic name, the place of manufacture of the product must be indicated beneath it, in a visible and clearly legible form.

SECTION II

Registration Procedure

Article 60. Applications for registration of a trademark must be presented to the respective competent national office, and must include:

a) Name and surname, or firm name, and address of applicant;

b) Precise and complete description of the trademark to be registered; and

c) Indication of the class or classes of the products or services for which registration of the trademark is being requested.

Article 61. The following must be attached to the application:

a) Receipts showing the corresponding payment of fiscal fees;

b) Any powers (of attorney) that may be necessary;

c) Documents that accredit the existence and representation of corporate entity applicants; and

d) Facsimiles of the trademark, if applicable.

Article 62. Upon filing of the application, the competent national office shall proceed to examine it to verify whether there has been compliance with the legal and regulatory requirements, and particularly if it conforms to the stipulations of Articles 56, 58, 59, 60 and 61 of the present Chapter.

Article 63. If the examination reveals that the application has failed to comply with the requirements of Article 60, or that the documents mentioned in Article 61 have not been attached, the competent national office shall notify the interested party that within a period of sixty work days he must make the corrections in point, or present the omitted documents, without prejudice to the priority right stipulated in the present Chapter.

Article 64. In cases of non-compliance with the stipulated requirements of Articles 56, 58 and 59, the competent national office may decide to reject the application after a previous hearing with the applicant.

Article 65. If the application merits no objections, or has been duly completed, its publication in extract form shall be ordered for a single time in the publicity organ stipulated by the domestic law of the respective Member Nation.

Within the thirty work days following the publication, any person may file objections to the registration of the trademark.

Article 66. If within a term of thirty work days, objections have been filed with the competent national office, these shall be processed pursuant to the domestic legislation of the respective Member Nation.

Article 67. If no objections are filed, or these have been rejected, the competent national office shall issue the corresponding certificate of registration.

Article 68. The registration of a trademark and its protection shall extend only to a single class. In order to register a mark covering several classes, individual applications are required for each, with respective fees payable on each, and the processing shall be made independently of each other.

The Member Nations agree to adopt the international classification signed in Nice on June 15, 1957.

The Member Nations that have not as yet adopted said classification shall have a term of one year in which to do so, computed from the enforcement date of the present Regulation.

Article 69.   The registration of a mark shall have a duration of five years computed from the date of the grant, and is renewable indefinitely for **periods** of **five years.**

Article 70.   In order to enjoy the right of renewal, the interested party must prove to the respective competent national office that the mark in question is being utilized in any Member Nation.

Article 71.   The competent national office shall order the publication of registered trademarks in an adequate publicity organ.

SECTION III

Rights Conferred by Registration

Article 72.   The exclusive right to a trademark shall be acquired by registration of same in the competent national office.

Article 73.   Acceptance of the application for registration of a trademark in a Member Nation shall give the applicant a priority right for a term of six months in order that he may, within that specified time, apply for registration in the remaining Member Nations.

Article 74.   The **owner or licensee of a trademark** shall have the right to use it in an exclusive manner, and may request protection measures in defense of his rights, as provided by the respective national laws.

Article 75.   The owner of a trademark may not object to the importation or entry of merchandise or products originating in another Member Nation, which carry the same trademark.   The competent national authorities shall require that the imported goods be clearly and adequately distinguished with an indication of the Member Nation where they were produced.

Article 76. The registration of a trademark shall be cancelled by the competent national office, ex officio or at the request of a party, when it is verified that the registration has been issued in contravention with the stipulations of Articles 56 and 58 of the present Regulation.

Article 77. A penalty of definitive cancellation of the trademark or license shall be imposed when the competent national authority verifies that the owner or licensee of the mark has speculated or made unlawful use price-wise or quality-wise of a product protected by the trademark to the detriment of the public or the economy of a Member Nation.

Article 78. Member Nations may require that products or services of similar character which are manufactured or rendered by the same owner and which are to be devoted to the same purpose, not be protected save by a single trademark.

SECTION IV

Conveyance and Assignment of Registration

Article 79. The owner of a trademark or service mark may assign its use or convey it by written contact.

Article 80. Conveyances, assignments, or transfers of marks which are subject to the laws of each Member Nation shall be recorded in the competent national office.

Article 81. All license contracts must be submitted by the competent organ of the respective Member Nation and shall not include restrictive classes stipulated in Article 25 of Decision 24 of the Commission of the Cartagena Agreement.

CHAPTER IV

MISCELLANEOUS PROVISIONS

Article 82. Every license contract must incorporate stipulations to insure the quality of the products made or of services rendered by the beneficiary of the license.

Article 83. The Member Nations shall refrain from unilaterally entering into agreements on industrial property with third countries or international organizations that contravene the provisions of the present Regulation.

Article 84. Matters relating to industrial property not covered under the present Regulation shall be governed by the domestic laws of the Member Nations.

Article 85. All rights in industrial property validly granted pursuant to the law of the respective Member Nations prior to the enforcement of the present Regulation shall continue in force for the term of the grant. The stipulations of the present Regulation shall govern these with respect to their use and enjoyment, their obligations and licenses, renewals and extensions.

The terms provided in Articles 30 and 34 shall be computed for patents already granted prior to the enforcement of this Regulation, as of the date of their grant. If this term has totally expired, an additional term of one year shall be granted from the date of enforcement of this Regulation.

Applications in process shall be governed by the provisions of this Regulation.

Article 86. The Governments of Member Nations agree to adopt all necessary provisions to incorporate the present Regulation in their respective domestic codes of law within the six months following approval of this Decision.

UNIFORM REGIME ON MULTINATIONAL ENTERPRISES AND REGULATIONS OF THE TREATMENT APPLICABLE TO SUBREGIONAL CAPITAL *

(Decision N° 46 of the Commission, December 18, 1971,
as amended) **

THE COMMISSION OF THE CARTAGENA AGREEMENT,

IN VIEW of Articles 28, 38, and 86 of the Cartagena Agreement, Article 30 and Transitory Article I of the Commission's Decision N° 24, and Proposal N° 17-18/Rev. 1 of the Board;

DECIDES:

To approve the following:

UNIFORM REGIME ON MULTINATIONAL ENTERPRISES AND REGULATIONS OF THE TREATMENT APPLICABLE TO SUBREGIONAL CAPITAL

CHAPTER I

General Provisions

Article 1. For the effects of this Decision and of Decision N° 24 of the Commission, the term "subregional investor" is understood to be a national investor of any Member Country other than the recipient country. In the case of multinational enterprises, the country of principal domicile shall be considered to be the recipient country.

---

* English version from International Legal Materials, Vol. XI, N° 2, March 1972.
** This text of Decision N° 46 incorporates the amendments introduced by Decision 70 (February 13, 1973) of the Commission.

Article 2. Subregional investors shall receive the treatment agreed upon in Chapters II to VIII, inclusive, of this Decision when they invest in multinational enterprises, and they shall be subject to the provisions of Decision No. 24 of the Commission in other cases.

On the recommendation of the Board, the Commission shall regulate the fourth paragraph of Article 30 of Decision No. 24 with reference to the authority to compute the contributions of subregional investors as being those of national investors. Until such regulations enter into force, the aforesaid paragraph shall not be applied with respect to the contributions of subregional investors.

Article 3. Each Member Country shall determine, according to their internal norms, the requirements to which their nationals must submit in order to invest in multinational enterprises or transfer capital to any other Member Country.

The appropriate national agencies shall not authorize the reexportation of capital or the transfer of profits of subregional investors except to the territory of the Member Countries where the capital originated.

Article 4. The appropriate national agencies shall not authorize the purchase by foreign investors of shares, participations, or ownership rights of subregional investors.

The sale of shares, participations, or rights of a subregional investor to another subregional investor of different nationality must be previously authorized by the appropriate national agency of the recipient country. If multinational enterprises are concerned, the rule of Article 11 of this Decision shall be observed.

Article 5. The appropriate national agencies referred to in Article 6 of Decision No. 24 shall not authorize transfers of capital belonging to their national investors, when such capital is intended for investment in other Member Countries in enterprises producing or exploiting products reserved for industrial programming, until the Commission adopts the pertinent programs.

Likewise, the appropriate national agencies of the recipient country shall not authorize investments belonging to subregional investors in enterprises that produce or exploit products reserved for industrial programming until the Commission adopts the pertinent programs.

Article 6. Subregional and foreign investors in a multinational enterprise shall be governed by all provisions on investment registration and control, and by the rules on reexportation of capital and transfer of profits contained in Decision No. 24, save for the exceptions provided in this regime.

CHAPTER II

Purposes of Multinational Enterprises

Article 7. With the installation and operation of multinational enterprises envisaged in this regime, the following purposes, among others, are sought:

a) To contribute to improvement of the process of economic integration called for in the Cartagena Agreement by strengthening the bonds among the Member Countries;

b) To help in implementing the principle of balanced harmonious development and equitable distribution of the benefits of integration, and in reducing the differences in the levels of development existing among the Member Countries of the Cartagena Agreement;

c) To contribute to the strengthening of subregional entrepreneurial capacity in order to take fuller advantage of the expanded market;

d) To channel subregional savings toward the priority productive centers and to make effective use of the investment opportunities of the expanded market;

e) To utilize the Subregion's resources adequately and efficiently;

f) To facilitate subregional programming;

g) To make possible the use of advanced technologies in the various fields in which they are engaged;

h) To facilitate the implementation of projects of subregional benefit whose cost, scope, or technological complexity prevent their realization by a single Member Country;

i) To strengthen the negotiating capacity of the Subregion for acquiring foreign technology.

j) To contribute to the generation of sources of employment in the Subregion;

k) To facilitate access to international capital markets and international financing agencies, and

l) To strengthen the Subregion's capacity to compete in the markets of third countries.

CHAPTER III

Requirements to be met by Multinational Enterprises

Article 8. For the effects of this regime, a multinational enterprise shall be understood to be an enterprise that meets the following requirements:

a) The contributions of subregional investors to the capital of the enterprises must meet the terms set forth in Article 10 and 11 of this regime;

b) In the judgment of the appropriate national agency of the country of principal domicile, the subregional majority of the capital must be reflected in the technical, financial, administrative, and commercial management of the enterprise;

c) The principal domicile of the enterprise must be located in the territory of one of the Member Countries;

d) It must have contributions of capital belonging to national investors of two or more Member Countries;

e) The corporate purpose of the enterprise must be of subregional interest, must be adapted to the conditions and procedures set forth in the programs indicated below, and must refer to the projects and products included therein:

1. Sectoral programs of industrial development;

2. Infrastructure projects, designed to solve problems that unfavorably affect the process of subregional integration;

3. Programs to rationalize production in existing industries; and

4. Joint agricultural development programs.

Article 9. On the recommendation of the Board, the Commission may declare the desirability of setting up multinational enterprises to carry out or develop projects of subregional interest relating to the production of goods and services other than those indicated in subparagraph (e) of the preceeding article.

In such cases the specific conditions to which the multinational enterprises will be subject in the pertinent field shall be set forth.

Until the conditions mentioned in the preceeding paragraph have been determined, the Commission, acting on the recommendation of the Board, may authorize the establishment of multinational enterprises in particular cases submitted to it for consideration.

Article 10. The participation of foreign investors in a multinational enterprise may not exceed 40 percent of the enterprise's capital.

Each Government shall be responsible for determining the maximum of foreign investment in the capital of multinational enterprises that establish their principal domicile in its territory, within the limit stipulated in the preceding paragraph.

In all cases the majority of capital belonging to national and subregional investors must be reflected in the technical, administrative, financial, and commercial management of the enterprise.

Article 11. The participation of the national investors of each Member Country in the capital of a multinational enterprise may not be less than 15 percent of the total subregional participation.

In special cases, the Commission, acting on the recommentation of the Board, may establish minimum percentages of national participation other than that provided in this article.

Article 12. Investors of Bolivia and Ecuador may pay in the capital corresponding to their percentage of participation within a period of not more than five years from the date on which the national investors of the other Member Countries will have paid their shares.

Article 13. Multinational enterprises shall set up establishments to engage in manufacturing, marketing, or other activities in the Member Countries whose nationals participate in their corporate capital, except when the conditions and nature of the enterprises do not justify such action.

Article 14. The capital of multinational enterprises shall be represented by registered stock.

Article 15. The value of the shares shall be expressed in the monetary unit of the country of principal domicile. The subregional investment must be made or priced in monetary units accepted by the country of principal domicile.

CHAPTER IV

Establishment of Multinational Enterprises

Article 16. Multinational enterprises shall be established in the form of stock companies and add to their firm or business name the words "multinational enterprise."

Nevertheless, on the recommendation of the Board, the Commission may adopt special standard rules for other types of entrepreneurial organization.

Article 17. Only enterprises established in conformity with the provisions of this regime may use the name "multinational enterprise."

Article 18. The bylaws of multinational enterprises must be adapted to the provisions of this regime and, in all respects not specified herein, to the provisions of the legislation of the country where their principal domicile is established.

Article 19. Multinational enterprises shall be constituted in the Member Country where they establish their principal domicile and shall be subject to the procedure set forth in the national laws of that country.

For those effects, the founders or promoters shall attach to the background or other documents required by the pertinent national legislation an authenticated copy of the Decision of the Commission referred to in Articles 8 and 9 of this regime.

Article 20. Upon receipt of the documents mentioned in the preceding article, the appropriate national authority of the country of principal domicile shall send to the Board and to the competent authorities of the other Member Countries authenticated copies of the draft bylaws, the enterprise's plan of work, and the accompanying background documents.

Article 21. If the competent authorities of the other Member Countries whose nationals participate in the capital of the enterprise should find that the enterprise does not conform to the specifications of the program or to the conditions referred to in Articles 8 and 9 of this regime, they shall submit their comments to the authorities of the country of principal domicile within 60 days after receipt of the background documents mentioned in the preceding article.

In contrary cases they shall communicate their approval within the same period of time and shall transmit certificates authorizing the transfer of the contributions of capital which their nationals are to make to establish the enterprise.

Within the same time period specified in this article the Board may present observations to the national authorities of the country of principal domicile and shall bring the case before the Commission, if in its judgment the terms of the program or the conditions referred to in Articles 8 and 9 of this regime are infringed.

For such purposes the Board shall seek the opinion of the administrative organs of the programs, if such organs exist.

Article 22. Once the observations have been duly cleared up, or upon the expiration of the time limit set in the preceding article without any observations having been made, the appropriate authorities of the country of principal domicile shall conclude the process of establishing the multinational enterprise in the manner prescribed in its legislation.

Article 23. When the process of establishing the enterprise in the country of principal domicile is completed, the pertinent authorities shall request the authorities of the other Member Countries to register the articles of incorporation in their national registers and to publish them in the form prescribed in their legislation.

From the date of publication or of registration of the multinational enterprise in the national registers in accordance with the requirements of the respective national laws, the enterprise shall be vested with the full legal capacity recognized for juristic persons by such laws and shall receive the treatment accorded a corporation of national law.

The registration of multinational enterprises shall be subject to the general legal provisions that regulate economic activity in each country.

Article 24. Multinational enterprises shall be governed by the following standards:

a)   Their bylaws; and

b)   This code in all matters not determined in their bylaws.

Article 25. In matters not regulated by the enterprise's bylaws or by this regime, the following provisions shall be applied:

a)   The legislation of the country of principal domicile when matters relating to the rules of Chapter VII of this regime are involved; and

b)   In other cases, the legislation of the country where legal status is established, or the legislation of the country where the legal acts of the multinational enterprises are to have effect, as provided by the applicable rules of private international law.

CHAPTER V

External Supervision of
Multinational Enterprises

Article 26. The Office of Superintendents of Corporations or of similar companies or organizations in the countries where the multinational enterprises have establishments shall be responsible for exercising their supervision and control, without prejudice to that exercised by the national agencies referred to in Article 6 of Decision No. 24 of the Commission in their fields of competence.

Article 27. When a Member Country considers that a multinational enterprise has violated the conditions established for its creation, or the aims or corporate purpose that gave rise to it, it shall so notify the Board, which will make a report to the Commission.

If proof of the violation charged is given, it shall be the duty of the Commission, following the general voting procedure established in Article 11 of the Cartagena Agreement, to set a time limit for the violation to be corrected or to nullify the multinational status of the enterprise concerned.

In the latter case, the enterprise shall lose its right to the benefits of the provisions of this regime and shall be subject to the provisions of the national laws, Decision No. 24, and Article 2 of this Decision.

CHAPTER VI

Special Treatment of
Multinational Enterprises

Article 28. The products of multinational enterprises shall enjoy the advantages deriving from the liberalization program of the Cartagena Agreement.

Article 29. Member Countries, individually or collectively, shall adopt the necessary measures to facilitate the transfers of capital intended for operation of the multinational enterprises, and of the capital contributions being made by their nationals to establish the enterprises.

Article 30. Multinational enterprises shall enjoy treatment no less favorable than that provided for national enterprises in respect of preference for State purchases of goods or services.

Article 31.   Investors in a multinational enterprise shall not be subject to the obligation stipulated in Decision No. 24, of transferring their shares, participations, or rights to investors who are nationals of the country where the enterprise operates.

Article 32.   In the matter of internal national taxes, multinational enterprises shall enjoy the treatment now or in the future determined for most favored enterprises in their field of economic activity, provided they comply with the requirements of the pertinent legislation.

Article 33.   Multinational enterprises shall not be required to obtain authorization to reinvest their profits. In these cases, the obligation for registration shall be applicable.

Article 34.   Multinational enterprises shall have access to domestic credit and, in general, to the financial treatment now or in the future determined for national most favored enterprises in their field of economic activity, provided they comply with the requirements of the pertinent legislation.

Article 35.   Subregional investors shall be entitled, with the authorization of the competent national agency, to transfer to the country of origin of capital the net profits proved to have come from the direct investment of such capital, upon payment of the applicable taxes.

Article 36.   Upon authorization of the appropriate national agency, multinational enterprises may participate in sectors of economic activity which the Member Countries have reserved for national enterprises.

In all cases the enterprises must have participation in their corporate capital, in the minimum percentage provided in Article 11 of this regime, by investors of the country in which the authorization referred to in this article is requested.

Article 37.   Multinational enterprises shall enjoy the treatment provided in Articles 28 and 29 of this Chapter in all Member Countries, and that indicated in Articles 30 to 36, inclusive, only in those Member Countries whose nationals participate in their corporate capital, in the terms of Article 11 of this regime.

CHAPTER VII

Domicile and Administration of Multinational Enterprises

Section I: Domicile

Article 38. The principal domicile of a multinational enterprise shall be located in the Member Country where it engages in its principal activity pursuant to the terms of the pertinent project or program, and it must be stated in the enterprise's bylaws. The principal domicile shall be the headquarters of the Board of Directors and General Management.

Section II: General Meeting of Shareholders

Article 39. The General Meeting shall be the enterprise's principal organ and shall be comprised of the shareholders assembled according to the following articles.

Article 40. The General Meeting may assemble in regular and special sessions, according to the provisions of the bylaws.

Article 41. The meetings shall be held at the principal domicile of the enterprise and the calls for meetings shall be issued as determined by the bylaws.

Article 42. Special meetings shall be held when convoked by the General Manager, ex officio, by decision of the Meeting or the Board of Directors, or at the request of shareholders who represent no less than ten percent of the corporate capital.

Special meetings may also be convoked by the persons indicated in Article 48 of this regime.

Article 43.   Shareholders may participate in the meetings either personally or by duly appointed proxies, according to the requirements of the legislation of the country in which the powers of representation are issued.

Article 44.   Holders of one half plus one of the paidin shares shall constitute a quorum for regular and special meetings, except in the cases indicated below, when the quorum shall consist of holders of at least 60 percent of the paid-in shares:

a)   Amendment of the bylaws;

b)   Anticipated dissolution of the enterprise;

c)   Participation in one or more other corporations; and

d)   Issuance of obligations.

Article 45.   Decisions of the Meeting shall be adopted by the favorable vote of holders of half plus one of the shares present or represented, except in the cases mentioned in a), b), c), and d) of the preceding article, when the favorable vote of at least 60 percent of the holders of the paidin shares shall be required.

Article 46.   Amendments to the bylaws must meet all the fomalities required for establishment of the enterprise.

Article 47.   In addition to the powers and duties determined in Article 44, the General Meeting shall:

a)   Issue its rules and regulations;

b)   Examine the condition of the enterprise;

c)   Examine the annual report and approve or reject the balance sheets;

d)   Decide on the distribution of profits and determine the funds to be allocated to the reserve;

e) Appoint and dismiss directors and fix their sala-
ries; and

f) Such other powers and duties as may be necessary
for proper implementation of the bylaws and preservation of the corporate interest.

Article 48. The General Meeting of Shareholders shall
designate the persons to be responsible for supervising the
enterprise's administration, in the terms established in
the bylaws.

Section III: Board of Directors

Article 49. The Board of Directors shall be the administrative organ of the enterprise.

Article 50. The number of directors, their functions,
the form in which they issue opinions, and the quorum required for their functioning and voting shall be as specified
in the bylaws of the enterprise.

Article 51. The responsibility of the directors shall
be governed by the provisions of the legislation of the country of principal domicile.

Article 52. When there is participation of foreign
capital in a multinational enterprise, the subregional shareholders and those of third countries shall separately designate the directors corresponding to them, according to the
proportion indicated in the bylaws.

In any case there must be at least one director for
each Member Country whose nationals participate in the
corporate capital of the enterprise.

Article 53. The Board of Directors shall have the
following powers and duties, among others:

a) To issue its rules and regulations and other instruments necessary for the progress of the enterprise;

b)   To appoint the General Manager and the legal representatives referred to in Article 54 of this regime;

c)   To direct the financial and commercial policy of the enterprises;

d)   To present the annual report and balance sheets of the enterprise to the Meeting;

e)   To propose to the Meeting the distribution of profits and the formation of reserve or other funds;

f)   To propose amendments of the bylaws to the Meeting; and

g)   To delegate powers and duties to the General Manager.

Article 54. Multinational enterprises shall have a General Manager, who shall represent it in legal matters in the place of its principal domicile. They shall also have a legal representative in the other Member Countries where they engage in their activities.

Article 55. The functions, rights, and obligations of the General Manager and the legal representatives shall be those established in the enterprise's bylaws.

Section V: Annual Report and Balance Sheets

Article 56. The general balance sheet, the statement of profit and loss and its annexes, the annual report of the Board of Directors, and the report of the person or persons responsible for auditing the corporate activities shall be available to the shareholders at all offices of the enterprise for their information and examination at least 15 days before the date of the General Meeting that is to consider them.

Furthermore, the bylaws of the enterprise must contain provisions that will ensure that shareholders residing in Member Countries other than the country of the enterprise's principal domicile are adequately informed of the documents referred to in this article.

Article 57. A multinational enterprise may change the terms of the objective for which it was established only if it maintains the conditions set forth in the Decisions of the Commission referred to in Articles 8 and 9 of this regime.

Section VI: Miscellaneous Provisions

Article 58. The duration of the enterprise must be stated in the bylaws, except in those cases when it is determined by the nature of the corporate objective itself.

Article 59. The dissolution and liquidation of the enterprise shall be carried out according to the provisions of the bylaws and the legislation of the country of principal domicile.

Article 60. Any conflict that may arise among shareholders or between shareholders and the enterprise shall be settled according to the rules on the matter existing in the legislation of the country of principal domicile.

Article 61. In case of an increase in the capital, the national investors of any Member Country who hold a smaller number of shares than do the investors who are nationals of other countries shall have first option to subscribe to new shares up to the number held by the major shareholder. The procedure for exercising this right shall be set forth in the bylaws of the enterprise.

CHAPTER VIII

Participation of the Andean Development

Corporation in Multinational Enterprises

Article 62. Contributions of the Andean Development Corporation to a multinational enterprise may be computed in the same manner as those of any Member Country, for the purpose of completing the minimum percentage established in Article 11 of this regime. The corresponding agreement of the Board of Directors of the aforesaid institution must be adopted by the favorable vote of the Series A

Director of the country or countries concerned and it shall indicate the procedure by which investors of the aforesaid countries may acquire such contributions.

CHAPTER IX

Transitory Provisions

Article a. Before November 30, 1972, the Commission, acting on the recommendation of the Board, shall approve the rules that will govern the merger of enterprises for the purpose of establishing and operating multinational enterprises.

Article b. Before November 30, 1972, the Commission, acting on the recommendation of the Board, shall approve the conditions to which multinational enterprises must be subject when they are established in the sector of services, especially banking, financial institutions, insurance and reinsurance, tourism, transportation, consulting services, and technical assistance.

Article c. This regime shall enter into force when all of the Member Countries have deposited with the Secretariat of the Board the instruments by which they put it into practice in their respective territories, in accordance with the provisions of the last paragraph of Article 28 of the Cartagena Agreement.

STANDARDS ON COMPETITION

(Decision 45 of the Commission, December 18, 1971)

THE COMMISSION OF THE CARTAGENA AGREEMENT:

HAVING SEEN: Chapter VIII of the Cartagena Agreement
and Resolution 65 (II) of the Conference of the Contracting Parties of the Montevideo Treaty; and

CONSIDERING: That the Commission should, prior to December 31, 1971, adopt "the necessary norms for preventing or correcting practices that can distort competition within the Subregion";

That the member countries lack systematic, general
legislation on the matters dealt with in Chapter VIII of the
Agreement;

That the Liberalization Program of the Agreement began to be applied on December 31, 1970;

That for the reasons explained there is insufficient experience regarding the situations that can arise as a consequence of practices that distort competition in the Subregion;

That it is necessary to gain experience in order to have
guidelines that will make it possible to define with precision
the practices mentioned and apply the treatment required in
each case;

That the treatment of the problem is closely linked to the
program for harmonization of economic and social policies
dealt with in Chapter III of the Agreement;

That it is necessary to adopt general norms and principles in order to expand and pinpoint them as the integration process requires;

That the principal aim of the Liberalization Program
of the Cartagena Agreement is to place at the disposal of
subregional consumers an increased volume of goods in the

Subregion under consistently more favorable conditions as regards quality and price;

That in these matters distinction should be made between situations arising in the territory of the member countries and situations originating in the territory of a third country;

That it is necessary for the member countries to coordinate their action in the international sphere in determining the rules of competition that are in consonance with subregional interests;

THE COMMITTEE ON THE CARTAGENA AGREEMENT

DECIDES THAT:

Article 1. The measures provided for in the present Decision should be applied in order to prevent or correct practices that can distort competition within the Subregion, either from the territory of the member countries or from the territory of a third country.

Article 2. The following, among others, are considered practices that distort competition:

a) Dumping;

b) Improper manipulation of prices;

c) Practices intended to disturb the normal supply of raw materials;

d) Other practices with equivalent results.

Article 3. When a member country considers itself affected by practices that distort the competition emanating from the territory of another member country, he may present the case to the Board (Junta), explaining the facts on which he bases his complaint.

Article 4. Within 48 hours following receipt of the complaint, the Board (Junta) shall communicate it to the member country from whose territory the practices leading to the complaint emanate and shall request whatever information is considered pertinent, which must be submitted within 15 days following the date of the corresponding communications.

The Board (Junta) may take whatever action is considered necessary to study and solve the problem, including the convocation of a meeting of the interested countries, if warranted, for the purpose of collecting more information and reaching a direct solution to the problem, in which case an additional 15 days may be made available.

Article 5. If a direct arrangement is not reached between the interested countries, and the Board (Junta) feels that the application of measures to correct the situation presented would be justified, it shall authorize such action by special resolution. The Board (Junta) shall have 30 days, following expiration of the time periods referred to in the preceding article, in which to transmit such a resolution.

Article 6. The Board (Junta) shall communicate its resolution to the interested countries and the other member countries and shall report it to the Commission at its next meeting.

Article 7. When a member country considers itself affected by a situation which in its opinion seriously distorts competition and requires the adoption of urgent corrective measures, it may present the case to the Board (Junta) showing cause for its request.

If the Board (Junta) considers that the situation so requires, it may authorize, by resolution, at a time compatible with the urgency of the case and after duly notifying the interested countries, the adoption of temporary corrective measures without prejudice to continuing the study of the situation presented in the manner provided for in the preceding articles.

The Board (Junta) shall communicate its resolution at once to the interested countries and to the other member countries.

408

Article 8.   In conformance with the procedure indicated
in Articles 5 and 7, the Board (Junta) may, among other
measures, authorize the affected member countries to impose duties and/or restrictions of a discriminatory nature
on imports of the commodities affected by the distortion of
competition.

Also, the Board (Junta) shall request the member
country from which or in whose territory the practices involved in the complaint emanate to adopt the necessary
measures to eliminate the distortion.

Article 9.   In determining which of the measures mentioned in Article 8 are necessary to correct the situation
presented, the Board (Junta) shall give special consideration
to:

a)   The norms for harmonization of the economic and
     social policies adopted in the Subregion in compli-
     ance with the provisions of Chapter III of the
     Agreement; and

b)   The conditions for production in the Subregion of
     the commodities referred to, the placement of these
     commodities in the Liberalization Program of the
     Agreement, the application of the Common Exter-
     nal Tariff, the Sectorial Industrial Development
     Programs, the Special Policy for Bolivia and Ecua-
     dor, and the provisions on origin contained in
     Chapter X.

Article 10.   Within 60 days after the date of the resolution of the Board (Junta) any of the member countries may
request the Commission to review the situation. The Commission shall decide on the request for review by the date
of the next meeting.

Article 11.   Without prejudicing the provisions of Article 7, the measures authorized by the Board (Junta) by
virtue of Article 8 of the present Decision shall not be applicable in situations resulting from non-harmonized legal
norms so long as the Commission does not act favorably on
the resolution of the Board (Junta). The Commission shall

409

act at the next regular or special meeting; if it does not, or if it fails to meet on the occasion of its convocation, the measures authorized by the Board (Junta) shall be fully applicable.

Article 12. When practices emanating from a country outside the Subregion affect the interests of a member country and it becomes necessary to apply corrective measures that might result in modification of the obligations contracted by virtue of the Agreement, the affected country should request the Board (Junta) to apply the measures referred to in Article 8, which shall apply the procedure indicated in the present Decision for study and solution.

If the measures would not result in modification of the obligations contracted, the affected member country could adopt them unilaterally and report on them to the Commission and the Board (Junta).

Article 13. As soon as the Board (Junta) can verify that the causes that led to the measures referred to in Article 8 no longer exist, it shall notify the member country concerned that the authorization granted by that article has been terminated.

Article 14. In harmonizing economic and social policies the organs of the Agreement shall take into consideration the experiences resulting from situations of distortion of competition that have arisen within the Subregion.

Article 15. On the basis of the experience resulting from application of the present Decision, the Commission shall, at the proposal of the Board (Junta), approve basic principles for defining the practices that distort or can distort competition within the Subregion as well as new norms that may be necessary to prevent or correct those practices.

Article 16. The member countries shall act coordinately in the various international forums and bodies in which questions relating to the prevention or correction of practices that distort competition are debated.

DIRECTIVES FOR THE HARMONIZATION OF
LEGISLATION ON INDUSTRIAL DEVELOPMENT

(Decision N° 49 of the Commission, December 18, 1971)

HAVING SEEN: The provisions of Articles 7, 15, 26, 28, 30, 31, 34 (d), 42, 53, 55, 56, 92, 102, 104, 105, and the Chapter on Common External Tariff of the Agreement; Decisions 24, 26, 27, 29 and 34 of the Commission, and Proposal 25 of the Board,

THE COMMISSION OF THE CARTAGENA AGREEMENT DECIDES:

To approve the following directives, which will serve as a basis for the harmonization of legislation on industrial development in the member countries.

CHAPTER I

Tariff Policy

PROVISIONS APPLICABLE TO
COLOMBIA, CHILE AND PERU

Article 1. The exemptions, reductions and rebates on import duties contained in the national legislation of Colombia, Chile and Peru on the products indicated in Decision 27 shall be eliminated on an annual, linear and automatic basis until the levels established in the Common Minimum External Tariff have been reached.

This process shall begin December 31, 1972 and be completed December 31, 1975. After the latter date Colombia, Chile and Peru may not apply reductions that would imply levels lower than those of the Common Minimum External Tariff.

Article 2. If the levels of the Common External Tariff
are lower than those of the Common Minimum External
Tariff, Colombia, Chile and Peru may apply reductions up
to the levels of the Common External Tariff for the duration
of the period of approximation.

If the levels of the Common External Tariff are higher
than those of the Common Minimum External Tariff, these
countries shall eliminate the reductions on an annual, linear
and automatic basis from December 31, 1976 to December
31, 1980. After the latter date Colombia, Chile and Peru
may not apply returns that would imply lower levels than
those of the Common External Tariff.

Article 3. Colombia, Chile and Peru shall cease
applying exemptions, reductions and rebates on duties on
June 30, 1972 for products included in Decision 26 and for
those included in the first section of the Common List.

Article 4. Products reserved for Industrial Development Sectorial Programs that were not included in them
shall be governed by the following rules:

a) In the case of products not produced in any country
    of the Subregion, Colombia, Chile and Peru shall
    cease applying exemptions, reductions and rebates
    from the moment that the product concerned is no
    longer reserved.

b) In the case of the other products, Colombia, Chile
    and Peru shall carry out the process of elimination
    of exemptions, reductions and rebates in accor-
    dance with the provisions of Articles 1 and 2 of
    that Decision. In such cases the process will begin
    at the level that would apply if the elimination had
    begun December 31, 1972.

Article 5. From December 31, 1972 on, Colombia,
Chile and Peru shall no longer apply reductions, exemptions
and rebates on import duties of products included in the
lists indicated in Decisions 29 and 34.

Article 6. Without prejudicing the provisions of Articles 56, 65 and 67 of the Agreement, Colombia, Chile and Peru may not apply exemptions, reductions or rebates on duties that would imply levels lower than those of the Common Minimum External Tariff on imports of products whose trade was significant between one of them and Bolivia or Ecuador during the last three years or that have certain prospects of significant trade in the immediate future.

The Board shall determine when trade has been significant or when there are certain prospects that it will be.

PROVISIONS APPLICABLE TO BOLIVIA AND ECUADOR

Article 7. The exemptions, reductions and rebates contained in the national legislation of Bolivia and Ecuador on the products indicated in Article 1 of the present Decision shall be eliminated on an annual, linear and automatic basis until the levels established in the Common External Tariff have been reached. This process shall begin December 31, 1976 and be completed December 31, 1985.

After December 31, 1985, Bolivia and Ecuador may not apply to the imports indicated in the present article reductions on duties that would imply levels lower than those of the Common External Tariff.

Article 8. Bolivia and Ecuador shall eliminate exemptions, reductions and rebates on products included in Decision 26 on a linear and automatic basis. This process shall be completed within a period of three years from the date on which the production concerned has begun in the Subregion.

Article 9. When the Commission, at the proposal of the Board, determines that Bolivia and Ecuador shall adopt the minimum levels in accordance with the provisions of the third and fourth subparagraphs of Article 104 of the Agreement, these countries shall cease applying exemptions, reductions and rebates in the manner stated in the corresponding Decision.

Article 10. In the case of products contained in the first section of the Common List, Bolivia and Ecuador shall eliminate the exemptions, reductions and rebates according to the procedure mentioned in Article 7 of that Decision.

If the Conference of the Contracting Parties of the Treaty of Montevideo agrees to the liberalization of Common List products by all the member countries, Bolivia and Ecuador shall cease applying exemptions, reductions and rebates to those products from the date on which that liberalization takes place.

Article 11. The products reserved for Industrial Development Sectorial Programs that are not included in them should be governed by the following rules:

a) In the case of products not produced in any country of the Subregion, Bolivia and Ecuador shall eliminate their exemptions, reductions and rebates by a linear and automatic process to be completed within a period of three years from the date on which the production concerned has begun in the Subregion.

b) In the case of the other products, Bolivia and Ecuador shall carry out the process of elimination of exemptions, reductions and rebates in accordance with the provisions of Article 7 of that Decision.

Article 12. Without prejudice to the statement made in the preceding article with respect to the products mentioned therein, the Commission, at the proposal of the Board, may agree to the elimination of exemptions, reductions and rebates under different conditions and time periods, although the period established may not go beyond December 31, 1985.

Article 13. Without prejudice to the provisions of Article 105 of the Cartagena Agreement, the Commission at the proposal of the Board, shall, by no later than December 31, 1976, approve a list of products for which Bolivia and

Ecuador may apply the exemptions, reductions and rebates on import duties contained in their industrial promotion legislation. These exemptions, reductions and rebates may not be applied in any case after December 31, 1985.

At the proposal of the Board, the Commission may, within the two dates indicated, approve additional lists whenever technological changes or other reasons of economic significance make it convenient to do so.

The products included in the industrial development sectorial programs dealt with in Chapter IV of the Cartagena Agreement are exempted from the above provisions.

COMMON PROVISIONS

Article 14. In its evaluations the Board shall consider the repercussions involved in the application of the norms of the present Decision in the industrial development of the member countries, and especially of Bolivia and Ecuador, and shall propose to the Commission whatever measures may be necessary to promote such development in light of the objectives of the Agreement.

Article 15. At any time that in fulfillment of the Liberalization Program a product becomes liberalized from duties and other restrictions, there shall be applied to it fully and simultaneously the duties established in the Common Minimum External Tariff or in the Common External Tariff, according to the case.

Therefore, from that time on no member country may continue applying to such products exemptions, reductions and rebates on duties below those common levels.

Article 16. Products included in the reserve list for industrial development sectorial programs shall be exempted from the provisions of that Decision so long as they remain in it.

Article 17. The exemptions, reductions and rebates that favor the importation of products included in the lists of exceptions of the member countries shall cease to be applied totally on December 31, 1985 by Colombia, Chile and Peru and by December 31, 1990 by Bolivia and Ecuador, in conformance with the provisions of Article 55 and 102 of the Agreement.

The dates specified in the previous paragraph shall be understood to be extended in cases authorized by the Board, in conformance with the provisions of the above-cited articles.

Products withdrawn from the lists of exceptions prior to the dates specified above shall be regulated according to the rules for elimination of exemptions, reductions and rebates under the conditions and at the levels that apply in accordance with the provisions of the present Decision, and they shall begin to enjoy at the same time the advantages of the Liberalization Program of the Agreement.

Article 18. The member countries undertake not to authorize the signing of contracts between governments and enterprises engaged in productive activities in the respective country granting the latter the right to enjoy exemptions, reductions or rebates that may be contrary to the rules of the present Decision.

When the governments of the member countries must proceed with granting exemptions, reductions or rebates that contravene the rules of the present Decision as a consequence of rights acquired by the enterprises by virtue of contracts entered into with the governments, these enterprises may not enjoy the benefits of the Liberalization Program of the Agreement. The products processed by these enterprises will not be considered to be of subregional origin.

Article 19. If, in use of the powers established in Article 66 of the Agreement, the Commission at the proposal of the Board should modify common tariff levels, the process of elimination of exemptions, reductions and rebates shall be carried out in the following manner:

a) If the new common levels are higher than the previous ones, the elimination process will continue to develop from the level reached up to that date and in a way that the new levels will be reached on an annual, linear and automatic basis.

b) If the new common levels are lower than the previous ones, the following situations may arise:

    i) If the process of elimination of exemptions, reductions and rebates has not reached the new common levels on the date of modification, the procedure mentioned in subparagraph (a) above will be followed.

    ii) If the process of elimination has exceeded the new common levels, the member countries may apply reductions up to the limit of these new levels.

Article 20. The Commission, at the proposal of the Board, may agree to procedures to accelerate the elimination of exemptions, reductions and rebates established in this chapter. For that purpose, it should particularly consider the cases of products of special interest to Bolivia and Ecuador.

Article 21. Without prejudice to the provisions of previous articles of this chapter, any member country, by virtue of the provisions of Articles 65 and 67 of the Agreement, may resort to the procedures of exception indicated below:

a) In the case of products that are not produced in the Subregion, each country may defer the the application of common tariffs until the Board can verify that their production has begun in the Subregion.

b) However, if in the opinion of the Board the new production is insufficient to meet the needs of the Subregion, it will propose to the Committee whatever measures are necessary to conciliate the need to protect the subregional production with the need to insure a normal supply.

c) To meet the temporary insufficiencies of supply that can affect any member country, the problem may be presented by the country affected to the Board for verification of the situation within a period compatible with the urgency of the case. As soon as the Board has verified that the problem exists and has notified the affected country of this fact, the latter may take such measures as a temporary reduction or suspension of the duties of the External Tariff within the limits necessary to correct the problem.

In such cases, the affected country may apply the exemptions, reductions and rebates considered in its national legislation until the Board notifies it that subregional production has begun or that the insufficiency has been corrected.

Article 22. Prior to November 30, 1972, the Commission, at the proposal of the Board, shall approve the procedures necessary to apply the measures indicated in Article 21.

Article 23. The member countries may maintain the exemptions and rebates that benefit imports of the diplomatic corps and international organizations and those that favor donations and aid sent by foreign public or private institutions to governments, municipalities, public or private educational establishments, institutions of charity or social welfare, or scientific or technological research institutes.

Article 24. The member countries may maintain the exemptions, reductions or rebates on import duties established for the benefit of depressed areas or areas separated from national or subregional centers of supply, and other geographic areas of special tariff treatment until a definitive policy to which such areas should be subjected is established by virtue of what is decided in this respect in the harmonization referred to in Articles 30 of the Agreement or 28 of the present Decision.

Products processed in those areas under protection of the exemptions, reductions or rebates mentioned may not enjoy the advantages of the Liberalization Program of the Agreement until a policy to which they should be subjected definitively is established. Therefore, during this period they may not be protected by certificates of origin.

Article 25. The member countries may keep in force their pending tax policies which favor the following situations:

a)   Products intended for fairs and expositions;

b)   Products introduced as commercial samples;

c)   Products intended for educational, artistic or circus shows;

d)   Molds and matrices.

General warehouses may continue to function in accordance with the provisions of the current laws of the member countries until a policy to which they must definitively be subjected is established, according to which a determination will be made in the harmonization referred to in Article 30 of the Agreement.

CHAPTER II

Fiscal, Exchange, Monetary and Financial Policies

Article 26. In matters relating to taxes, fees and other internal charges, the original products of a member country shall enjoy in the territory of the other member countries treatment no less favorable than that which is applied to similar national products.

Article 27. Instruments of industrial promotion relating to the fiscal, exchange, monetary and financial policies of the member countries shall be harmonized to accord with what the Commission decides, in compliance with the obligation set forth in Article 26 (d) of the Agreement.

For that purpose, prior to November 30, 1973 the Commission shall decide on Board proposals intended to orient or initiate the process of harmonization of the instruments of industrial promotion mentioned in the preceding paragraph.

CHAPTER III

The Promotion of Exports

Article 28. Prior to December 31, 1972 the Commission, at the proposal of the Board, shall approve a subregional system for promotion of intrasubregional exports.

In the program dealt with in Article 30 of the Agreement, the Commission shall decide at what moment to approve a subregional promotion system covering all exports of the member countries.

Article 29. Until the system mentioned in the first paragraph of Article 28 is approved, the member countries may maintain the exemptions, reductions and rebates of internal taxes and other direct aids intended to promote intrasubregional exports.

Article 30. With respect to exports outside the Subregion, until the system for promoting exports mentioned in the second paragraph of Article 28 is adopted, the member countries may apply their national legislation on promotion of exports. If the application of these mechanisms should create production or exportation problems in the rest of the member countries, the Commission, at the request of the country affected, shall decide what measures should be taken.

Article 31. The Board shall present to the Commission programs permitting joint negotiations to be carried on with countries or groups of countries either directly or through international forums, leading to the growth of subregional exports.

CHAPTER IV

Joint Action Leading to
Industrial Promotion

Article 32. Prior to November 31, 1972, the Commission shall approve at the proposal of the Board, a mechanism that will make it possible to utilize, for the benefit of the production of the Subregion, the demand of the governments of the member countries in the exercise of their public function.

Article 33. The Commission, at the proposal of the Board, shall approve measures permitting joint action by the member countries in the following matters:

a) Industrial reporting and research; and

b) Provision of engineering services and an economic evaluation of an industrial nature.

Article 34. In drafting the Proposal to which Article 33 refers, the Board shall especially consider:

a) The need to prepare systematic studies of the existing natural resources that can be industralized in the Subregion;

b) The desirability of coordinating the action of national and subregional organisms in the study of investment opportunities and possibilities in the Subregion

c) The benefits that can be derived from the utilization of subregional technical resources for, among other things:

  i) The preparation and evaluation of projects;

  ii) Production analysis and selection of productive processes and production techniques;

  iii) The preparation of studies on industrial safety and on control against contamination of the environment.

Article 35. The Commission, at the proposal of the Board, shall approve a program intended to strengthen action of the member countries in the formulation of technical norms and the establishment of quality control systems.

In drafting the proposal the Board shall act in coordination with the competent national organisms of each member country.

CHAPTER V

Technology and Industrial Promotion

Article 36. In conformance with the provisions of Decision 24, the Commission, at the proposal of the Board, shall approve a program intended to promote and protect the development of subregional technology, make optimum use of foreign technology from the technical and economic points of view, and control their utilization in the Subregion.

Article 37. In line with preparing the proposal indicated in Article 36 and in close relation to its content, the Commission, at the proposal of the Board, shall approve a program leading to the establishment of a reporting and price control system for intermediate products furnished by the providers of foreign technology.

CHAPTER VI

Other Provisions

Article 38. Without prejudice to what may be decided in compliance with the provisions of Chapters III and VIII of the Agreement, any member country may resort to the Commission when it considers that the benefits it was granting to one of the others is detracting from its objectives.

Article 39. The industrial development sectorial programs may consider norms that are different from those set forth in the present Decision whenever the characteristics of the program in question so require.

Article 40. In drafting the proposals dealt with in the present Decision, the Board shall give preferential consideration to the situation of Bolivia and Ecuador so that the mechanisms it is proposed to establish will contribute effectively to the industrial development of these countries.

Article 41. For purposes of application in the member countries of internal legal or administrative norms of industrial promotion that demand the use of domestic consumer goods and capital assets, or condition that use to the enjoyment of certain privileges, or limit or prohibit the importation of foreign products when they are produced domestically, consumer goods and capital assets of subregional origin shall be considered as domestic production.

Countries in which provisions of this nature already exist shall adopt the measures necessary to make them compatible with the provisions of this article.

Transitory Provisions

Article 1. The obligation entered into by the member countries by virtue of Transitory Article H of Decision 24 shall cease in accordance with what the Commission decides in this respect while the harmonization process to which this Decision refers is being carried out.

Article 2. The Commission, at the proposal of the Board, shall approve whatever regulations may be necessary for application of the present Decision.